Raspberry Pi OS System Administration with systemd and Python

The second in a new series exploring the basics of Raspberry Pi Operating System administration, this installment builds on the insights provided in Volume 1 to provide a compendium of easy-to-use and essential Raspberry Pi system administration for the novice user, with specific focus on Python and Python3.

The overriding idea behind system administration of a modern, 21st-century Linux system such as the Raspberry Pi OS is the use of systemd to ensure that the Linux kernel works efficiently and effectively to provide these three foundation stones of computer operation and management: computer system concurrency, virtualization, and secure persistence. Exercises are included throughout to reinforce the readers' learning goals with solutions and example code provided on the accompanying GitHub site.

This book is aimed at students and practitioners looking to maximize their use of the Raspberry Pi OS. With plenty of practical examples, projects, and exercises, this volume can also be adopted in a more formal learning environment to supplement and extend the basic knowledge of a Linux operating system.

Robert M. Koretsky is a retired lecturer in Mechanical Engineering at the University of Portland School of Engineering. He previously worked as an automotive engineering designer at the Freightliner Corp. in Portland, Oregon. He's married, and has two kids and two grandkids.

Raspberry Pi OS System Administration with systemd
A Practical Approach
Series Editor: Robert M. Koretsky

Raspberry Pi OS System Administration with systemd: A Practical Approach
Robert M. Koretsky

Raspberry Pi OS System Administration with systemd and Python: A Practical Approach
Robert M. Koretsky

Raspberry Pi OS System Administration with systemd and Python

A Practical Approach

Robert M. Koretsky

CRC Press
Taylor & Francis Group
CHAPMAN & HALL

First edition published 2024
by CRC Press
4 Park Square, Milton Park, Abingdon, Oxon, OX14 4RN

and by CRC Press
2385 NW Executive Center Drive, Suite 320, Boca Raton FL 33431

CRC Press is an imprint of Informa UK Limited

British Library Cataloguing-in-Publication Data
A catalogue record for this book is available from the British Library

ISBN: 978-1-032-59689-1 (hbk)
ISBN: 978-1-032-59688-4 (pbk)
ISBN: 978-1-003-45580-6 (ebk)

DOI: 10.1201/b23421

Typeset in Palatino
by Newgen Publishing UK

To my family.

Bob Koretsky

Contents

Series Preface

This series of books covers the basics of Raspberry Pi Operating System administration, and is geared towards a novice user. Each book is a complete, self-contained introduction to important system administration tasks, and to other useful programs. The foundation of all of them is the systemd super-kernel. They guide the user along a path that gives the "why" and "how to" of those important system administration topics, and they also present the following essential application facilities:

1) Raspberry Pi OS System administration with systemd, Volume 1

2) Raspberry Pi OS System administration with systemd and Python, Volume 2

3) Raspberry Pi OS Text Editing, git, Virtualization with LXC/LXD, Volume 3

They can be used separately, or together, to fit the learning objectives/pace, and interests of the individual, independent learner, or can be adopted in a more formal learning environment to supplement and extend the basic knowledge of a Linux operating system in a classroom environment that uses the Raspberry Pi OS.

In addition, each book has In-Chapter Exercises throughout, and a Question, Problems, and Projects addendum to help reinforce the learning goals of the individual student, or reader.

An online Github site, with further materials and updates, program code, solutions to both In-Chapter Exercises and End-of-Chapter Problems, Questions, and Projects, plus other supplements, is provided for each volume. It can be found at:

www.github.com/bobk48/RaspberryPiOS

The fundamental prerequisites of each volume are 1) knowledge of how to type a syntactically correct Linux command on the command line, 2) having access to a dedicated Raspberry Pi computer with the latest Raspberry Pi Operating System already installed and running on it, 3) being a privileged user on the system that is able to execute the **sudo** command to assume superuser status, and 4) having a basic knowledge of how to edit and save text files in the **nano** text editor.

All instructions in these volumes were tested on either a Raspberry Pi 4B, or a Raspberry Pi 400, both with 4 GB of memory, and the latest version of the Raspberry Pi OS at the time.

Volume 2 Preface

Background

This book is a compendium of easy-to-use, and essential Raspberry Pi system administration tasks for the beginner. The Raspberry Pi OS is derived from the Debian branch of Linux, and as of this writing, Debian Bullseye was the most current version of that operating system. To present the system administration topics and commands here, I have selected some very basic stuff, and a few more advanced concepts, topics, commands, and details that might not appear in a more complete system administration book.

The overriding idea behind system administration of a modern, 21st-century Linux system such as the Raspberry Pi OS is the use of systemd to ensure that the Linux kernel works efficiently and effectively to provide these three foundation stones of computer operation and management: computer system concurrency, virtualization, and secure persistence.

And this control of the kernel by a "super-kernel", which is what systemd essentially is, must also promote the highest level of system performance and speed, given the use cases the computer might be put to, and the perceived needs of the target user base that the computer serves. Unless that novice user, or even a more seasoned system professional, has not only a basic, but also a more complete knowledge of how systemd controls and oversees every process and operation of a modern Linux system, they will never be able to master administrating and implementing the kind of functionality that their use case(s) might ultimately require. Particularly for the user base on the system, and the demands that user base makes.

Certainly out of the multitude of possible topics we could have presented, the ones you find detailed here have basically been selected in somewhat of a subjective way. That selective way was mainly guided by these concerns:

a. The secure maintenance, in terms of concurrency, virtualization, and persistence, of a single Raspberry Pi system that an ordinary novice user can install on her own dedicated hardware.

b. How important the topics are, in a perceived ranking of essential system administration tasks.

c. How systemd plays into the maintenance regimen of the Raspberry pi OS, and the hardware it's installed on, as chosen by that ordinary user.

d. The overall pedagogic integration of the selected topics presented on system administration with each other.

e. How well these topics serve to prepare a student for entry into any chosen Information Technology or Computer Science profession, or how someone already in those professions can use this book to better conform to the best practices of that profession. In other words, for educational and continuing education audiences.

f. To some degree, make it possible to extrapolate these topics (for audiences in e) from a single Raspberry Pi system environment to a broader and larger-scaled computing environment, such as is found on small-to-medium-sized servers, or to cloud-based, virtual computing.

How to Read and Use This Book

Note

The premise and prerequisite of this book is that you understand what the correct form, or structure, of a Linux command is, and how to type one in on the console or terminal command line of a Raspberry Pi!

Just to review that here, the general syntax, or structure of a single Linux command (often referred to as a *simple command*) as it is typed on the command line, is as follows:

$ **command [[-]option(s)] [option argument(s)] [command argument(s)]**

where:

$ is the command line or shell prompt from the Raspberry Pi OS;
anything enclosed in [] is not always needed;
command is the name of the valid Linux command for that shell in lowercase letters;
[-option(s)] is one or more modifiers that change the behavior of command;
[option argument(s)] is one or more modifiers that change the behavior of
  [-option(s)]; and
[command argument(s)] is one or more objects that are affected by **command**.

Note the following seven essentials:

1. A space separates command, options, option arguments, and command arguments, but no space is necessary between multiple option(s) or multiple option arguments.

2. The order of multiple options or option arguments is irrelevant.

3. A space character is optional between the option and the option argument.

4. Always press the <Enter> key to submit the command for interpretation and execution.

5. Options may be preceded by a single hyphen - or two hyphens --, depending on the form of the option. The short form of the option is preceded by a single hyphen, the long form of the option is preceded by two hyphens. No space character should be placed between hyphen(s) and option(s).

6. A small percentage of commands (like **whoami**) take *no* options, option arguments, or command arguments.

7. Everything on the command line is case sensitive!

Also, it is possible, and *very* common, to type *multiple* Linux commands (sometimes called *compound* commands, to differentiate them from simple commands) on the same command line, before pressing the **<Enter>** key. The components of a multiple Linux command are separated with input and output redirection characters, to channel the output of one into the input of another.

As stated in the Series Preface, the fundamental prerequisites of this volume are:

1) Knowledge of how to type a syntactically correct Linux command on the command line (as detailed above)

2) Having access to a dedicated Raspberry Pi computer with the latest Raspberry Pi Operating System already installed and running on it

3) Being a privileged user on the system, and as such, being able to execute the **sudo** command to assume superuser status, and

4) Having a basic knowledge of how to edit and save text files in the **nano** text editor. We give no instruction on how to use the nano text editor in this volume, but there is a brief overview of it in Volume 3, Raspberry Pi OS Text Editing, git, Virtualization with LXC/LXD.

An online Github site, with further materials and updates, program code, solutions to both In-Chapter Exercises and End-of-Chapter Problems, Questions, and Projects, plus other supplements, is provided for this book. It can be found at:

www.github.com/bobk48/RaspberryPiOS

All command line instructions in this volume were tested on either a Raspberry Pi 4B, or a Raspberry Pi 400, both with 4 GB of memory, and the latest version of the Raspberry Pi OS at the time.

Routes through the Book

Browse the Contents.

Select a topic that interests you.

Do the examples, or all the command line materials presented for that topic.

Maybe pick another topic that interests you, and do the examples and all the command line materials there.

Finally, go back to the beginning of the book. Do everything, from start to finish.

Rinse and repeat the above as necessary.

Refer as much as possible to the systemd materials in Volume 1, using them as an encyclopedic source for the material you select out of Chapter 1.

Have fun!

0

"Quick Start" into Sysadmin for the Raspberry Pi OS

In this introductory chapter, duplicated in the first volume of this series, we cover the essential Raspberry Pi OS commands that allow a system administrator to do file maintenance and perform other useful operations. This is a mandatory set of essentials that even an ordinary, non-administrative user would need to know to work efficiently in a character- or text-based interface to the operating system. It should be evident to the reader, after completing this chapter, that correctly deployed, text-based commands are the predominant means that a system administrator has at her disposal to maintain the integrity of the system. We give a set of core examples, and show the basic format of essential commands and primitives here.

Objectives:

To explain how to manage and maintain files and directories
To show where to get system-wide help for Raspberry Pi OS commands
To demonstrate the use of a beginner's set of utility commands
To cover the basic commands and operators:

cat cd cp exit hostname -l ip login lp lpr ls man mesg mkdir more mv passwd PATH pwd rm rmdir telnet unalias uname whatis whereis who whoami

0.1 Introduction

To start working productively with system administration on the Raspberry Pi OS, the beginner needs to have some familiarity with these sequential topics, as follows:

1. How to maintain and organize files in the file structure of the operating system. Creating a tree-like structure of folders (also called directories), and storing files in a logical fashion in these folders, is critical to working efficiently in the Raspberry Pi OS.
2. How to get help on text-based commands and their usage. With keyboard entry, in a command-based, Character User Interface (CUI)

DOI: 10.1201/b23421-1

environment, being able to find out, in a quick and easy way, how to use a command, its options, and arguments by typing it on the keyboard correctly, is imperative to working efficiently.

3. How to execute a small set of essential utility commands to set up or customize your working environment. Once a beginner is familiar with the right way to construct file maintenance commands, adding a set of utility commands makes each session more productive.

To use this chapter successfully as a springboard into the remainder of the book, you should carefully read, follow, and execute the instructions and command line sessions we provide, in the order presented. Each section in this chapter, and the two subsequent chapters as well, builds on the information that precedes it. They will give you the concepts, command tools, and methods that will enable you to do system administration using the Raspberry Pi OS.

Throughout this book, we illustrate everything using the following version of the Raspberry Pi OS, on the hardware listed:

System: raspberrypi Kernel: 6.1.21-v8+ aarch64 bits: 64 compiler: gcc v: 10.2.1 Console: tty0 Distro: Debian GNU/Linux 11 (bullseye)

Machine: Type: ARM Device System: Raspberry Pi 400 Rev 1.0

In this chapter, the major commands we want to illustrate are first defined with an abbreviated syntax description, which will clarify general components of those commands. The syntax description format is as follows:

Syntax: The exact syntax of how a command, its options, and its arguments are correctly typed on the command line

Purpose: The specific purpose of the command

Output: A short description of the results of executing the command

Commonly used options/features: A listing of the most popular and useful options and option arguments

In addition, the following web link is to a site that allows you to type-in a single or multiple Raspberry Pi OS command, and get a verbose explanation of the components of that command:

https://explainshell.com/

In-Chapter Exercises

1. Type the following commands on your Raspberry Pi system's command line, and note the results. Which ones are syntactically incorrect? Why? (The Bash prompt is shown as the $ character in each, and we assume that **file1** and **file2** exist)

   ```
   $ la -ls
   $ cat
   $ more -q file1
   $ more file2
   $ time
   $ lsblk-a
   ```

2. How can you differentiate a Raspberry Pi OS command from its options, option arguments, and command arguments?

3. What is the difference between a single Raspberry Pi OS command, and a multiple Raspberry Pi OS command, as typed on the command line before pressing **<Enter>**?

4. If you get no error message after you enter a Raspberry Pi OS command, how do you know that it actually accomplished what you wanted it to?

0.2 File Maintenance Commands and Help On Raspberry Pi OS Command Usage

After your first-time login to a new Raspberry Pi OS, one of your first actions will be to construct and organize your workspace environment, and the files that will be contained in it. The operation of organizing your files according to some logical scheme is known as *file maintenance*. A logical scheme used to organize your files might consist of creating *bins* for storing files according to the subject matter of the contents of the files, or according to the dates of their creation. In the following sections, you will type file creation and maintenance commands that produce a structure similar to what is shown in Figure 0.1. Complete the operations in the following sections in the order they are presented, to get a better overview of what file maintenance really is. Also, it is critical that you review what was presented in the Preface regarding the structure of a Raspberry Pi OS command, so that when you begin to type commands for file maintenance, you understand how the syntax of what you are typing conforms to the general syntax of any Raspberry Pi OS command.

0.2.1 File and Directory Structure

When you first open a terminal, or console, window, you are working in the *home directory*, or folder, of the autonomous user associated with the user-name and password you used to log into the system with. Whatever directory you are presently in is known as the *current working directory*, and there is only one current working directory active at any given time. It is helpful to visualize the structure of your files and directories using a diagram. Figure 0.1 is an example of a home directory and file structure for a user named **bob**. In this figure, directories are represented as parallelograms and plain files (e.g., files that contain text or binary instructions) are represented as rectangles. A *pathname*, or path, is simply a textual way of designating the location of a directory or file in the complete file structure of the Raspberry Pi system you are working on.

For example, the path to the file **myfile2** in Figure 0.1 is **/home/bob/myfile2**. The designation of the path begins at the root (/) of the entire file system, descends to the folder named **home**, and then descends again to the home directory of the user named **bob**.

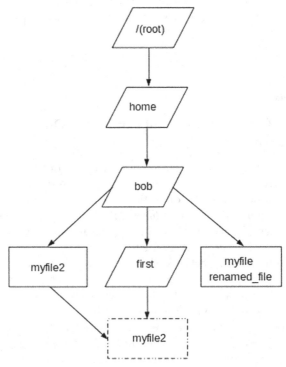

FIGURE 0.1
Example Directory Structure.

As shown in Figure 0.1, the files named **myfile, myfile2,** and **renamed_file** are stored under or in the directory **bob.** Beneath **bob** is a *subdirectory* named **first.** In the following sections, you will create these files, and the subdirectory structure, in the home directory of the username that you have logged into your Raspberry Pi system with.

In-Chapter Exercise

5. Type the following two commands on your Raspberry Pi OS:

   $ **cd /**
   $ **ls**

Similar to Figure 0.1, sketch a diagram of the directories and files whose names you see listed as the output of the second command. Save this diagram for use later.

0.2.2 Viewing the Contents of Files

To begin working with files, you can easily create a new text file by using the **cat** command. The syntax of the **cat** command is as follows:

cat [options] [file-list]

Purpose: Join one or more files sequentially or display them in the console window

Output: Contents of the files in **file-list** displayed on the screen, one file at a time

Commonly used options/features:

+E Display $ at the end of each line

-n Put line numbers on the displayed lines

-- help Display the purpose of the command and a brief explanation of each option

The **cat** command, short for concatenate, allows you to join files. In the example you will join what you type on the keyboard to a new file being created in the current working directory. This is achieved by the redirect character >, which takes what you type at the *standard input* (in this case the keyboard) and directs it into the file named **myfile.** You can consider the keyboard, and the stream of information it provides, as a file. As stated in the Preface, this usage is an example of a command, **cat** with no options, option arguments, or command arguments. It simply uses the command, a redirect character, and a target, or destination, named **myfile,** where the redirection will go.

This is the very simplest example of a *multiple command* typed on the command line, as opposed to a single command, as shown and briefly described in the Preface. In a multiple command, you can string together single Raspberry Pi OS commands in a chain with connecting operators, such as the redirect character shown here.

$ **cat > myfile**
This is an example of how to use the cat command to add plain text to a file
<Ctrl+D>
$

You can type as many lines of text, pressing **<Enter>** on the keyboard to distinguish between lines in the file, as you want. Then, on a new line, when you hold down **<Ctrl+D>**, the file is created in the current working directory, using the command you typed. You can view the contents of this file, since it is a plain text file that was created using the keyboard, by doing the following:

$ **more myfile**
This is an example of how to use the cat command to add plain text to a file
$

This is a simple example of the syntax of a single Raspberry Pi OS command.

The general syntax of the **more** command is as follows:

more [options] [file-list]

Purpose: Concatenate/display the files in **file-list** on the screen, one screen at a time

Output: Contents of the files in **file-list** displayed on the screen, one page at a time

Commonly used options/features:

+E/str   Start two lines before the first line containing **str**

-nN   Display N lines per screen/page

+N   Start displaying the contents of the file at line number N

The **more** command shows one screen full of a file at a time by default. If the file is several pages long, you can proceed to view subsequent pages by pressing the **<Space>** key on the keyboard, or by pressing the **Q** key on the keyboard to quit viewing the output.

In-Chapter Exercise

    6.   Use the **cat** command to produce another text file named **testfile**. Then join the contents of **myfile** and **testfile** into one text file, named **myfile3**, with the **cat** command.

0.2.3 Creating, Deleting, and Managing Files

To copy the contents of one file into another file, use the **cp** command. The general syntax of the **cp** command is as follows:

cp [options] file1 file2

Purpose: Copy **file1** to **file2**; if **file2** is a directory, make a copy of **file1** in this directory

Output: Copied files

Commonly used options/features:

-**i**   If destination exists, prompt before overwriting

-**p**   Preserve file access modes and modification times on copied files

-**r**   Recursively copy files and subdirectories

For example, to make an exact duplicate of the file named **myfile**, with the new name **myfile2**, type the following:

$ cp myfile myfile2
$

This usage of the **cp** command has two required command arguments. The first argument is the source file that already exists and which you want to copy. The second argument is the destination file or the name of the file that will be the copy. Be aware that many Raspberry Pi OS commands can take plain, ordinary, or regular files as arguments, or can take directory files as arguments. This can change the basic task accomplished by the command. It is also worth noting that not only can file names be arguments, but *pathnames* as well. A pathname is the route to any particular place in the file system structure of the operating system. This changes the site or location, in the path structure of the file system, of operation of the command.

In order to change the name of a file or directory, you can use the **mv** command. The general syntax of the **mv** command is as follows:

mv [options] file1 file2
mv [options] file-list directory

Purpose: First syntax: Rename **file1** to **file2**

Second syntax: Move all the files in file-list to directory

Output: Renamed or relocated files

Commonly used options/features:

-**f**   Force the move regardless of the file access modes of the destination file

-**i**   Prompt the user before overwriting the destination

In the following usage, the first argument to the **mv** command is the source file name, and the second argument is the destination name.

```
$ mv myfile2 renamed_file
$
```

It is important at this point to notice the use of spaces in Raspberry Pi OS commands. What if you obtain a file from a Windows system that has one or more spaces in one of the file names? How can you work with this file in Raspberry Pi OS? The answer is simple. Whenever you need to use that file name in a command as an argument, enclose the file name in double quotes ("). For example, you might obtain a file that you have "detached" from an e-mail message from someone on a Windows system, such as **latest revisions october.txt**.

   In order to work with this file on a Raspberry Pi OS—that is, to use the file name as an argument in a Raspberry Pi OS command—enclose the whole name in double quotes. The correct command to rename that file to something shorter would be:

```
$ mv "latest revisions october.txt" laterevs.txt
$
```

In order to delete a file, you can use the **rm** command. The general syntax of the **rm** command is as follows:

rm [options] file-list
Purpose: Removes files in **file-list** from the file structure (and disk)
Output: Deleted files
Commonly used options/features:
-f   Remove regardless of the file access modes of **file-list**
-i   Prompt the user before removing files in **file-list**
-r   Recursively remove the files in **file-list** if **file-list** is a directory; use with caution!
To delete the file **renamed_file** from the current working directory, type:

```
$ rm renamed_file
$
```

In-Chapter Exercise

   7.   Use the **rm** command to delete the files testfile and myfile3.

The most important command you will execute to do file maintenance is the **ls** command. The general syntax for the **ls** command is as follows:

ls [options] [pathname-list]

Purpose: Sends the names of the files and directories in the directory specified by **pathname-list** to the display screen

Output: Names of the files and directories in the directory specified by
pathname-list, or the names only if **pathname-list** contains file
names only

Commonly used options/features:

-F   Display a slash character (/) after directory names, an asterisk
(*) after binary executables, and an "at" character (@) after symbolic links

-a   Display names of all the files, including hidden files

-i   Display inode numbers

-l   Display long list that includes file access modes, link count,
owner, group, file size (in bytes), and modification time

The **ls** command will list the names of files or folders in your current working
directory or folder. In addition, as with the other commands we have used
so far, if you include a complete pathname specification for the **pathname-list**
argument to the command, then you can list the names of files and folders
along that pathname list. To see the names of the files now in your current
working directory, type the following:

$ **ls**
Desktop Documents Downloads Dropbox Music Pictures Public Templates
Videos
$

Please note that you will probably not get a listing of the same file names as
we showed above, because your system will have placed some files automatically in your home directory, as in the example we used, aside from the ones
we created together named **myfile** and **myfile2**. Also note that this file name
listing does not include the name **renamed_file**, because we deleted that file.

The next command you will execute is actually just an alternate or modified way of executing the **ls** command, one that includes the command name
and options. As shown in the Preface, a Raspberry Pi OS command has
options that can be typed on the command line along with the command to
change the behavior of the basic command. In the case of the **ls** command, the
options **l** and **a** produce a longer listing of all ordinary and system (dot) files,
as well as providing other attendant information about the files.

Don't forget to put the space character between the **s** and the - (dash).
Remember again that spaces delimit, or partition, the components of a
Raspberry Pi OS command as it is typed on the command line!
Now, type the following command:

$ **ls -la**

```
total 30408
drwxr-xr-x   25   bob bob     4096    May 5 07:53 .
drwxr-xr-x   5    root root   4096    Oct 20 2022..
drwxr-xr-x   5    bob bob     4096    Apr 23 16:32   .audacity-data
-rw-------   1    bob bob     36197   May 5 07:51    .bash_history
-rw-r--r--   1    bob bob     220     Apr 4 2022     .bash_logout
-rw-r--r--   1    bob bob     3523    Apr 4 2022     .bashrc
-rw-r--r--   1    bob bob     47329   Sep 19 2022    Blandemic.txt
drwxr-xr-x   2    bob bob     4096    Apr 4 2022     Bookshelf
drwxr-xr-x   15   bob bob     4096    Apr 17 14:05   .cache
drwx------   32   bob bob     4096    Apr 28         07:08          .config
drwx------   3    root root   4096    Jun 29 2022    .dbus
drwxr-xr-x   7    bob bob     4096    Apr 27 05:21   Desktop
Output truncated...
```

As you see in this screen display (which shows the listing of files in our home directory and will not be the same as the listing of files in your home directory), the information about each file in the current working directory is displayed in eight columns. The first column shows the type of file, where **d** stands for directory, **l** stands for symbolic link, and - stands for ordinary or regular file. Also in the first column, the access modes to that file for user, group, and others is shown as r, w, or x. In the second column, the number of links to that file is displayed. In the third column, the username of the owner of that file is displayed. In the fourth column, the name of the group for that file is displayed. In the fifth column, the number of bytes that the file occupies on disk is displayed. In the sixth column, the date that the file was last modified is displayed. In the seventh column, the time that the file was last modified is displayed. In the eighth and final column, the name of the file is displayed. This way of executing the command is a good way to list more complete information about the file. Examples of using the more complete information are (1) so that you can know the byte size and be able to fit the file on some portable storage medium, or (2) to display the access modes, so that you can alter the access modes to a particular file or directory.

In-Chapter Exercise

8. Use the **ls -la** command to list all of the filenames in your home directory on your Raspberry Pi system. How does the listing you obtain compare with the listing shown above? Remember that our listing was done on a Raspberry Pi system.

You can also get a file listing for a single file in the current working directory by using another variation of the ls command, as follows:

```
$ ls -la myfile
-rw-r--r-- 1 bob bob 797 Jan 16 10:00 myfile
$
```

This variation shows you a long listing with attendant information for the specific file named **myfile**. A breakdown of what you typed on the command line is (1) **ls**, the command name; (2) **-la**, the options; and (3) **myfile**, the command argument.

What if you make a mistake in your typing, and misspell a command name or one of the other parts of a command? Type the following on the command line:

```
$ lx -la myfile
lx: not found
$
```

The lx: not found reply from Raspberry Pi OS is an error message. There is no **lx** command in the Raspberry Pi OS, so an error message is displayed. If you had typed an option that did not exist, you would also get an error message. If you supplied a file name that was not in the current working directory, you would get an error message, too. This makes an important point about the execution of Raspberry Pi OS commands. If no error message is displayed, then the command executed correctly and the results might or might not appear on screen, depending on what the command actually does. If you get an error message displayed, you must correct the error before Raspberry Pi OS will execute the command as you type it.

Note
Typographic mistakes in commands account for a large percentage of the errors that beginners make!

0.2.4 Creating, Deleting, and Managing Directories

Another critical aspect of file maintenance is the set of procedures and the related Raspberry Pi OS commands you use to create, delete, and organize directories in your Raspberry Pi OS account on a computer. When moving through the file system, you are either ascending or descending to reach the directory you want to use. The directory directly above the current working directory is referred to as the *parent* of the current working directory. The directory or directories immediately under the current working directory are referred to as the *children* of the current working directory. The most common mistake for beginners is misplacing files. They cannot find the file names listed with the **ls** command because they have placed or created the files in a directory either above or below the current working directory in the file structure. When you create a file, if you have also created a logically organized set of directories beneath your own home directory, you will know where to store the file. In the following set of commands, we create a directory beneath the home directory and use that new directory to store a file.

To create a new directory beneath the current working directory, you use the **mkdir** command. The general syntax for the **mkdir** command is as follows:

mkdir [options] dirnames
Purpose: Creates directory or directories specified in **dirnames**
Output: New directory or directories
Commonly used options/features:
-m MODE   Create a directory with given access modes
-p   Create parent directories that don't exist in the pathnames
           specified in **dirnames**

To create a child, or subdirectory, named **first** under the current working directory, type the following:

```
$ mkdir first
$
```

This command has now created a new subdirectory named **first** under, or as a child of, the current working directory. Refer back to Figure 0.1 for a graphical description of the directory location of this new subdirectory.

In order to change the current working directory to this new subdirectory, you use the **cd** command. The general syntax for the **cd** command is as follows:

cd [directory]
Purpose: Change the current working directory to **directory** or return to the
          home directory when **directory** is omitted
Output: New current working directory

To change the current working directory to **first** by descending down the path structure to the specified directory named **first**, type the following:

```
$ cd first
$
```

You can always verify what the current working directory is by using the **pwd** command. The general syntax of the **pwd** command is as follows:

pwd
Purpose: Displays the current working directory on screen
Output: Pathname of current working directory

You can verify that **first** is now the current working directory by typing the following:

```
$ pwd
/home/bob/first
$
```

The output from the Raspberry Pi OS on the command line shows the pathname to the current working directory or folder. As previously stated, this path is a textual route through the complete file structure of the computer that Raspberry Pi OS is running on, ending in the current working directory. In this example of the output, the path starts at /, the root of the file system. Then it descends to the directory **home**, a major branch of the file system on the computer running Raspberry Pi OS. Then it descends to the directory **bob**, another branch, which is the home directory name for the user. Finally, it descends to the branch named **first**, the current working directory.

On some systems, depending on the default settings, another way of determining what the current working directory is can be done by simply looking at the command line prompt. This prompt may be prefaced with the complete path to the current working directory, ending in the current working directory.

You can ascend back up to the home directory, or the parent of the subdirectory **first**, by typing the following:

```
$ cd
$
```

An alternate way of doing this is to type the following, where the tilde character (~) resolves to, or is a substitute for, the specification of the complete path to the home directory:

```
$ cd ~
$
```

To verify that you have now ascended up to the home directory, type the following:

```
$ pwd
/home/bob
$
```

You can also ascend to a directory above your home directory, sometimes called the parent of your current working directory, by typing the following:

```
$ cd ..
$
```

In this command, the two periods (**..**), represent the parent, or branch above the current working directory. Don't forget to type a space character between the **d** and the first period. To verify that you have ascended to the parent of your home directory, type the following:

```
$ pwd
/home
$
```

To descend to your home directory, type the following:

```
$ cd
$
```

To verify that there are two files in the home directory that begins with the letters my, type the following command:

```
$ ls my*
myfile myfile2
$
```

The asterisk following the y on the command line is known as a *metacharacter*, or a character that represents a pattern; in this case, the pattern is any set of characters. When Raspberry Pi OS interprets the command after you press the **<Enter>** key on the keyboard, it searches for all files in the current working directory that begin with the letters my and end in anything else.

In-Chapter Exercise

9. Use the **cd** command to ascend to the root (/) of your Raspberry Pi file system, and then use it to descend down each sub-directory from the root recursively to a depth of two sub-directories, sketching a diagram of the component files found on your system. Make the named entries in the diagram as complete as possible, listing as many files as you think necessary. Retain this diagram as a useful map of your particular Raspberry Pi distribution's file system.

Another aspect of organizing your directories is movement of files between directories, or changing the location of files in your directories. For example, you now have the file **myfile2** in your home directory, but you would like to move it into the subdirectory named **first**. See Figure 0.1 for a graphic description to change the organization of your files at this point. To accomplish this, you can use the second syntax method illustrated for the **mv file-list directory** command to move the file **myfile2** down into the subdirectory named **first**. To achieve this, type the following:

```
$ mv myfile2 first
$
```

To verify that **myfile2** is indeed in the subdirectory named first, type the following:

```
$ cd first
$ ls
myfile2
$
```

You will now ascend to the home directory, and attempt to remove or delete a file with the **rm** command.

Caution: you should be very careful when using this command, because once a file has been deleted, the only way to recover it is from archival backups that you or the system administrator have made of the file system.

```
$ cd
$ rm myfile2
rm: myfile2: No such file or directory
$
```

You get the error message because in the home directory, the file named **myfile2** does not exist. It was moved down into the subdirectory named first.

Directory organization also includes the ability to delete empty or non-empty directories. The command that accomplishes the removal of empty directories is **rmdir**. The general syntax of the **rmdir** command is as follows:

rmdir [options] dirnames
Purpose: Removes the empty directories specified in **dirnames**
Output: Removes directories
Commonly used options/features:
-p   Remove empty parent directories as well
-r   Recursively delete files and subdirectories beneath the current directory

To delete an entire directory below the current working directory, type the following:

```
$ rmdir first
rmdir: first: Directory not empty
$
```

Since the file **myfile2** is still in the subdirectory named **first**, **first** is not an empty directory, and you get the error message that the **rmdir** command will not delete the directory. If the directory was empty, **rmdir** would have accomplished the deletion. One way to delete a nonempty directory is by using the **rm** command with the -**r** option. The -**r** option recursively descends down into the subdirectory and deletes any files in it before actually deleting the directory itself. Be cautious with this command, since you may inadvertently delete directories and files with it. To see how this command deletes a nonempty directory, type the following:

```
$ rm -r first
$
```

The directory **first** and the file **myfile2** are now removed from the file structure.

0.2.5 Obtaining Help with the man Command

A very convenient utility available on Raspberry Pi systems is the online help feature, achieved via the use of the **man** command. The general syntax of the **man** command is as follows:

man [options][-s section] command-list
man -k keyword-list
Purpose: First syntax: Display Raspberry Pi OS Reference Manual pages for
             commands in **command-list** one screen at a time
             Second syntax: Display summaries of commands related to
             keywords in **keyword-list**
Output: Manual pages one screen at a time
Commonly used options/features:
-**k**   **keyword-list** Search for summaries of keywords in **keyword-list**
             in a database and display them
-**s sec-num**   Search section number **sec-num** for manual pages
             and display them

To get help by using the **man** command, on usage and options of the **ls** command, for example, type the following:

$ man ls

```
LS(1)                          User Commands                          LS(1)

NAME
       ls - list directory contents
```

```
SYNOPSIS
       ls [OPTION]... [FILE]...

DESCRIPTION
       List information about the FILEs (the current
       directory by default).
       Sort entries alphabetically if none of -cftuvSUX
       nor -sort is specified.

       Mandatory arguments to long options are manda-
       tory for short options too.

       -a, --all
              do not ignore entries starting with .

       -A, --almost-all
              do not list implied . and ..

       --author
Manual page ls(1) line 1 (press h for help or q to quit)
```

This output from Raspberry Pi OS is a Raspberry Pi OS *manual page,* or *manpage,* which gives a synopsis of the command usage showing the options, and a brief description that helps you understand how the command should be used. Typing **q** after one page has been displayed, as seen in the example, returns you to the command line prompt. Pressing the space key on the keyboard would have shown you more of the content of the manual pages, one screen at a time, related to the **ls** command.

To get help in using all the Raspberry Pi OS commands and their options, use the **man man** command to go to the Raspberry Pi OS reference manual pages.

The pages themselves are organized into eight sections, depending on the topic described, and the topics that are applicable to the particular system. Table 0.1 lists the sections of the manual and what they contain. Most users find the pages they need in Section 2.2. Software developers mostly use library and system calls and thus find the pages they need in Sections 2.3 and 2.3. Users who work on document preparation get the most help from Section 2.7. Administrators mostly need to refer to pages in Sections 2.2, 2.5, 2.6, and 2.9.

The manual pages comprise multi-page, specially formatted, descriptive documentation for every command, system call, and library call in Raspberry Pi OS. This format consists of eight general parts: name, synopsis, description, list of files, related information, errors, warnings, and known bugs. You can use the **man** command to view the manual page for a command. Because

TABLE 0.1

Sections of the Raspberry Pi OS Manual

Section	What It Describes
1	User commands
2	System calls
3	Language library calls (C, FORTRAN, etc.)
4	Devices and network interfaces
5	File formats
6	Games and demonstrations
7	Environments, tables, and macros for troff
8	System maintenance-related commands

of the name of this command, the manual pages are normally referred to as Raspberry Pi OS man pages. When you display a manual page on the screen, the top-left corner of the page has the command name with the section it belongs to in parentheses, as with LS(1), seen at the top of the output manual page.

The command used to display the manual page for the **passwd** command is:

$ **man passwd**

The manual page for the **passwd** command now appears on the screen, but we do not show its output. Because they are multi-page text documents, the manual pages for each topic take up more than one screen of text to display their entire contents. To see one screen of the manual page at a time, press the space bar on the keyboard. To quit viewing the manual page, press the **Q** key on the keyboard.

Now type this command:

$ **man pwd**

If more than one section of the man pages has information on the same word and you are interested in the man page for a particular section, you can use the **-S** option. The following command line therefore displays the man page for the read system call, and not the man page for the shell command read.

$ **man -S2 read**

The command **man -S3 fopen fread strcmp** sequentially displays man pages for three C library calls: **fopen, fread,** and **strcmp.**

To exit from the display of these system calls, type **<Ctrl-C>**.

Using the **man** command and typing the command with the **-k** option, allows specifying a keyword that limits the search. It is equivalent to using the **apropos** command. The search then yields useful man page headers from all the man pages on the system that contain just the keyword reference. For example, the following command yields the on-screen output on our Raspberry Pi system:

$ **man -k passwd**

chgpasswd (8)	- update group passwords in batch mode
chpasswd (8)	- update passwords in batch mode
exim4_passwd (5)	- Files in use by the Debian exim4 packages
exim4_passwd_client (5)	- Files in use by the Debian exim4 packages
fgetpwent_r (3)	- get passwd file entry reentrantly
getpwent_r (3)	- get passwd file entry reentrantly
gpasswd (1)	- administer /etc/group and /etc/gshadow
openssl-passwd (1ssl)	compute password hashes
pam_localuser (8)	- require users to be listed in /etc/passwd
passwd (1)	- change user password
passwd (1ssl)	- compute password hashes
passwd (5)	- the password file
passwd2des (3)	- RFS password encryption
update-passwd (8)	- safely update /etc/passwd, /etc/shadow and /etc/group
vncpasswd (1)	- VNC Server password utility

Output truncated...

0.2.6 Other Methods of Obtaining Help

To get a short description of what any particular Raspberry Pi OS command does, you can use the **whatis** command. This is similar to the command **man -f**. The general syntax of the **whatis** command is as follows:

whatis keywords

Purpose: Search the whatis database for abbreviated descriptions of each keyword

Output: Prints a one-line description of each keyword to the screen

The following is an illustration of how to use **whatis-**
The output of the two commands are truncated.

$ whatis man
man (7)   - macros to format man pages
man (1)   - an interface to the on-line
              reference manuals
$

You can also obtain short descriptions of more than one command by entering multiple arguments to the **whatis** command on the same command line, with spaces between each argument. The following is an illustration of this method:

$ whatis login set setenv
login (1)   - begin session on the system
login (3)   - write utmp and wtmp entries
setenv (3)   - change or add an environment variable
set: nothing appropriate.
$

The following in-chapter exercises ask you to use the **man** and **whatis** commands to find information about the **passwd** command. After completing the exercises, you can use what you have learned to change your login password on the Raspberry Pi OS that you use.

In-Chapter Exercises

10. Use the **man** command with the **-k** option to display abbreviated help on the **passwd** command. Doing so will give you a screen display similar to that obtained with the **whatis** command, but it will show all apropos command names that contain the characters passwd.

11. Use the **whatis** command to get a brief description of the **passwd** command shown above, and then note the difference between the commands **whatis passwd** and **man -k passwd**.

0.3 Utility Commands

There are several important commands that allow the beginner to be more productive when using a Raspberry Pi OS. A sampling of these kinds of utility commands is given in the following sections, and is organized as system setups, general utilities, and communications commands.

0.3.1 Examining System Setups

The **whereis** command allows you to search along certain prescribed paths to locate utility programs and commands, such as shell programs. The general syntax of the **whereis** command is as follows:

whereis [options] filename

Purpose: Locate the binary, source, and man page files for a command

Output: The supplied names are first stripped of leading pathname components and extensions, then pathnames are displayed on screen

Commonly used options/features:

-b   Search only for binaries

-s   Search only for source code

For example, if you type the command **whereis bash** on the command line, you will see a list of the paths to the Bash shell program files themselves, as follows:

$ whereis bash
bash: /bin/bash /etc/bash.bashrc /usr/share/man/man1/bash.1.gz

Note that the paths to a "built-in", or internal, command cannot be found with the **whereis** command.

When you first log on, it is useful to be able to view a display of information about your **userid**, the computer or system you have logged on to, and the operating system on that computer. These tasks can be accomplished with the **whoami** command, which displays your **userid** on the screen. The general syntax of the **whoami** command is as follows:

whoami

Purpose: Displays the effective user id

Output: Displays your effective user id as a name on standard

The following shows how our system responded to this command when we typed it on the command line.

$ whoami
bob
$

To find out the IP address of the Raspberry Pi you are working on, you can use the **ip** command. The general syntax of the **ip** command is as follows:

ip [OPTIONS] OBJECT {COMMAND | help}

Purpose: Show/manipulate routing, network devices, interfaces, and tunnels

Output: Information about your LAN

To find out the IP address of the computer you are working on, type the following command in a terminal, or console window:

$ **ip addr**
1: lo: <LOOPBACK,UP,LOWER_UP> mtu 65536 qdisc noqueue state UNKNOWN group default qlen 1000
    link/loopback 00:00:00:00:00:00 brd 00:00:00:00:00:00
    inet 127.0.0.1/8 scope host lo
     valid_lft forever preferred_lft forever
    inet6::1/128 scope host
     valid_lft forever preferred_lft forever
2: eth0: <BROADCAST,MULTICAST,UP,LOWER_UP> mtu 1500 qdisc mq state UP group default qlen 1000
   link/ether dc:a6:32:ee:c6:6b brd ff:ff:ff:ff:ff:ff
   inet 192.168.1.2/24 brd 192.168.1.255 scope global dynamic noprefixroute eth0
   valid_lft 65558sec preferred_lft 54758sec
   inet6 fe80::78d9:c72e:75e2:82c/64 scope link
   valid_lft forever preferred_lft forever
3: wlan0: <BROADCAST,MULTICAST> mtu 1500 qdisc noop state DOWN group default qlen 1000
link/ether dc:a6:32:ee:c6:6c brd ff:ff:ff:ff:ff:ff
$

In the above output, the IP address 192.168.1.2 is the address on the LAN of this computer.

The following In-Chapter Exercises give you the chance to use **whereis**, **whoami**, and two other important utility commands, **who** and **hostname**, to obtain important information about your system.

In-Chapter Exercises

12. Use the **whereis** command to locate binary files for the Korn shell, the Bourne shell, the Bourne Again shell, the C shell, and the Z shell. Are any of these shell programs not available on your system?
13. Use the **whoami** command to find your username on the system that you're using. Then use the **who** command to see how your username

is listed, along with other users of the same system. What is the on-screen format of each user's listing that you obtained with the **who** command? Try to identify the information in each field on the same line as your username.

14. Use the **hostname -I** command to find out the IP address of host computer you are logged on to, on your LAN. Compares this to the output of the **ip addr** command on that same system.

0.4 Printing Commands

A very useful and common task performed by every user of a computer system is the printing of text files at a printer. This is accomplished using the configured printer(s) on the local, or a remote, system. Printers are controlled and managed with the Common UNIX Printing System (CUPS). We show this utility in detail in Chapter 1.

The common commands that perform printing on a Raspberry Pi OS are **lpr** and **lp**. The general syntax of the **lpr** command is as follows:

lpr [options] filename
Purpose: Send files to the printer
Output: Files sent to the printer queue as print jobs
Commonly used options/features:
-P printer   Send output to the named printer
-# copies   Produce the number of copies indicated for each named file

The following **lpr** command accomplishes the printing of the file named **order.pdf** at the printer designated on our system as **spr**. Remember that no space is necessary between the option (in this case **-P**) and the option argument (in this case **spr**).

```
$ lpr -Pspr order.pdf
$
```

The following **lpr** command accomplishes the printing of the file named **memo1** at the default printer.

```
$ lpr memo1
$
```

The following multiple command combines the **man** command and the **lpr** command, and ties them together with the Raspberry Pi OS pipe (|)

redirection character, to print the man pages describing the **ls** command at the printer named **hp1200**.

```
$ man ls | lpr -Php1200
$
```

The following shows how to perform printing tasks using the **lp** command. The general syntax of the **lp** command is as follows:

lp [options][option arguments] file(s)

Purpose: Submit files for printing on a designated system printer, or alter pending print jobs

Output: rinted files or altered print queue

Commonly used options/features:

-d destination   Print to the specified destination

-n copies   Sets the number of copies to print

In the first command, the file to be printed is named **file1**. In the second command, the files to be printed are named **sample** and **phones**. Note that the **-d** option is used to specify which printer to use. The option to specify the number of copies is **-n** for the **lp** command.

```
$ lp -d spr file1
request id is spr-983 (1 file(s))
$ lp -d spr -n 3 sample phones
request id is spr-984 (2 file(s))
$
```

0.5 Chapter Summary

In this introductory chapter, we covered essential Raspberry Pi OS commands that allow a system administrator to do file maintenance, and perform other useful operations. This is a mandatory set of essentials that even an ordinary, non-administrative user would need to know to work efficiently in a character, or text-based interface to the operating system. Text-based commands are the predominant means that a system administrator uses to maintain the integrity of the system. We gave examples and showed the basic format of the following commands and primitives:

TABLE 0.2

Useful Commands for the Beginner

Command	What It Does
<Ctrl+D>	Terminates a process or command
alias	Allows you to create pseudonyms for commands
biff	Notifies you of new e-mail
cal	Displays a calendar on screen
cat	Allows joining of files
cd	Allows you to change the current working directory
cp	Allows you to copy files
exit	Ends a shell that you have started
hostname	Displays the name of the host computer that you are logged on to
ip	Displays IP information of the current host
login	Allows you to log on to the computer with a valid username/password pair
lpr or lp	Allows printing of text files
ls	Allows you to display names of files and directories in the current working directory
man	Allows you to view a manual page for a command or topic
mesg	Allows or disallows writing messages to the screen
mkdir	Allows you to create a new directory
more	Allows viewing of the contents of a file one screen at a time
mv	Allows you to move the path location of, or rename, files
passwd	Allows you to change your password on the computer
pg	Solaris command that displays one screen of a file at a time
pwd	Allows you to see the name of the current working directory
rm	Allows you to delete a file from the file structure
rmdir	Allows deletion of directories
talk	Allows you to send real-time messages to other users
telnet	Allows you to log on to a computer on a network or the Internet
unalias	Allows you to undefine pseudonyms for commands
uname	Displays information about the operating system running the computer
whatis	Allows you to view a brief description of a command
whereis	Displays the path(s) to commands and utilities in certain key Directories
who	Allows you to find out login names of users currently on the system
whoami	Displays your username
write	Allows real-time messaging between users on the system

cat cd cp exit hostname -I ip login lp lpr ls man mesg mkdir more mv passwd PATH pwd rm rmdir telnet unalias uname whatis whereis who whoami

Table 0.2 summarizes a basic set of useful commands necessary for the beginner.

1

Raspberry Pi OS System Administration Fundamentals

1.0 Objectives

1. Do various kinds of installation of a 64-bit Raspberry Pi OS, onto Raspberry Pi hardware, and do a preliminary configuration of those systems and the OS.
2. Illustrate booting strategies, and how to gracefully bring the system down.
3. Detail the basics of using systemd to manage system services.
4. Add additional users and groups to the system, and show how to design and maintain user accounts.
5. Add persistent media to the system, in particular externally mounted, USB3 types. We also established a framework for connecting and maintaining the file system on that media, which classifies the file system as either existing on a physical medium (physically connected to the computer), a virtual medium (NFSv4, iSCSI), or as a specialized pseudo-file system that was not on a medium at all (cgroups, proc).
6. Provide strategies using traditional and generic commands, to backup and archive the system files and user files.
7. Update and maintain the operating system, and add/upgrade/remove user application package repository software to both increase functionality and upgrade existing packages.
8. Monitor the performance of the system, and tune it for optimal performance characteristics.
9. Provide strategies for system security to harden the individual Internet-connected Raspberry Pi system.
10. Provide network connectivity strategies, both on a LAN and the Internet.
11. Give an overview of system virtualization, using LXD/LXC.

DOI: 10.1201/b23421-2

12. To cover the following commands and primitives:

ACL addgroup adduser APT apt apt-get BIOS capabilities cgroups chgrp chmod chown cipher text clone Clonezilla cpio CUI DAC dd delgroup deluser df Docker du ext4 fail2ban fdisk Filezilla find firewalld free GID git Github Gparted GRUB2 GUI gunzip gzip halt IDS ifdown ifup inxi ip IPS iSCSI journalctl LIO ls lsblk LVM LXC LXD MAC MBR mdadm mirror mkfs newusers NFSv4 nice NIDS openssh passwd passwd persistent cgroup pgrep plain text POSIX1.e ACL ps RAID RBAC renice repositories rsync SAN shutdown SSD ssh su sudo system.slice systemctl systemd systemd-cgls systemd-run tar top transient cgroup UEFI ufw UID umount untar update upgrade usermod vdev Webmin ZFS

1.1 Introduction

This chapter is central to a major component of Raspberry Pi OS use: system administration.

In order to install, maintain, and effectively use a Raspberry Pi system composed of both hardware and software components, it is often necessary to perform the set of common tasks shown in the following sections. In this chapter, we target an individual, novice user, who performs these tasks exclusively for her own use, on her own personal desktop/laptop computer. The common tasks may also be performed by an appointed administrator, for a more complex system used by many people. It is possible to divide these common tasks into those performed by an administrator, and those performed by a single user, or a group of ordinary, autonomous users.

Even though we show the basics of those common tasks, it is possible to extrapolate from what is presented to the wider context of much larger-scaled computer systems, run by a system administrator.

Additionally, at the book website, we provide other materials that supplement our presentation of these tasks here in the printed book.

In order to do many of the system administration tasks in this chapter, it is absolutely necessary to either have superuser or root user privileges on the system. That means you need to know the superuser password, which you (or a designated system administrator) can establish at installation of your Raspberry Pi system.

Both the **su** and **sudo** commands are used to execute programs and other commands with root permissions. The root user has maximum permissions, and can do anything to the system that a system administrator needs to. Normal users execute programs and commands with reduced permissions.

To execute something that requires maximum permissions, you must first execute the **su** or **sudo** commands. Using the **su** command makes you the super user—or root user—when you execute it with no additional options.

You are prompted to enter the root account's password. Also, the **su** command allows you to switch to any user account. If you execute the command **su**, you'll be prompted to enter the password, and the command shell current working directory will be your home directory. Once you're done running commands in the root shell, you should type **exit** to leave the root shell and go back to limited-privileges mode.

Note
The root shell is *not* the login shell.

In contrast, **sudo** runs a single command with root privileges. When you execute

$ **sudo command**

the system prompts you for your current user account's password before running **command**, whatever it happens to be, as the root user. In order to use the **sudo** command, you must be part of the sudoers group. More information on the **sudo** command, and its details, can be found in Volume 1, Section 1.13.

In our "learning-by-doing" approach, we have selected a common set of system administration tasks aimed specifically at an individual novice Raspberry Pi OS user, as stated above in Section 1.0.

Besides these common tasks we have selected to present, there are numerous extensions, and also many additional tasks that Linux system administration encompasses.

You must realize that we have listed all of the tasks above based upon the use cases we target.

To extend some of the system administration topics covered in this book so that they are reflective of modern Linux systems, and to anticipate other use cases you might have, we provide some additional materials and references in this volume, as follows:

If you want to install another Linux OS, for example, Ubuntu, in a virtual environment (such as in a container), so that it runs simultaneously with the Raspberry Pi OS on your computer's hardware, we give specific instructions on how to do this in Volume 3, "Raspberry Pi OS Text Editors, git, and Virtualization with LXC/LXD". There we give the specifics of efficient ways of installing a "guest" operating systems using LXC/LXD container virtualization.

In Section 1.14.1.2, we show details of the use of Control Groups (cgroups) in systemd. cgroup techniques, executed on the command line, allow an administrator to more explicitly set and view the limits of the three major functions performed by the modern Linux kernel (or the Linux super-kernel, systemd): concurrency, virtualization, and persistence.

In Volume 1, Sections 1.14 and 1.15, "Raspberry Pi OS POSIX.1e Access Control Lists (ACL's)", and "Raspberry Pi OS NFS Server and Client Install, and Setting NFSv4 ACLs on the Client", we fully illustrate the use of POSIX.1e and Network File System, version 4 (NFSv4) Access Control Lists (ACLs). We show the application of these facilities, which further extend the Discretionary Access Control (DAC) methods of the traditional Linux permissions model. We apply ACLs to file system objects mounted as NFSv4 "shared" network drives. In addition, we provide an extended example of using ACLs on NFSv4 network drives.

1.1.1 System Administration the Easy Way

How can you do the majority of what is shown in this chapter in an easy way? Use Webmin.

Webmin is a modern Linux web browser-based, GUI system administration tool that allows you to do many of the system administration tasks shown in this chapter in a very intuitive, fast, and simple way. We strongly encourage you to first download and install Webmin on your Linux system, following the instructions we give in Volume 1, Section 1.2. Then you can explore the Webmin facilities before you begin the rest of this chapter, and even go back to Webmin to find out how something which we show in the rest of this chapter can be done (or can't be done!) in Webmin.

1.2 Installation of the Raspberry Pi OS onto Various Media, and Preliminary System Configuration

This section has four paths through it, as follows:

Section 1.2.1—Shows how to download and install a 64-bit version of the Raspberry Pi OS onto a microSD card, so that you can insert that card into Raspberry Pi hardware, and operate that hardware with it.

Section 1.2.2—Shows how to create a 32-bit version of the Raspberry Pi OS desktop to install on an older PC, so that you can test drive the operating system to get a good feel for how it works.

Section 1.2.3—Shows how to run the Raspberry Pi OS, created on a microSD card, from an externally mounted USB SSD or M2 PCIe medium, instead of from the microSD card.

Section 1.2.4—Shows how to download and install a 64-bit version of Ubuntu 23.04 onto a microSD card mounted on Raspberry Pi hardware.

The above sections assume that you will be using a release of the software system that is designed for either the 64-bit ARM-architecture Raspberry Pi hardware, or a 32-bit X-86 architecture machine, but be aware that some of the functionality we show in this chapter is limited to a 64-bit architecture machine. Also be aware that some of the systems administration tasks illustrated in this book are, or may, be done in a different way in earlier (or later) releases of the software! And, this section assumes that you will running the Raspberry Pi OS from persistent media (either a microSD card mounted in the provided slot on the Raspberry Pi hardware, from a USB3 thumb drive, SATA SSD, or M.2 PCIe module drive, or from the hard drive on an older PC,) rather than from some other source.

If you want to install another Linux operating system in a virtual environment created on the Raspberry Pi, so that it runs simultaneously with the Raspberry Pi OS on your Raspberry Pi computer's hardware, we give specific instructions on how to do this in Volume 3, entitled "Raspberry Pi OS Text Editors, git, and Virtualization with LXC/LXD" . There we give the specifics of installing Ubuntu Linux as a "guest" operating systems, using LXC/LXD.

1.2.1 Imager Download and Install of 64-Bit Version of Raspberry Pi OS onto a microSD Card

This section is probably the easiest, and most-often used means of getting the Raspberry Pi OS onto your hardware. At the time this book was written, specific instructions for doing this were found at the following website:

www.raspberrypi.com/documentation/computers/getting-started.html

They are summarized here as follows:

1) From another Linux computer, perhaps a Raspberry Pi that's already working with an installed operating system on it, type the following at the command prompt:

   $ **sudo apt install rpi-imager**

2) Connect an SD card reader to that computer with an adequately sized microSD card in it.

3) Run the Raspberry Pi Imager, and choose the desired operating system from a presented list.

4) Choose the microSD card from step 2).

5) At this point, while running the Imager, choose "Advanced Options", and enable things like SSH, and hostname.

6) When finished with the Imager, quit it, take out the microSD card, and place it into the Raspberry Pi hardware you want the operating system to run on. Boot into that microSD card, and follow the instructions.

1.2.2 Installing the Raspberry Pi Desktop OS on an Older X86 Architecture PC

Prerequisites:

1. A USB drive (8 GB or more)
2. An X86 architecture processor computer to create the USB drive installer on.
3. A computer to install Raspberry Pi Desktop on.

Note

You can use *one* computer to do both. You have the option to create the installer using one computer, and to then install the Raspberry Pi Desktop on that same computer.

4. The computer you're going to install the Raspberry Pi Desktop OS onto must be able to boot from a USB thumb drive! That means that you may have to edit the boot sequence on that computer, and possibly change the boot device order.

This section shows how to download and install a 32-bit version of the Raspberry Pi OS onto an older computer with an X86 architecture processor, so that you can use that PC to run the Raspberry Pi OS. At the time this book was written, specific instructions for doing this were found at the website listed in Step 1):

1) Download the Raspberry Pi Desktop

   On a PC, or Linux machine, go to

   www.raspberrypi.org/downloads/raspberry-pi-desktop/

   and download, and save the .iso of the specific version of the software you want to install.

   For our purposes in this book, we downloaded the 32-bit Desktop version of the Raspberry Pi OS.

2) Download and Install Etcher

   From the following website,

   https://etcher.io/

   download and install the Etcher program on your X86 architecture machine. This will allow you to take the .iso file you obtained in step 1) and install it on a USB thumb drive.

3) Use Etcher to burn the .iso image onto the USB thumb drive.

4) Boot your X86 architecture computer from the USB thumb drive.

5) Install the 32-bit Raspberry Pi OS Desktop onto the X86 architecture computer.

After booting from your USB drive installer, the Debian installation menu will appear.

Select Graphical install from the Debian GNU/Linux menu.

Note

If you don't select Graphical install quickly enough, the installer will start using the default option. If this happens, turn off the computer, restart it, and boot from the USB drive again.

6) Follow the multiple steps of the Debian installation procedure, and then when it's done, remove the thumb drive from the X86 architecture computer, and reboot into the Raspberry Pi Desktop from the boot medium you installed it on.

You now have an X86 architecture machine with the Raspberry Pi OS Desktop on it!

1.2.3 How to Boot from and Run a Raspberry Pi OS from a USB3-Mounted SSD

Objectives: To detail how to boot from and run your Raspberry Pi OS from a USB3-mounted SSD.

Prerequisites:

Having your storage model conform to our recommendation.

Note

We do the operations in this Example on the following Raspberry Pi system:

System: Host: raspberrypi Kernel: 6.1.21-v8+ aarch64 bits: 64 compiler: gcc v: 10.2.1 Console: tty 0

Distro: Debian GNU/Linux 11 (bullseye)

Machine: Type: ARM Device System: Raspberry Pi 400 Rev 1.0 details: BCM2835

rev: c03130

serial: 10000000fdd89bf2

Background:

As recommended in our storage model in the next section, the Raspberry Pi OS is traditionally booted from, and run, from a microSD card mounted on the hardware. With the operating system kernel at release 6.1.21-v8, as shown in the above system description, it is possible, and highly advantageous, to boot and run the system from a USB3-mounted SSD, or other external device. There are several advantages to doing this, chiefly among them a performance speed increase, and a storage capacity increase as well.

Requirements: Do the steps below, in the order shown, to complete the requirements for this example.

1. Update your package manager on your system, using the following commands:

   $ **sudo apt update**
   Output truncated...
   $ **sudo apt upgrade**
   Output truncated...

2. Insert an SSD, or other suitable device that has a SATA-to-USB3 cable connection capability, into a USB3 port on your Raspberry Pi hardware. On our Raspberry Pi 400, the USB3 ports had a blue-colored tab inside them, visible from the outside. We connected a 128 GB Silicon Power SSD, which was inside an Orico SATA-to-USB tool less enclosure. We previously had formatted the SSD in Gparted, with a FAT32 partition on it.

3. The SSD mounted automatically. We then used the Raspberry Pi Accesories Menu > SD Card Copier to copy the microSD Raspberry Pi OS to the USB3-mounted SSD.

Note

In the SD Card Copier, make sure that you copy the system from the microSD card to the SSD!

4. When the copying is done, shut down the system, and remove the microSD card from its slot in the hardware.

5. Disconnect the power, and then reconnect it to reboot the system.

6. The Raspberry Pi OS now boots from, and runs on the USB3-mounted SSD. It is an exact clone of what was on the microSD card as you did the above steps.

Conclusion: At the time of the writing of this book, the Raspberry Pi OS is able to boot from and run from an external USB3 SSD. To gauge the performance speed advantages of using an SSD, we encourage you to use the Accessories

Menu> Raspberry Pi Diagnostics program to gauge the relative performance speed advantages of an SSD over a microSD card. The log readings of SSD versus microSD card provide that information.

1.2.4 How to Install Ubuntu Desktop onto Raspberry Pi Hardware

In preparation for showing exterior media additions that can use the Zettabyte File System (ZFS), we provide you with a technique in this section that allows you to install another operating system, 64-bit Ubuntu 23.04 Desktop, onto either a Raspberry Pi 4B or Pi 400 hardware. We do this using a microSD card to boot and run the system from.

Although this presentation might seem antithetical to the theme of the volumes of this book (after all, they are about the Raspberry Pi OS!), there is great value in learning about ZFS, and its use as a modern file system for Linux, and the Raspberry Pi OS itself. Currently, with the upstream operating system (Debian Bullseye), and the 6.X Linux kernel, the downstream Raspberry Pi OS does *not easily* support the installation of ZFS, especially for beginners. But that will more than likely change, particularly when the Raspberry Pi 5 is released, and the Raspberry Pi OS version for it stabilizes.
Background:

Probably the most popular, and well supported downstream release of the Debian family of Linux, is Ubuntu. And Canonical, the stewards of that system, have made a concerted effort to not only have the latest release of their software available for Raspberry Pi hardware, but also have very strongly supported ZFS on their releases. In what follows, we show a step-by-step installation of 64-bit Ubuntu 23.04 Desktop onto a Raspberry Pi 4B. These steps work just as well for the Pi 400.
Prerequisites:

a. A microSD card with a minimum size of 9 GB. We used a 32 GB microSD card.

b. A Raspberry Pi with a microSD USB-connected card reader and cable, or attached drive bay.

c. A Raspberry Pi 4B or Pi 400 that recognizes the mounted microSD card from the above steps!

d. An HDMI Monitor connected to the Raspberry Pi, and a USB keyboard.

Requirements: Do the steps below, in the order shown, to complete the requirements for this example.

1. At the command line, type the following command:

    $ **sudo snap install rpi-imager**

On our Raspberry Pi, the latest version of the Imager was already installed!

2. Launch the Imager, and in the Raspberry Pi Imager window, click on the box that says CHOOSE OS.

3. Scroll down in the menu presented, and click on "Other general-purpose OS".

4. The menu presented has a variety of choices available. Scroll down to "Ubuntu Desktop 23.04 (Rpi 4/400)", and click on it.

5. In the Raspberry Pi Imager window, click on the Choose Storage box. Choose the microSD card you have mounted on your system, and then click WRITE. It will take a few minutes for the image to be written to the microSD card.

6. Shutdown your Raspberry Pi, and insert the microSD card that you've written Ubuntu onto into the Raspberry Pi microSD card slot.

7. Restart the Raspberry Pi, and follow the onscreen instructions to prepare your Ubuntu system on the Raspberry Pi hardware. Once the full system is installed, play around with it to gain some familiarity with the facilities of another Linux distribution. For example, enable ssh, install some of your favorite Linux apps, etc..

8. ***Optional*** Follow the steps of the example in Section 1.2.3 above to be able to boot and run this Ubuntu-running-on-Raspberry Pi from an USB3-mounted external medium, such as an SSD.

Conclusion:
In Section 1.8 below, we will show how to take advantage of ZFS when adding additional media to your Raspberry Pi. This example prepared you for doing that.

1.3 Pre- and Post-Installation Considerations and Choices

Your Raspberry Pi is a System-on-a-Chip (SoC) computer, with an Advanced RISC Machine (ARM) chip in it, which probably makes it significantly different from the other types of traditional X-86 architecture machines that you might have used for computing, whether that was for education, business, or entertainment. And as such, the considerations you make before and after the installation of the Raspberry Pi OS on it, are somewhat different as well. The sections below detail these. At the time this book was written, there was no easy way to add RAM, or include other bus architecture connections to the circuit board that you purchased. You could use Power Over Ethernet (POE) to supply power to a Raspberry Pi, but as far as using the GPIO 40-pin topology, and any number of hats or additions to it, the internal circuit board, and the external connector options, were limited to what's available on the printed circuit board. If you format a microSD card to exFAT or NTFS, you can use larger than 32 GB cards as the system storage medium. Given our use cases, for example, we've only had to use Etcher, not NOOBS or the Imager, and deploy 32 GB microSD cards in our Pi 3, Pi 4B, or Pi 400. We run both our Pi 4B and 400 off of a USB3, externally mounted SSD that is the boot/system disk, and used the procedure in Section 1.2.3 above to accomplish this.

1.3.1 Pre-Installation Considerations

Once you've determined exactly what you want to use your Raspberry Pi hardware and software for, you need to carefully consider the following listing of questions that suggest very important aspects of your envisioned usage. Considerations you can make over and above the default installation choices presented to you by the operating system, as you proceed with the installation. Rather than viewing these suggestions as highly formal constraints, you should consider them as informally presented guides as to how you can choose certain aspects of a prospective purchase of hardware, for example, that the installation will serve on, in the very subjective light of how you actually will use your Raspberry Pi.

1) Where will the system boot from? There are several options here, especially if you are going to add additional equipment to your base Raspberry Pi hardware on the General Purpose Input/Output (GPIO) 40-pin header, like HATS such as a Compute Module, etc.. Are you always going to boot from a microSD card that you used the Imager to create, from a USB3-connected SSD, from a network connection, or from some connected NVME M.2 device? All of these things affect performance and boot speed. And booting the system using one of these options usually dictates that that medium becomes the primary *system disk*, where the operating system resides, and runs from.

2) Are you going to be a casual user of a Raspberry Pi, making only light demands on it in terms of computational tasks, or graphics? Are you going to be a gamer who needs not only heavy computational power, but also extreme graphics capabilities? Or are you going to cluster Raspberry Pi hardware together in a server array, and rely upon free or commercial NAS software to service your customer and user base?

Given the way that you want to use your Raspberry Pi, does the hardware that you already have, or intend to purchase, have an adequate amount of physical memory, or RAM, for your intended use case? This consideration is basically a performance concern. For example, the Raspberry Pi model 4B comes with 1, 2, 4, or 8 GB of RAM. The Raspberry Pi 400 we do all of our work on only comes with 4 GB of RAM. When the Raspberry Pi 5 is released, how much optional installed RAM will be offered with it? Which one are you going to buy, or which one do you have? In any situation, you should always first consider whether you have, or will have, an adequate amount, or size of physical memory installed on the Raspberry Pi hardware, if that is a viable option.

How would you know that? Read reviews online, look at benchmark tests performed by reputable sources, and talk to other Raspberry Pi users that would have similar use cases as yourself. The Raspberry Pi Forums is a good place to start:

https://forums.raspberrypi.com/

3) Two of the most integral and important considerations you must make are a) what persistent media data storage model are you going to use given your use case, and b) how much, and what type of external USB-mounted media can or does your computer have physically connected to it?

a) With regard to the first consideration, are you going to need to attach virtual storage media, via protocols such as NFSv4 or iSCSI? Are you going to connect and work within the contexts of Network Attached Storage (NAS), or a Storage Area Network (SAN)?

b) With regard to the second consideration, if you are only going to use the microSD card, or one external USB-mounted disk drive as the system disk as detailed in Section 1.2.3, that microSD card, or USB-mounted disk will most likely be the bootable system disk *and* the user file system data disk. If it is foreseeable that you will have additional USB-mounted disk media installed on the system, what strategies will you use to backup or "clone" the bootable system disk, and perhaps "mirror" all other user data on the multiple data disk hard drives, with some dependable and robust strategy of backup?

Note

Our Data Storage Model Recommendation:

If your hardware can support multiple USB, externally mounted media, we recommend that you install the operating system on one medium (traditionally, a microSD card, or preferably a Solid State Drive [SSD], or a USB3-adaptor-connected M.2 PCIe device), and store all of the user data on *another* single medium, or an array of external media. That way, if the operating system and its bootable medium become corrupted, or unusable for some reason, your user data is on a separate medium or array of media. This technique, or storage model, dovetails very well with the most practical methods of operating system upgrades. Using it, you can then simply replace the operating system medium, and reinstall either the current version of the operating system or a newer version, without significantly impacting your user data storage. This will allow you to reattach the data media to the new operating system and its medium, whatever that might be. This is highly valuable not only for single-user desktops, but also for NAS server-class systems as well. The way that your data is deployed on your media is a critical design consideration when you are building your system, and is highly dependent on the particular use case that is guiding it.

One caveat you must consider when using the above recommended storage model is some applications software, most prominently LXC/LXD containers, store required files in both the system area and in the data storage area. We supply some useful backup strategies for LXC/LXD containers in Volume 3, that work with our recommended data storage mode.

4) Do you want to have a wireless connection to a local area network and the Internet? A wired connection through DHCP is *not* automatically done on installation by the Raspberry Pi OS 64-bit Desktop version, so you must configure the network settings during the default install procedure. This wired connection can also be configured post-installation, as shown below in Section 1.3.2, item 4). What is the IP address of your Raspberry Pi, and is it automatically assigned by the DHCP server on your network?

5) How many users are you going to initially establish at installation, and what are their user profiles going to be? For example, what users will have administrative privileges other than yourself, and what kind of security will each profile have? Integral with these questions are the considerations of the storage model you will establish after the initial installation of the operating system on a single medium, as defined in 1)b). For example, will all users' home directories be on separate media from the system medium? Also, what user groups are you going to establish at installation, and how are you going to manage groups in a post-installation environment?

6) Who will be responsible for the items of systems administration tasks listed above in Section 1.0? For example, that will influence your media management tasks concerning file systems for users and projects, according to the data storage model you employ.

7) What kind of software tools do you want to include, given the version of the Raspberry Pi OS you are going to install, for the kinds of tasks you and your user base will be doing? For example, during installation, you are able to add packages on top of the default package installation to help accomplish those tasks. How are the user groups established in item 5) above going to have access privileges to this

software? What are your policies with respect to group access to software tools, and how do you enforce these policies?

8) Will you have a GUI windowing system after you install your system? You have a choice of installing either a GUI Desktop version, *or* Raspberry Pi OS Lite, which has a Command Line Interface (CUI) only, no graphical or desktop environment, a minimal set of application packages, and is the equivalent of a server operating system. Your previous experience and preferences with a particular style of computer environment can be implemented at installation, and dictated by your use case. Will you need a server install, based on your use case? A server install, and the management of a server system, involves another whole universe of considerations and design decisions.

In-Chapter Exercise

1. Make a detailed listing on paper of your answers to the above eight sets of questions before you begin to install your operating system. Then, read through the sections below referencing the procedures for actual installation, and for each of your answers, determine ahead of time how you will proceed through the procedures. This exercise is meant to serve as a "dry run" through any particular path you might take through the purchase, installation, and usage procedures.

1.3.2 Post-Installation Choices and Actions

The highly practical things you do to your Raspberry Pi OS after it is installed successfully are *very* dependent upon your individual pre-installation considerations, as outlined above in Section 1.3.1, and how you implemented those considerations in detail. As presented in the pre-installation considerations, you should view the suggested post-installation considerations here as informally presented guides to how you can choose certain post-installation aspects of your operating system.

Our minimal set of recommendations for post-installation tasks are specific to our Raspberry Pi 4B and 400 systems, and their hardware configurations. They follow directly from pre-installation considerations we made above in Section 1.3.1.

1. Our boot/system medium for our Raspberry Pi 4B is a 128 GB SSD, and for the Pi 400 a 512 GB SSD, which we connect through the USB3 ports, further described below in item 4.

2. Since we installed a desktop system on our Pi 400, which was going to heavily rely on a very convenient and easy-to-use GUI environment, it wasn't possible on those particular models of the hardware to increase the amount of installed physical memory, to speed up this

kind of usage. See the output of the **inxi** commands shown immediately following these recommendations listing, and In-Chapter Exercise 2, to gain more information and insight into how to view physical memory size on your Raspberry Pi system.

As stated above, your particular physical memory needs depend upon how you use your Linux system. We had to go with the defaults affecting the size of virtual memory, paging, and swap space, although these may be important considerations for you depending on the model of Raspberry Pi you have.

3. Use the Pi Menu Preferences > Add/Remove Software to install absolutely essential applications that you need to use that are not already pre-installed. For us, the pre-installed required software was the Chromium Web Browser, and the LibreOffice suite on our version of the operating system. Additionally for us, the post-install software included, in priority order, Filezilla, Gparted, Webmin, and the GNU Image Manipulation Program. We also put desktop icons on our desktop for all of our important applications.

4. Our highly recommended storage model dictates the use of **mdadm**, so we installed that package, using the instructions given in Volume 1. Our Raspberry Pi OS was originally built on 32 GB microSD cards, but then we rebuilt it on the above-indicated capacity SSDs, using the Pi Menu Accessories > SD Card Copier, as shown in Section 1.2.3. We then added additional USB3-mounted media later, in order to conform to our recommended storage model.

5. Since printing documents was an essential operation that our system needed to perform, we attached and setup (via CUPS) a laser printer directly to the hardware of the Raspberry Pi 400, with a USB connection (as shown in detail in Volume 1).

6. We used the Raspberry Pi Configuration tool, selecting the "System" tab, to configure our network settings and connect to a wired intranet network. We then exposed our system on the local intranet as a basic ssh server, so we immediately modified the sshd configuration file, and constructed ufw firewall rules, according to what we show below in this chapter, to secure the system.

7. We minimally exposed our system as a web server using nginx, and our custom web programs, but went with the default security measures for those applications.

8. We needed only a very sparse set of additional users and groups on the system, so we immediately set those up using the method shown in the sections below, and added to them as necessary. This method of adding new users and groups is shown below. The primary advantage this confers is that users, and their data files, which

for us are on their own redundant pair of hard drives, are discreet and maintained separately from the operating system installation. We feel that this model is useful for a single-user computer desktop system, a shared multi-user computer, or low-to-mid-level enterprise-level servers as well.

There are various text-based Raspberry Pi OS commands that survey system hardware, in order to provide you with a basis for doing performance tuning and post-installation modification of the system. Some of these are lscpu, lshw, hwinfo, lspci, lspci, lsusb, inxi, lsblk, df, fdisk, mount, free, hdparm, and examining the relevant contents of the /proc directories. We detailed the use of some of these below, and in Volume 1.

But, in order to get a very useful summary of the actual post-installation configuration of their system, we have found that the **inxi** command is the most useful and expedient way for beginners. We show three uses of that command, on three different machines in order: a Raspberry Pi 400, a Raspberry Pi 4B, and an HP Proliant Microserver with X-86 processor architecture.

Note
On our HP Proliant Microserver running the 32-bit Desktop version of the Raspberry Pi OS, we had to install **inxi** as superuser first, with the command **sudo apt install inxi**.

We utilize various options that yield our specific required outputs for those machines, as follows:

Raspberry Pi 400

```
$ sudo inxi -GSCMm -t c -P -x
[sudo] password for bob: qqqqq
System:    Host: raspberrypi Kernel: 6.1.21-v8+ aarch64 bits: 64 com-
           piler: gcc v: 10.2.1 Console: tty 0
           Distro: Debian GNU/Linux 11 (bullseye)
Machine:   Type: ARM Device System: Raspberry Pi 400 Rev 1.0
           details: BCM2835 rev: c03130
           serial: 10000000fdd89bf2
Memory:    RAM: total: 3.78 GiB used: 1.01 GiB (26.8%) gpu: 76 MiB
           RAM Report: unknown-error: Unknown dmidecode error.
           Unable to generate data.
CPU:       Info: Quad Core model: N/A variant: cortex-a72 bits:
           64 type: MCP arch: ARMv8 rev: 3
           features: Use -f option to see features bogomips: 432
Speed:     1800 MHz min/max: 600/1800 MHz Core speeds (MHz): 1: 1800
           2: 1800 3: 1800 4: 1800
```

Graphics: Device-1: bcm2711-hdmi0 driver: vc4_hdmi v: N/A bus ID: N/A
Device-2: bcm2711-hdmi1 driver: vc4_hdmi v: N/A bus ID: N/A
Device-3: bcm2711-vc5 driver: vc4_drm v: N/A bus ID: N/A
Display: server: X.Org 1.20.11 driver: loaded: modesetting
unloaded: fbdev
resolution: 1920x1080~60Hz
OpenGL: renderer: V3D 4.2 v: 2.1 Mesa 20.3.5 direct render: Yes

Partition: ID-1: / size: 438.79 GiB used: 11.56 GiB (2.6%) fs: ext4 dev:
/dev/sda2
ID-2: /boot size: 252 MiB used: 30.4 MiB (12.1%) fs: vfat dev:
/dev/sda1

Processes: CPU top: 5 of 217
1: cpu: 7.8% command: soffice.bin pid: 57392 mem: 321.3
MiB (8.4%)
2: cpu: 2.0% command: xorg pid: 727 mem: 227.2 MiB (5.9%)
3: cpu: 0.3% command: mutter pid: 919 mem: 81.8 MiB (2.1%)
4: cpu: 0.2% command: [irq/37-mmc0] pid: 100 mem: 0.00
MiB (0.0%)
5: cpu: 0.2% command: [v3d_bin] pid: 245 mem: 0.00 MiB (0.0%)

$

Raspberry Pi 4B

```
$ sudo inxi -DRGSCMm -t c -P -x
```

System: Host: raspberrypi Kernel: 6.1.21-v8+ aarch64 bits:
64 compiler: gcc v: 10.2.1 Console: tty 0
Distro: Debian GNU/Linux 11 (bullseye)

Machine: Type: ARM Device System: Raspberry Pi 4 Model B Rev 1.1
details: BCM2835 rev: c03111
serial: 100000006ec81c99

Memory: RAM: total: 3.78 GiB used: 552.2 MiB (14.3%) gpu: 76 MiB
RAM Report: unknown-error: Unknown dmidecode error.
Unable to generate data.

CPU: Info: Quad Core model: N/A variant: cortex-a72 bits:
64 type: MCP arch: ARMv8 rev: 3
features: Use -f option to see features bogomips: 432
Speed: 1500 MHz min/max: 600/1500 MHz Core speeds
(MHz): 1: 1500 2: 1500 3: 1500 4: 1500

Graphics: Device-1: bcm2711-hdmi0 driver: vc4_hdmi v: N/A bus ID: N/A
Device-2: bcm2711-hdmi1 driver: vc4_hdmi v: N/A bus ID: N/A
Device-3: bcm2711-vc5 driver: vc4_drm v: N/A bus ID: N/A
Display: server: X.org 1.20.11 driver: loaded: modesetting
unloaded: fbdev tty: 115x60

Message: Advanced graphics data unavailable in console for root.

Partition: ID-1: / size: 116.56 GiB used: 9.23 GiB (7.9%) fs: ext4 dev:
/dev/sda2
ID-2: /boot size: 252 MiB used: 30.4 MiB (12.1%) fs: vfat dev:
/dev/sda1
Processes: CPU top: 5 of 201
1: cpu: 3.0% command: sudo pid: 324622 mem: 4.25 MiB (0.1%)
2: cpu: 1.5% command: sshd: pid: 324602 mem: 7.73 MiB (0.2%)
3: cpu: 1.2% command: cubenetic pid: 324549 mem: 43.3
MiB (1.1%)
4: cpu: 0.4% command: -bash pid: 324609 mem: 4.60 MiB (0.1%)
5: cpu: 0.3% command: mutter pid: 833 mem: 69.4 MiB (1.8%)
$

HP Proliant X-86 architecture

$ sudo inxi -DGSCMm -t c -P -x
System:	Host: raspberry Kernel: 5.10.0-22-686-pae i686 bits:
32 compiler: gcc v: 10.2.1 Console: tty 0
Distro: Debian GNU/Linux 11 (bullseye)
Machine:	Type: Desktop System: HP product: ProLiant MicroServer v:
N/A serial: 5C7142P200
Mobo: N/A model: N/A serial: N/A BIOS: HP v: O41 date: 07/29/2011
Memory:	RAM: total: 5.73 GiB used: 718.4 MiB (12.2%)
Array-1: capacity: 8 GiB slots: 2 EC: Single-bit ECC max module
size: 4 GiB note: est.
Device-1: DIMM0 size: 4 GiB speed: 1333 MT/s type: Other
Device-2: DIMM1 size: 2 GiB speed: 1333 MT/s type: Other
CPU:	Info: Dual Core model: AMD Turion II Neo N40L bits:
64 type: MCP arch: K10 rev: 3 L2 cache: 2 MiB
flags: lm nx pae sse sse2 sse3 sse4a svm bogomips: 5990
Speed: 800 MHz min/max: 800/1500 MHz Core speeds
(MHz): 1: 800 2: 1500
Graphics:	Device-1: Advanced Micro Devices [AMD/ATI] RS880M
[Mobility Radeon HD 4225/4250]
vendor: Hewlett-Packard ProLiant MicroServer N36L
driver: radeon v: kernel bus ID: 01:05.0
Display: server: X.org 1.20.11 driver: loaded: ati,radeon
unloaded: fbdev,modesetting,vesa
tty: 113x59
Message:	Advanced graphics data unavailable in console for root.
Partition:	ID-1: / size: 438.1 GiB: used 7.85 GiB (1.8%) fs: ext4 dev:
/dev/sda1
ID-2: swap-1 size: 976 MiB used: N/A (0.0%) fs: swap dev:
/dev/sda5

Processes: CPU top: 5 of 137
         1: cpu: 2.0% command: sudo pid: 9741 mem: 4.68 MiB (0.0%)
         2: cpu: 0.6% command: sshd: pid: 8657 mem: 7.61 MiB (0.1%)
         3: cpu: 0.3% command: [kworker/0:3-events] pid: 8574
            mem: 0.00 MiB (0.0%)
         4: cpu: 0.1% command: -bash pid: 8664 mem: 4.32 MiB (0.0%)
         5: cpu: 0.0% command: init pid: 1 mem: 9.20 MiB (0.1%)
$

As you can see from the above output, **inxi** shows system hardware, CPU, drives, and partitions, among other information. For all three machines, which were running a GUI desktop system, kernel information, disk information and statistics, in our cases the top five processes, RAM usage, and other useful information about the three systems. For more information about the **inxi** command, see the man page for **inxi** on your Raspberry Pi system.

In-Chapter Exercise

2.   Part a) Following up on your answer to In-Chapter Exercise 1, completely list and detail how you implemented your pre-installation considerations on the system you have installed. Or, if you did not implement them because you didn't do an installation, how you *would* implement them on an actual hardware platform of your choice. Use our set of minimal recommendations for post-installation tasks as a guide for how to fulfill the requirements of this exercise. In addition, you could consult with the person that actually installed your system on the hardware, if that person is available.

        Part b) From looking at the output of the three **inxi** commands, which system has the slowest memory modules installed? Can you infer what the memory bus speed is from the speed of the CPU on that system? What is ECC memory? Why would these machines have that kind of memory? Given your system and hardware, what options of the **inxi** command would be most useful and revealing for you to use?

1.4 System Services Administration, Startup, and Shutdown Procedures

What you have to think about first, in terms of system "booting" as it's generally called, is:
  "How do you want the system to boot?"

As stated above in Section 1.3, that is one of the most important pre-installation considerations you have to make. There are a few options, and the details of them, especially for an ARM-architecture machine, are complex.

This section gives an overview of the general procedures for booting, managing the startup process, and gracefully shutting down the Raspberry Pi OS, given how you've answered the above question. It gives a brief summary overview of the steps that the operating system and hardware go through in successfully starting up and shutting down. It then gives some further references to the basic but important systemd services administration utilities available to a system administrator. In those further references, we give examples of commands for manipulating and changing system services by enabling and running new services.

1.4.1 The Boot and Startup Processes

The Raspberry Pi 4B and 400 use an EEPROM to boot the system. Here are the general steps that the Raspberry Pi OS goes through to boot up:

1) When the Raspberry Pi is first turned on, the ARM core is off, and the GPU core is on. At this point the SDRAM is disabled.
2) The ROM on the SoC initiates the first stage of booting.
3) The boot behavior for a microSD or USB boot is controlled by a configuration file in the EEPROM, and can be edited via the rpi-eeprom-config tool, with the command **sudo -E rpi-eeprom-config --edit**

The EEPROM second stage consists of the following steps:
   a. Initialize clocks and SDRAM.
   b. Read the EEPROM configuration file.
   c. Determine if booting should be a restart/stop, or from microSD card, the network, a USB device, or an PCIe NVME device.

The Raspberry Pi 400's boot process, for example, is similar to other Linux-based computers, with the main differences being that:

a. it traditionally, by default, uses a microSD card as its primary storage device, and boot medium, or alternate sources, and
b. is controlled by an EEPROM.

The term "booting" is used here to mean bringing the operating system from a complete power-off condition to a point where systemd can take over. Then in "startup", systemd brings the computer to a steady-state, fully normal operating condition.

When a system hangs up during the shutdown procedure, a contemporary way of diagnosing the problem is to examine the systemd journal, with the **journalctl** command, as shown in Volume 1. This way, if some process or program is preventing the system from reaching a powered-off condition, the journal logs will allow you to see what that process or program that's causing the problem is. On shutdown, systemd attempts to stop all services, and unmount all file systems. The system is finally powered down. We give more details of how a Raspberry Pi system using systemd shuts down in the next section.

In-Chapter Exercises

3. How can you boot into an alternative environment found on another boot medium on your Raspberry Pi, and in which phase of the bootup process shown in Figure 1.1 might this alternative method be presented to you? Why would you want to do this? Make note of exactly how

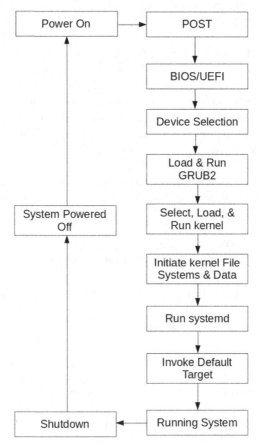

FIGURE 1.1
Traditional Linux Boot Process Steps.

this might be done on the Raspberry Pi OS. Also, draw an arrow, or arrows, in Figure 1.1 that would specify what path would be followed if the system were to be rebooted rather than powered-off.

4. Which methodology of booting (from a traditional microSD, USB3-mounted SSD, NMVe M.2 device, or a network) would allow you to test drive different Raspberry Pi OS versions in the quickest and easiest way on the same piece of hardware? **And not necessarily on Raspberry Pi hardware.** Sketch exactly how this would be accomplished, given your choice. (Note: *Not simultaneously, but sequentially!*)

1.4.2 systemd and Traditional System Reboot or Shutdown

systemd is in charge of taking the system from the normal operating condition to a power-off state, or to reboot the system. The relevant systemd **systemctl** commands, with their options, that achieve shutting the system down or rebooting it, and briefly what they accomplish, are shown in Table 1.1. We described these commands and the systemd shutdown process further in Volume 1. The systemd shutdown path through possible target states, from a normal operating condition, to a powered-off state, is described in Figure 1.2.

Traditionally, the graceful shutdown or reboot procedures can be done graphically from the active window system, or from the command line or console window, using the **halt** or **shutdown** commands and their options. The **shutdown** command has the advantage of allowing you to specify a time when shutdown processes are initiated.

Graceful shutdown procedures are generally done as follows:

1. Shutdown system and user processes
2. Flush system memory to disk
3. Unmount file systems
4. Power off

TABLE 1.1

systemd systemctl Shutdown Commands

Command	Description
systemctl halt	Halts the system
systemctl poweroff	Powers off the system
systemctl reboot	Restarts the system
systemctl suspend	Suspends the system
systemctl hibernate	Hibernates the system
systemctl hybrid-sleep	Hibernates and suspends the system

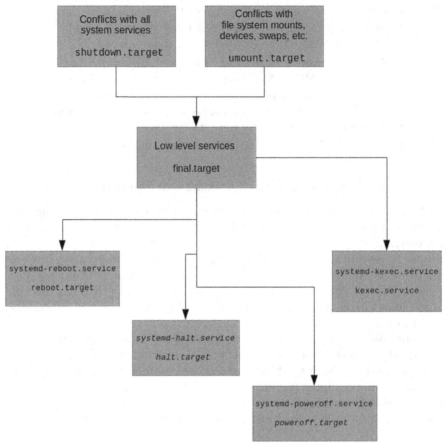

FIGURE 1.2
systemd Shutdown Path.

An example of using the **shutdown** command on a Raspberry Pi system is as follows:

$ **shutdown –h now**

where **–h** means halt the processor, and **now** is the time option, and means immediately.

To get a more complete description of the **shutdown** command, particularly the format of the time option, see the man page on your Raspberry Pi system.

1.4.3 Preliminary Considerations When Managing System Services with systemd

The system service manager that is available in our base Raspberry Pi OS is systemd. In fact, systemd is the system service manager for all distributions in the three major branches of Linux, and all important downstream Linux distributions as well, including Raspberry Pi OS.

We detail system service management with systemd completely in Volume 1, and provide several examples there of how to effectively control operating system services in a modern systemd-controlled Linux system.

We first pose a couple of preliminary questions about "system services" on the Raspberry Pi OS.

Question: What is a daemon?

Answer: Basically a daemon is a background, ongoing process that is not linked or controlled by a terminal. Particularly not connected in the usual way to standard output or stand error.

Question: Is a "service" a daemon?

Answer: Sometimes. More accurately and generally, a service can be a process or collection of processes, the overall state of the system, or the state of a physical device, a virtual device, a dataset, etc. And as a provider of resources, or a collection of an applications' capabilities, it can have more than one instance. For example, the many layered file systems present on the system, or the multiple means of remote login to the system.

1.4.4 Further References For System Service Management Using systemd

In this section we provide further references for the uses of systemd for service management, which are presented fully, with numerous examples, in Volumes 1 and 3. Our primary reference is the example detailed in Volume 1, Example 1.2, of how to enable server-side host services for a secure ftp daemon, known as vsftpd. That is a complete primary, basic example of using systemd to manage system services.

In addition, Volume 3, "Raspberry Pi OS Text Editors, git, and Virtualization with LXC/LXD", also shows examples of how you can implement the vsftpd service securely inside of an LXC/LXD container.

As noted in the references, you should be cautious when executing these examples, particularly if you are *not* using one of the virtualization methodologies shown in Volume 3, and are on an insecure network connected to the Internet. You must have root privileges on the computer to execute the examples we show in the above references as well.

In-Chapter Exercise

    5.   What is the danger of using ftp, telnet, rlogin, or rsh from a remote site on the Internet into your home computer?

1.5 User Administration

The two most important objectives of user administration are service and security. First, providing service to ensure that the user base has access to and can fully take advantage of the resources that the Raspberry Pi OS can provide. Second, securing the files and processes that the user base needs to utilize those resources. Later in this chapter we go over some of the security methodologies that a system administrator can deploy to keep the system secure. In Volume 3, in the chapter entitled "Virtualization with LXC/LXD", we also show security methods that utilize various virtualization technologies such as LXC/LXD containers.

The traditional Linux technique for providing service and security to users is through read, write, and execute (rwx) access privileges, for the individual user, the group, or all others (u,g,o) on the system, to specific objects on the system, such as directories, or folders, and most importantly, to the files contained in them. Designing and implementing user groups, and access privileges for user groups, are the most important parts of this technique.

Certainly, user account and group creation and configuration are the first steps in providing maximum service and security to the user base. That is true even if you are the only user of the system!

A very integral part of designing user accounts and groups is the detailed consideration given to the recommended user data storage model we showed in Section 1.4.1, item 3. This is done by securing user files on a second, possibly redundant, storage medium, so that they can be kept separate from the operating system boot medium itself. It can be practically achieved by properly creating user accounts so that they have their home directories on that second hard drive. As we show in Section 1.8 below, various ways of adding redundant persistent media very easily and effectively implement the model.

We concentrate here on how to manage user accounts and groups on Raspberry Pi OS with the **adduser, addgroup, deluser, delgroup, newusers, passwd,** and **usermod** commands. These activities are usually done a significant time after the initial installation of your Raspberry Pi system, but can be done during installation and initialization of the system as well. Following is Table 1.2 showing brief descriptions of these commands.

TABLE 1.2

Basic User Administration Commands

Command	Description
adduser	Add a new user account
deluser	Delete a user account
addgroup	Add a new group
delgroup	Delete a group
newusers	Update and create new users in batch mode
passwd	Manage user passwords
usermod	Modifies user accounts

The examples in this section illustrate:

* simple cases of text-based user account creation and configuration,
* text-based group creation and configuration, and
* text-based deletion of a user account and a group.

In-Chapter Exercise

6. Make a table or chart of what users and groups need to be added to your system, and what their default account parameters and group memberships should be. What command can you use to identify all existing groups on the system?

1.5.1 Adding a User and Group in a Text-Based Interface

The commands **adduser** and **addgroup**, by default, add a "normal" (non-system) user or group to the system, using command line options and option arguments. They take default configuration information from /etc/adduser.conf. They are a more developed front-end for the older, low-level commands, such as **useradd, groupadd**, and **usermod. Adduser** and **addgroup** utilize patented UID and GID values for creation of new accounts and groups. By default they create a home directory from a skeletal configuration file, etc.

adduser itself is a script file that interfaces to the following commands and their functionality:

useradd, groupadd, passwd, gpasswd, usermod, chfn, chage, edquota.

An abbreviated listing of the syntax of the **adduser** and **addgroup** commands, taken from the man page for adduser, is as follows:

```
***********************************************************************
adduser, addgroup - add a user or group to the system
Syntax:
    adduser [options] [--home DIR] [--shell SHELL] [--no-create-home]
    [--uid ID] [--firstuid ID] [--lastuid ID] [--ingroup GROUP | --gid ID]
    [--disabled-password] [--disabled-login] [--gecos GECOS]
    [--add_extra_groups] [--encrypt-home] user

    adduser --system [options] [--home DIR] [--shell SHELL] [--no-create-
    home] [--uid ID] [--group | --ingroup GROUP | --gid ID] [--disabled-
    password] [--disabled-login] [--gecos GECOS] user

    addgroup [options] [--gid ID] group

    addgroup --system [options] [--gid ID] group

    adduser [options] user group
```

Purpose:
> adduser and addgroup add users and groups to the system according to command line options and configuration information in /etc/adduser.conf. They are friendlier front ends to the low-level tools like useradd, groupadd, and usermod programs, by default choosing Debian policy conformant UID and GID values, creating a home directory with skeletal configuration, running a custom script, and other features. adduser and addgroup can be run in one of five modes:

Output: New or modified user accounts or groups.

Commonly Used Options:
```
    [--quiet] [--debug] [--force-badname] [--help|-h] [--version] [--conf FILE]
***********************************************************************
```

The basic, simple usage as superuser of the following **adduser** command, does the following five things:

```
$ sudo adduser username
```

1. Create the user named username.
2. Create the user's home directory (the default is /home/username), and copy the files from /etc/skel into it.

3. Create a group with the same name as the user, and place the user in it.

4. Prompt for a password for the user (by default not shown on-screen), and its confirmation.

5. Prompt for personal information about the user, such as telephone, office contact, etc.

Below are two simple examples of how to add a new user in a text-based, command line interface. The first example illustrates how to interactively create a single user account from the command line as superuser. If you make a mistake in creating a user account, you can always remove the account immediately by using the **deluser** command, shown in Section 1.5.3.

Example 1.1 **adduser** Command for a Single User Account

```
$ sudo adduser sarwar
[sudo] password for bob: qqq
Adding user `sarwar' ...
Adding new group `sarwar' (1002) ...
Adding new user `sarwar' (1002) with group `sarwar' ...
Creating home directory `/home/sarwar' ...
Copying files from `/etc/skel' ...
Enter new UNIX password: www
Retype new UNIX password: www
passwd: password updated successfully
Enter the new value, or press ENTER for the default
      Full Name []: ENTER
      Room Number []: ENTER
      Work Phone []: ENTER
      Home Phone []: ENTER
      Other []: ENTER
Is the information correct? [Y/n] Y
$
```

In-Chapter Exercise

7. Create a single new account on your Raspberry Pi system, with the **adduser** command as shown above. Be sure to use the entries you made in your answer to In-Chapter Exercise 6 to override the defaults for user account configurations on your system!

The second example uses the command **newusers**, which allows "batch" mode creation of new users, in conjunction with a file that contains a listing of several user accounts that can be added all at one time. A brief description of the **newusers** command, taken from the man page, is as follows:

```
*********************************************************************
```

newusers - update and create new users in batch mode

Syntax: newusers [options] [file]

Purpose: The newusers command reads a file (or the standard input by default) and uses this information to update a set of existing users or to create new users. Each line is in the same format as the standard password file, as follows:
pw_name:pw_passwd:pw_uid:pw_gid:pw_gecos:pw_dir:pw_shell
where pw_name is the name of the user you want to create,
pw_passwd is the password,
pw_uid is the UID,
pw_gid is the GID,
pw_gecos is an identifying comment,
pw_dir is the home directory path,
pw_shell is the new users default shell.

Common Options:
  -h, --help
    Display help message and exit.
  -r, --system
    Create a system account.
```
*********************************************************************
```

Example 1.2 Creating Several New Users in "Batch" Mode

1.   Use your favorite text editor to create the following file, named "dev_grp.txt" in your home directory. Feel free to add more lines similar to the one shown to add more new users to the listing.

hassan:QQQ:2001:2001:CFO of Accounting:/home/hassan:/bin/bash

The seven fields of the above line, separated by colons (:), are the new user accounts name, password, UID, GID, GECOS commentary, default home directory, and default shell.

2.   Use the following command to create the user(s) encoded in the file dev_grp.txt:

    $ sudo newusers dev_grp.txt
    [sudo] password for bob: **qqq**
    $

3. Check the addition of the new user(s) using the following command:

    $ **more /etc/group**
    Output truncated…
    hassan:x:2001:
    $

In-Chapter Exercise

8. According to the table or chart of user accounts and their configur-
    ation requirements you did for In-Chapter Exercise 6 above, create a
    file of new user accounts. *Don't recreate the user account you added in
    In-Chapter Exercise 7!* As shown in Example 1.2, for each user account,
    you must have a single line in the file with seven colon-delimited
    fields that contain the configuration for each user. The table, or chart
    design with its entries, determines what is in the file.

1.5.2 Adding and Maintaining Groups in a Text-Based Interface

The easiest and most efficient way to create and manage user accounts and
groups is by using Webmin. From Webmin's main menu, you can make the
System > Users and Groups choice to view, create, and delete both. We certainly recommend that, but for text-based interaction in a console or terminal window, you can use the **addgroup** and **adduser** commands to manage
groups.

Following is an example of how to add and manage groups.

Example 1.3 Adding and managing groups and users from the command line

Objectives: To add a new group, and manage those users that are in
               that group.
Prerequisites: Having completed Examples 1.1 and 1.2, having default
               groups available on your system.
Background: Text-based management of groups is accomplished with the
               addgroup command, and its options.
Requirements: Do the following steps, in the order presented, to complete
               the requirements of this example:

1. Create a group named "development", using the **addgroup** command
    as follows:

    $ **sudo addgroup development**
    [sudo] password for bob: GGG
    Adding group `development' (GID 1003) …
    Done.
    $

2. Add the user sarwar to the group named "development" using the
    adduser command as follows:

    $ **sudo adduser sarwar development**
    Adding user `sarwar' to group `development' ...
    Adding user sarwar to group development
    Done.
    $

3. List the groups on the system, and verify sarwar as a member of the
    group named "development":

    $ **cd /etc**
    /etc$ **more group**
    Output truncated...
    sarwar:x:1002:
    development:x:1003:sarwar
    /etc $

4. Remove the user sarwar from the group named "development":

    /etc $ **sudo deluser sarwar development**
    Removing user `sarwar' from group `development' ...
    Done.
    /etc $

5. Verify that sarwar has been removed from the group named
    "development":

    /etc $ **more group**
    Output truncated...
    sarwar:x:1002:
    development:x:1003:

    In-Chapter Exercise
9. You have an air-gapped Raspberry Pi in a room. You want only certain
    users in a defined group named "proj" to be able to access files in a dir-
    ectory named "proj1" in your account on the file system of that com-
    puter. Use the above command line commands to add those certain
    users, and yourself, to the group "proj". Create the "proj1" directory.
    Then, set the permission bits appropriately on your home directory,
    the "proj1" directory, and any files put in that directory, so that only
    those certain users can read, write, and execute the files in it. The room
    is open to the public, but to login to the computer, each individual user
    has to use her own password.

1.5.3 Modifying and Deleting a User Account and Group from the Command Line

To effectively delete a user account or a group from the system using the command line, use the **deluser** or **delgroup** commands. A brief description of those commands, taken from the man pages on the Raspberry Pi OS is as follows:

```
*************************************************************
```

deluser, delgroup - remove a user or group from the system

Syntax:
deluser [options][--force][--remove-home] [--remove-all-files]
        [--backup] [--backup-to DIR] user
deluser --group [options] group
delgroup [options] [--only-if-empty] group
deluser [options] user group

Purpose: deluser and delgroup remove users and groups from the system according to command line options and configuration information in /etc/deluser.conf and /etc/adduser.conf.

Common Options:
    [--conf FILE] Use FILE instead of /etc/deluser.conf
    --version Display version and copyright information.
```
*************************************************************
```

To modify an existing user account from the command line, you can use the **usermod** command. A brief description of that command, taken from the man page on the Raspberry Pi OS, is as follows:
```
*************************************************************
```

usermod - modify a user account

Syntax:
usermod [options] LOGIN

Purpose: usermod modifies the system account files to reflect the changes that are specified on the command line, for LOGIN name.
Common Options: ·
  -a, --append
  Add the user to the supplementary group(s). Use only with the -G option.
  -d, --home HOME_DIR
  he user's new login directory.

-G, --groups GROUP1[,GROUP2,...[,GROUPN]]]

A list of supplementary groups which the user is also a member of. Each group is separated from the next by a comma, with no intervening whitespace.

-l, --login NEW_LOGIN

The name of the user will be changed from LOGIN to NEW_LOGIN. Nothing else is changed. In particular, the user's home directory should probably be renamed manually to reflect the new login name.

-m, --move-home

Move the content of the user's home directory to the new location.

-s, --shell SHELL

The name of the user's new login shell. Setting this field to blank causes the systemto select the default login shell.

****

Following is an example of deleting a user account named sarwar from the system, using the **deluser** command:

Example 1.4 User Account Deletion with deluser

Objectives: To delete a user account from the command line.
Pre-Requisites: Having completed Examples 1.1 through 1.3, or having a user account on your system that you want to permanently delete.
Background: Similar to the **adduser** command, **deluser** deletes a user account from the system.

Requirements:
Do the following steps, in the order shown, to complete the requirements of this example:

1. To delete the user account sarwar we created in Example 1.1, type the following command:

    $ **sudo deluser sarwar**
    [sudo] password for bob: WXYZ
    Removing user `sarwar' ...
    Warning: group `sarwar' has no more members.
    Done.
    $

1.5.4 A Method of User and Group Creation on a Second Storage Medium

According to our recommended storage model from Section 1.3.1, item 3, it would be advantageous to install the operating system on one bootable medium (preferably a fast but not necessarily large-capacity USB3 Solid State

Drive [SSD], or a USB3-adaptor-connected M.2 PCIe device), and store all of the user data on *another* single medium of a similar type, but with much larger capacity, or even some kind of array of external media. In this section, we show a simple way of conforming to that model when new users are created on your Raspbeery Pi OS.

Note that this technique does *not* show how to transfer an already-existing user, with their entire home directory, over to a newly-added medium. Although we do leave that as an In-Chapter Exercise for you to accomplish outside of the scope of this section.

The prerequisites, and the steps we took to accomplish this technique, are as follows:

0. You have a USB3-mountable medium, formatted to ext4, that you want to use for the new user's home directory, and it is mountable and recognized by your Raspberry Pi system.

1. The new user in our case is named sarwar.

2. The home directory of the administrative user that will execute this technique in our case is /*home*/bob.

3. The home directory of the new user in our case will be /*media/sarwar*.

4. The pathname to the external medium, in our case a USB3 thumb drive drive, is **/media/bob/04fd2202-8879-46f2-8040-446753ed077c**.

5. We will be putting the new user's login directory on an ext4 file system.

Follow these steps sequentially to achieve the desired result:

0. Add the external medium to the system. Find out its device name and UUID with the **blkid** command, and then unmount it (if indeed it is mounted!) with the command:

   $ **sudo umount /media/bob/04fd2202-8879-46f2-8040-446753ed077c**

1. Show the results of the command in step 0 (in /dev) of unmounting the external medium, with the following command:

$ **sudo blkid -o list**

device	fs_type	label	mount point	UUID
/dev/sda1	vfat	boot		/boot 5EA1-EC88
/dev/sda2	ext4	rootfs		/f0702b0a-e54b-4c34-bd2d-6e52a561898c
/dev/sdb1	ext4		(not mounted)	**04fd2202-8879-46f2-8040-446753ed077c**

$

On our system, it was */dev*/sdb1 with UUID of **04fd2202-8879-46f2-8040-446753ed077c**, and in the output showed as being not mounted.

2. Create a new directory on the system in /media for the new user.

     $ **sudo mkdir /media/sarwar**

3. Add the new user with the **adduser** command.

$ **sudo adduser sarwar**
Adding user `sarwar' ...
Adding new group `sarwar' (1001) ...
Adding new user `sarwar' (1001) with group `sarwar' ...
Creating home directory `/home/sarwar' ...
Copying files from `/etc/skel' ...
New password: **www**
Retype new password: **www**
passwd: password updated successfully
Changing the user information for sarwar
Enter the new value, or press ENTER for the default
         Full Name []:
         Room Number []:
         Work Phone []:
         Home Phone []:
         Other []:
Is the information correct? [Y/n] **Y**
$

Note that we've gone with all of the defaults, except supplying a new password for the new user.

4. Mount the external medium as an ext4 file system, at /media/sarwar

     $ **sudo mount -t ext4 -o defaults /dev/sdb1 /media/sarwar**

5. Use the **usermod** command to change the new user's home/login directory to /media/sarwar

     $ **sudo usermod --home /media/sarwar sarwar**
     $

6. Use the **chown** and **chgrp** commands to change the access privileges of the directory */media/*sarwar so that the new user can work in that directory when logging in.

```
$ sudo chown sarwar /media/sarwar
$ sudo chgrp sarwar /media/sarwar
$
```

7. Log into the system with the new user's login name and password. Verify that the current working directory upon login is /*media*/sarwar. Add files to Sarwar's home directory, and note their access privileges.

Conclusion:

The new user now has their home directory, or login directory, on the external medium, and on the boot/system medium. At this point, you can safely delete the new user's home/login directory on the boot/system medium.

Followup: Unmounting and Mount on boot

To unmount the external medium, while in the administrative account, use the following command:

$ **sudo umount /*dev*/sdb1**

If you want this user's home/login directory to mount, and be available after reboots of the system, you need the information from the column UUID from Step 1's output above, to be able to have this exact medium device mount on subsequent reboots of the system. Edit the file /etc/fstab with any editor, for example nano.

$ **sudo nano /etc/fstab**

Add the following line at the end of the file. Make sure to replace the UUID and the path of the mounted device with what is on your system, not what shows on ours here in this example!

UUID=04fd2202-8879-46f2-8040-446753ed077c /*media*/sarwar ext4 defaults 0

It's possible to use /dev/sdb1 instead of UUID=... in the above line in the file, but using the UUID ensures that you are mounting this *exact* external medium, and not another one that you could put in the same USB slot on the Raspberry Pi upon reboot.

In-Chapter Exercise

10. Using a hybrid version of the above technique, move the home/login directory of another user you have previously added to the system, from the boot/system medium to another post-installation medium. How would this affect the file system parameters of the files of the existing user?

1.6 Basic Password Management

It is often necessary for the person responsible for user and group account management, and for obvious security reasons, to make changes to passwords. This is accomplished most easily with the **passwd** command. We give a few basic examples of the use of this command in this section. For a more complete description of the **passwd** command, see the man page for the command on your Raspberry Pi system.

To reset the password for a user account, use the following command:

$ **sudo passwd mansoor**
[sudo] password for bob: **QQQ**
Enter new UNIX password: **ZZZ**
Retype new UNIX password: **ZZZ**
passwd: password updated successfully
$

To obtain a brief listing of the options available with the **passwd** command, use the following command:

$ **sudo passwd -h mansoor**
Usage: passwd [options] [LOGIN]

Options:
-a,	--all	report password status on all accounts
-d,	--delete	delete the password for the named account
-e,	--expire	force expire the password for the named account
-h,	--help	display this help message and exit
-k,	--keep-tokens	change password only if expired
-i,	--inactive	INACTIVE set password inactive after expiration to INACTIVE
-l,	--lock	lock the password of the named account
-n,	--mindays	MIN_DAYS set minimum number of days before password change to MIN_DAYS
-q,	--quiet	quiet mode
-r,	--repository	REPOSITORY change password in REPOSITORY repository
-R,	--root	CHROOT_DIR directory to chroot into
-S,	--status	report password status on the named account
-u,	--unlock	unlock the password of the named account
-w,	--warndays	WARN_DAYS set expiration warning days to WARN_DAYS
-x,	--maxdays	MAX_DAYS set maximum number of days before password change to MAX_DAYS

$

To see the status of a particular user's password, use the following command:

$ **sudo passwd -S mansoor**
mansoor P 11/15/2016 0 99999 7 -1
$

The output of the above command is described in the man page for **passwd** as follows:

"The status information consists of 7 fields. The first field is the user's login name. The second field indicates if the user account has a locked password (L), has no password (NP), or has a usable password (P). The third field gives the date of the last password change. The next four fields are the minimum age, maximum age, warning period, and inactivity period for the password. These ages are expressed in days".

1.7 Determining and Changing File Access Privileges

Once a user or group account has been added to the system, the next concern of a system administrator is how to maintain file access security, in terms of that user or group accounts' permissions to access and utilize system services, and all files in general.

Traditional UNIX and Linux permissions, which define secure access to file objects, such as regular files or directories, are the permissions of *read(r)*, *write(w)*, and *execute(x)*.

Additionally, there are other advanced techniques for setting permissions, such as setting the setuid, setgid, and sticky bit. Beyond these, the POSIX ACL model gives users finer-grained control over file and directory object security. Every file object can be thought of as having associated with it an access ACL, that controls the discretionary access to that object. For a directory, this ACL is referred to as a default ACL. Linux, by default, uses what is known as the POSIX.1e ACLS model. We show extensive methods of doing this model using POSIX.1e, and also the NFSv4 Access Control Lists (ACLs) model, in Volume 1. We discuss system security in general in Section 1.15 below, and follow that up with specific details of it in the sub-sections of that section.

1.7.1 How to Reveal File Access Privileges

The **ls** command, with the **-l** or **-la**, and **-ld**, options can display access permissions for an individual named file, or a list of files or directories.

A brief description of the **ls** command with the three options, taken from the man page on our Raspberry Pi OS, follows:

****
ls [options][file-list][directory-list]

Syntax
ls -l, ls -la [file-list]
ls -ld [directory-list]

Purpose   First syntax: Display the long list of files and/or directories in the space-separated file-list on the display screen; in the case where file-list contains directories, display long list of all the files in these directories Second syntax: Display the long list of directories in directory-list on the display screen.

Common Options

-a, --all	Display a long listing.
-d, --directory	List directories themselves, not their contents.
-g	Similar to -l, but do not list the owner of the file(s) or directories.
-l	Use a long listing format.

****

If no **file-list** is given, the **ls** command gives long lists for all the files (except hidden files, sometimes known as "dot" files) in the current working directory. If you include the **-l** and **-a** options on the command line, hidden files are displayed, as follows:

```
$ ls -la
total 59696
drwxr-xr-x   26   bob bob     4096    Jun 22    07:27 .
drwxr-xr-x   5    root root   4096    Oct 20    2022 ..
-rwxr--r--   1    bob bob     422     May 16    11:53   17_3_4.bash
-rw-r--r--   1    bob bob     7744    May 17    10:30   17_3_4.docx
drwxr-xr-x   5    bob bob     4096    Apr 23    1 6:32  .audacity-data
-rwxr--r--   1    bob bob     402     May 24    11:42   backup.bash
-rw-------   1    bob bob     31557   Jun 21    18:54   .bash_history
-rw-r--r--   1    bob bob     220     Apr 4     2022    .bash_logout
-rw-r--r--   1    bob bob     3523    Apr 4     2022    .bashrc
-rw-r--r--   1    bob bob     47329   Sep 19    2022    Blandemic.txt
drwxr-xr-x   2    bob bob     4096    Apr 4     2022    Bookshelf
Output truncated...
$
```

TABLE 1.3

Permissions of the Files for the Three Kinds of Users

File Name	User	Group	Other
17_3_4.bash	Read, write, execute	Read	Read
17_3_4.docx	Read, write	Read	Read
Blandedmic.txt	Read, write	Read	Read
Bookshelf	Read, write, execute	Read, execute	Read, execute

Following is a description of the fields in the output:

1) The leftmost character in the first field of the output is the file type (**d** for a directory and – [hyphen] for an ordinary file). The rest of the nine characters in the first field show the file access privileges for user, group, and others.

2) The second field shows the number of hard links to the file.

3) The third field shows the owner's login name.

4) The fourth field shows the file's group owner.

5) The fifth field displays the file's size (in bytes).

6, 7) The sixth and seventh fields display the date and time of file's creation (or last update).

8) The last field is the file's name.

Table 1.3 shows what constituent file in the displayed output has what type of access privileges, for the four files in the truncated output.

In the current working directory where the **ls -l** command is executed from, the command displays the long listing of all the files and directories in it, without showing hidden files. You can use the **ls -ld** command to display the long listing of *only* directories. When executed without an argument, this command displays the long listing for the current working directory, as shown in the first command below. The second and third commands show that when the **ls -ld** command is executed with a list of directories as its arguments, it displays the long listing for those directories only. If an argument to the **ls -ld** command is a file, the command displays the long listing for the file. The fourth command below, **ls -ld Bookshelf/***, displays the long listing for *all* the files and directories in the Bookshelf directory.

$ **ls -ld**
drwxr-xr-x 25 bob bob 4096 May 18 05:40.
$ **ls -ld remzi**
drwxr-xr-x 2 bob bob 4096 Nov 5 2022 remzi
$ **ls -ld ~/Downloads remzi**
drwxr-xr-x 2 bob bob 4096 May 14 10:23 /home/bob/Downloads
drwxr-xr-x 2 bob bob 4096 Nov 5 2022 remzi
$ **ls -ld test.py**
-rw-r--r-- 1 bob bob 106 Jun 5 07:00 test.py
$ **ls -ld Bookshelf/***
-rw-r--r-- 1 bob bob 35954684 Apr 4 2022 Bookshelf/BeginnersGuide-4thEd-Eng_v2.pdf
$

1.7.2 Changing File Access Privileges

The **chmod** command changes access privileges for files and directories, *if you have the permissions and system privilege to do so*. The following description is taken from the man page on our Raspberry Pi OS for the **chmod** command:

****

chmod [options][file(s)][directory]

Syntax
        chmod [OPTION]... MODE[,MODE]... FILE...
        chmod [OPTION]... OCTAL-MODE FILE...
        chmod [OPTION]... --reference=RFILE FILE...

Purpose Change/set permissions for files in file-list

Common Options
-R   Recursively descend through directories changing/setting permissions
      for all the files and subdirectories under each directory
-f   Force specified access permissions; no error messages are produced if you
      are the owner of the file
****

Symbolic mode, also known as "mode control", has the form [who][operator] [privilege], with possible values for "who", "operator", and "privilege", as shown in shown in Table 1.4. This table shows the use of the + and – operators for the **chmod** command, to respectively add, and remove designated permissions.

Note that u, g, or o can be used as a privilege with the = operator only. Multiple values can be used for "who" and "privilege", such as ug for the

TABLE 1.4

Values for Symbolic Mode Components

Who	Operator	Privilege
u User	+ Add privilege	r Read bit
g Group	– Remove privilege	w Write bit
o Other	= Set privilege	x Execute/search bit
a All		u User's current privileges
ugo All		g Group's current privileges
		o Others' current privileges
		l Locking Set-group-ID privilege bit
		s Sets user or group ID mode bit
		t Sticky bit

TABLE 1.5

Examples of the **chmod** Command and Their Meanings

Command	Meaning
chmod 700 *	Sets access privileges for all files, including directories, in the current directory to read, write, and execute for the owner, and provides no access privilege to anyone else
chmod 740 Bookshelf	Sets access privileges for Bookshelf to read, write, and execute for the owner and read-only for the group, and provides no access for others
chmod 751 ~/ Bookshelf	Sets access privileges for ~/Bookshelf to read, write, and execute for the owner, read and execute for the group, and execute-only permission for others
chmod 700 ~	Sets access privileges for the home directory to read, write, and execute (i.e., search) for the owner, and no privileges for anyone else
chmod u=rwx Bookshelf	Sets owner's access privileges for Bookshelf to read, write, and execute and keeps the privileges of group and others at their present values
chmod ugo-rw test or chmod a-rw test	Does not let anyone read or write test
chmod a+x test	Gives everyone execute permission for test
chmod g=u test	Makes test's group privileges match its user (owner) privileges
chmod go= test	Removes all access privileges to test for group and others

"who" field, and rx for the "privilege" field. Some useful examples of the **chmod** command, and their purposes, are listed in Table 1.5.

Also, the permission bits can be set as octal numbers, according to Table 1.6. The text explanations of the following commands are provided here to illustrate how access privileges for files can be interrogated and set. The **chmod** command is used to modify, or initially set, access privileges. The **ls -l** (or the **ls -ld** and **ls -la**) commands are used to show the results of the applied **chmod**

TABLE 1.6

Access Permissions for a File and Their Octal Equivalents and Meanings

r	w	x	Octal Digit	Meaning
0	0	0	0	No permission
0	0	1	1	Execute-only permission
0	1	0	2	Write-only permission
0	1	1	3	Write and execute permissions
1	0	0	4	Read-only permission
1	0	1	5	Read and execute permissions
1	1	0	6	Read and write permissions
1	1	1	7	Read, write, and execute permissions

command. After the **chmod 700 Bookshelf** command has been executed, the owner of the Bookshelf file has read, write, and execute access privileges for it, and no other user has any privilege. The **chmod g+rx Bookshelf** command adds read and execute access privileges to the Bookshelf file for the group. The privileges of the owner and others remain exactly the same. The **chmod o+r Bookshelf** command adds read access privilege to the Bookshelf file for others. The **chmod a-w *** command takes away the write access privilege from all users for all the files in the current working directory. The **chmod go+x, o+r *** command enables the execute permission for group and others, and read permission to others to all the files in the current working directory. The **chmod 700 [l-t]*** command sets the access permissions to 700 for all the files that start with letters "l" through "t", as illustrated by the output of the last **ls -l** command, which shows access privileges for the files labs and temp changed to 700.

```
$ ls -l
drwxr-x---    2    bob    bob    512    Apr    23    09:37 Bookshelf
-rwxrwxrwx    1    bob    bob    12     May    01    13:22 labs
-rwxr--r--    1    bob    bob    163    May    05    23:13 temp
$ chmod 700 Bookshelf
$ ls -ld Bookshelf
drwx------    2    bob    bob    512    Apr    23    09:37 Bookshelf
$ chmod g+rx Bookshelf
$ ls -ld Bookshelf
drwxr-x---    2    bob    bob    512    Apr    23    09:37 Bookshelf
$ chmod o+r Bookshelf
$ ls -ld Bookshelf
drwxr-xr--    2    bob    bob    512    Apr    23    09:37 Bookshelf
$ chmod a-w *
$ ls -l
dr-xr-x---    2    bob    bob    512    Apr    23    09:37 Bookshelf
-r-xr-xr-x    1    bob    bob    12     May    01    13:22 labs
```

```
-r-xr—-r--       1    bob    bob    163    May    05      23:13 temp
$ chmod go+x, o+r *
$ ls -l
dr-xr-xr--       2    bob    bob    512    Apr    23      09:37 Bookshelf
-r-xr-xr-x       1    bob    bob    12     May    01      13:22 labs
-r-xr—-xr--      1    bob    bob    163    May    05      23:13 temp
$ chmod 700 [l-t]*
$ ls -l
dr-xr-x---       2    bob    bob    512    Apr    23      09:37 Bookshelf
-rwx------       1    bob    bob    12     May    01      13:22 labs
-rwx------       1    bob    bob    163    May    05      23:13 temp
$ chmod +x *
$ ls -l
dr-xr-x--x       2    bob    bob    512    Apr    23      09:37 Bookshelf
-rwx--x--x       1    bob    bob    12     May    01      13:22 labs
-rwx--x--x       1    bob    bob    163    May    05      23:13 temp
$
```

The access permissions for the files and directories nested beneath one or more upper-level directories can be set by using the **chmod** command with the **-R** option. In the following commands, the first command sets access permissions for all the files and directories under the directory called Bookshelf to 711, *recursively*. The second command sets the permissions for all the files and directories under ~/temp/motions to 700, recursively. "Recursively" means by descending downward to all subdirectories under the specified directories, i.e., Bookshelf and ~/temp/motions on these two command lines.

```
$ chmod -R 711 Bookshelf
$ chmod -R 700 ~/temp/motions
$
```

If you set access privileges with a single octal digit in a **chmod** command, it is used by the command to set the access privileges for "others"; the access privileges for "user" and "group" are both set to 0 (i.e., no access privileges). If you specify two octal digits in a **chmod** command, the command uses them to set access privileges for "group" and "others". The access privileges for "user" are set to 0.

In the following two commands, the first **chmod** command sets "others" access privileges for the Bookshelf directory to 7 (rwx) and 0 (---) for owner and group. The second **chmod** command sets "group" and "others" access privileges for the temp directory to 7 (rwx) and 0 (---), respectively, and no access rights for the file owner. The **ls -l** command shows the results of these commands.

```
$ chmod 7 Bookshelf
$ chmod 70 temp
$ ls –l Bookshelf temp
d------rwx  2  bob  bob  512  Nov  10 09:43  Bookshelf
d---rwx---  2  bob  bob  512  Nov  10 09:43  temp
$
```

1.7.3 Access Privileges for Directories

The read permission on a directory lets you read the contents of the directory (the contents of a directory are the names of ordinary files and directories under it), the write permission allows you to create a file in the directory, or delete an existing file or sub-directory from it, and the execute permission for a directory allows searching the contents of the directory.

Note

Read and write permissions on directories are *not* meaningful without the search permission. You must have both read and execute permissions on a directory to be able to list the names of files under it. You must have both write and execute permissions on a directory to be able to create a file in it.

In the following commands, the write permission for the directory Bookshelf has been turned off. Thus, you cannot create a subdirectory ee345 in this directory by using the **mkdir** command or copy a file foo into it. Similarly, as you do not have search permission for the directory personal, you cannot use the **cd** command to enter (change directory to) this directory. If the directory test had a subdirectory, say foobar, for which the execute permission was turned on, you still could not change directory to foobar, because search permission for test is turned off. Finally, as read permission for the directory personal is turned off, you cannot display the names of files and directories in it by using the **ls** command, even though search permission on it is turned on.

```
$ chmod 600 sample
$ chmod 500 Bookshelf
$ chmod 300 personal
$ ls -ld Bookshelf personal sample
dr-x------    2    bob   bob   512   Aug 4 06:36    Bookshelf
d-wx------    2    bob   bob   62    Aug 4 06:36    personal
drw-------    2    bob   bob   88    Aug 4 06:36    sample
$ mkdir Bookshelf/Salinger
mkdir: Bookshelf/Salinger: Permission denied
$ cp foo Bookshelf
cp: Bookshelf/foo: Permission denied
$ cd sample
cd: sample: Permission denied
```

```
$ ls -l personal
total 0
ls: personal: Permission denied
$
```

The next set of commands show that having read or write permission on a directory is *not* adequate to read its contents (e.g., display them with the **ls** command), or create a file or sub-directory in it. For example, the directory dirtest has write permission turned on, but you cannot copy the morsel.txt file into it, because search permission on it is turned off. Similarly, you cannot remove the file steak.txt from dirtest2. After you turn on its search permission with the **chmod u+x dirtest2** command, you can remove the file steak.txt.

```
$ ls -ld dir?
d-w-------   2    bob bob   2 Aug 4 06:59      dirtest
d-w-------   2    bob bob   3 Aug 4 06:59      dirtest2
$ cp morsel.txt dirtest
cp: dirtest/morsel.txt: Permission denied
$ rm dirtest2/steak.txt
rm: dirtest2/steak.txt: Permission denied
$ chmod u+x dirtest2
$ ls -ld dirtest2
d-wx------   2    bob bob   3 Aug 4 06:59      dirtest2
$ rm dirtest2/steak.txt
$
```

1.8 File Systems, Connections to Persistent Media, and Adding Media to Your System

Question: What is a computer file system?

Answer: A way of logically ordering data, so that it is persistent, can be securely and easily located very quickly, and then accessed in a consistent way for use.

Providing data persistence, which is the third primary objective of an operating system, in large part involves establishing and maintaining connections to persistent media, such as the microSD card that may be the system/boot disk on your hardware. Alternative forms of this media, and the file systems found on them, can be physically connected via the USB3 ports on the Raspberry Pi itself, such as with SATA SSD's inside external enclosures, or USB3 thumb drives. They can also be some form of remote virtual drive, such as a network-available, and a mounted NFSv4 share, or remote volumes and complements of drives.

And in some cases, a file system may *not* make use of a persistent storage device or medium at all! At this higher level of abstraction, the file system can access, use, organize, and represent *any* form of data, whether it is persistent or volatile. We use the word volatile here to mean during the transient lifetime of some process or service. Of course, systemd and the Linux kernel control all processes and services running on the Raspberry Pi. *Pseudo,* and special-purpose file systems (sometimes called *synthetic file systems*), which can be thought of as virtual file systems, have this kind of characteristic.

There are also established protocols for connecting to and accessing either physical, virtual, or pseudo file systems, in the locations where they may reside. Two examples of access protocols that establish and maintain the connections to virtual, network-available media and file systems are the Network File System, version 4 (NFSv4), and the Internet Small Computer System Interface (iSCSI).

In this section, we first present an organizing scheme that you can use to think about types of media and file systems. A file system may be nominally assigned according to what medium it exists on: a directly connected physical medium (such as a USB3 SATA disk), a virtual medium (such as Network-Attached Storage or Storage Area Networks that use NFSv4 or iSCSI), or as a specialized pseudo-file system that is not on a persistent medium at all (such as the cgroups or proc file systems).

We then go on to give some particular examples of adding directly connected, physical media to a Raspberry Pi OS.

Additionally, we suggest a traditional approach, when using the recommended storage model we give in Section 1.3.1, to adding persistent media to your system. This is as follows:

Where you first properly connect the device to the Raspberry Pi via attaching it to a USB3 port, partition that medium, manually add a file system to it (typically the ext4 file system), and then finally create directories and files in the partition(s) on the media. The sections below detail this more traditional approach.

According to our organizing scheme, a file system can be separated into three hierarchically arranged layers that perform very particular functions. These layers, arranged from farthest-to-nearest to the actual hardware of the physical medium in question, are as follows:

The Logical Layer:
This layer is used for interaction with user application programs, and the processes they consist of, via Linux system calls. It provides the application programming interface (API) for file operations, for example system calls to **OPEN, CLOSE, READ,** etc., and connects with the layer below it for processing. The Logical Layer achieves efficient file access, logically organized directory

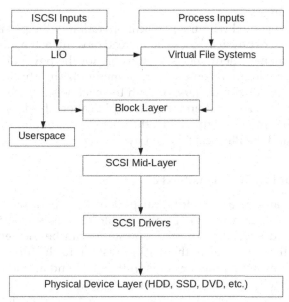

FIGURE 1.3
Linux Raspberry Pi OS File System Storage Layers.

operations, and provides user-autonomy and security. In Figure 1.3, this layer is represented by the ISCSI and Process Inputs blocks at the top of the figure.

The Virtual Layer:
This layer provides the interface mechanisms for maintaining multiple, simultaneously existing implementations of physical and virtual file systems on the same computer. For example, it makes possible mounting and transparently using NFSv4, btrfs, ext3, ext4, fat32, or ZFS at the same time on the same system, and operating with files from all of those implementations as if they were all of the same type.

The Linux IO (LIO) block shown in Figure 1.3 is known as an iSCSI "target", and represents Virtual Layer connectivity to persistent media from various network connections. These connections traditionally use high-speed fiber channel technology to create a storage area network (SAN), but most importantly can also be achieved using Ethernet and TCP/IP.

A more detailed architectural scheme of classifying Virtual Layer file systems further separates that layer into block-based, network, stackable, pseudo, and special purpose categories. In Figure 1.3, many of the different implementations of file systems, such as NFSv4, ext4, xfs, btrfs, initramfs, and the procfs, would be situated within the Virtual file systems block shown in that diagram. Two very contemporary and extremely important virtual file systems are the cgroups file system (cgroupsfs) used by systemd, and the userland, block-based file system, ZFS.

The Physical Layer:
This layer is concerned with the physical operation of the persistent storage device. It processes physical blocks being read or written. It handles buffering and memory management and is responsible for the physical placement of blocks in specific locations on the storage medium. The physical file system interacts with the device drivers, or with the channels that physical devices communicate over. At a certain level of simplification, this layer can be schematically represented in Figure 1.3 by the integrated grouping of Block Layer, SCSI Layers, and the Physical Device Layer.

1.8.1 Types of File System and ext4

Furthermore, and as a very integral part of the operation of the Linux kernel as it exists in a transient and volatile state as we have defined it, the pseudo and special purpose file systems can be viewed as a series of conduits through which the entire system itself "flows". Thinking along these lines, when the kernel is in the CPU and attendant RAM, the kernel code itself is organized as a file system. The kernel (or systemd super-kernel) can be viewed as a file system of transitory data structures, that maintains the steady state of the hardware and software using these conduits exclusively; this achieves the important controlling goals of virtualization, concurrency, user-autonomy, security, and the necessary archival, long-term data persistence on the file systems that are there to serve the user base.

Over the history of Linux, various file systems have been used to provide speed, efficiency, security, and utility to the ordinary user. The most contemporary and universal of these, across the three major branches of Linux, is the Linux Extended File System (ext). All of the representative downstream releases of Linux use it as the default file system.

The 4th version of ext, ext4, is the current and most robust version so far. It has several features, such as large scalability, the ability to map to very large disk array sizes, and other very critical features, such as journaling. Following is a compact listing of some of the features of ext4:

1. It can support volumes with sizes up to 1 exabyte, and files with sizes up to 16 terabytes.
2. It uses an "extents" mapping scheme, which replaces block mapping used by earlier versions of ext. An extent is a range of contiguous physical blocks.
3. It is backward-compatible with ext3 and ext2. Therefore ext3 and ext2 file systems can be mounted as ext4.
4. It delays block allocation until data is flushed to disk.
5. It has an unlimited number of sub-directories that can be created.

6. It has a multi-block allocator that can make better choices about allocating files contiguously on disk.

7. It provides timestamps, measured in nanoseconds.

Most importantly, from the perspective of our Raspberry Pi OS recommended data storage model, adding a second medium, for example, allows you to keep the operating system and the user data on two different physical persistent media. That way, if the operating system fails and the system disk is corrupted and unusable, the data survives on the user data disk, and can very easily be recovered.

There are many traditional, legacy methods of achieving the objective of this data storage model, using facilities such as Linux disk and file maintenance commands, utilities such as mdadm (a software RAID manager), and Linux Volume Management (LVM). But from our perspective, the modern and contemporary way of implementing the recommended data storage model is using ZFS on redundant additional persistent media. With ZFS, you get bit-level data integrity, volume management, RAID capabilities at all levels, and a failure-proof backup strategy, all rolled into one utility.

Note
Unfortunately, at the time this book was written, the Raspberry Pi OS did *not* easily and reliably support the installation and implementation of ZFS. Additionally, ZFS works best on systems that have Error Correction Code (ECC) memory.

1.8.2 Persistent Media and Devices

There are some very important reasons for adding persistent media to your system, aside from conforming to our recommended storage model. Your microSD card may be running out of space, or beginning to show signs of failure. In a traditional legacy scheme, these situations might involve downtime of the system in order to correct the problem. Whereas, with our storage model implementation, and some of the facilities shown in the sections below, they can be handled without bringing the system down.

1.8.2.1 Partitioning Schemes and Strategies

By now, it should be evident to you that the Raspberry Pi OS organizes everything in files, and uses a file system to organize those files. A disk partition can be most simply defined as a logical area of the disk that holds a file system.

Once you verify that your Raspberry Pi system can actually recognize and mount the additional media, there are several reasons to adopt a particular partitioning scheme for a newly added medium. Creating multiple partitions on a disk avoids full disk problems by segregating directories into those partitions, and gives the system administrator control over access to those directories and partitions. And you can maintain different file system structures simultaneously in different partitions.

When you are adding new media, you have the option of using the traditional method of doing disk partitioning with command line utilities such as **fdisk** or **gdisk**, or the option of using a GUI-based method, with a utility such as Gparted. We showed the basics of using Gparted in Volume 1. And, as we show in the sections below, you can implement our recommended data storage model with a traditional ext4 file system scheme. We present an example detailing how to do this using the traditional ext4 scheme.

To help the administrator of a Linux system with the task of adding persistent media, the following sections will also address these general concerns:

* The availability of software device drivers for the new hardware to be added.

* How the hardware will be recognized, configured, and deployed on the system.

* Identification of possible paths to replacement and upgrading of existing hardware, within the context of using our recommended data storage model.

As discussed in Item 3) of Section 1.3.1, our data storage model for a Raspberry Pi, used for our deployed models, is capable of mounting and using two or more external USB3-mounted media, and that implementation is made possible by what we show in the following sub-sections.

We show a further example of additions of persistent media, and their configuration, in Volume 1. That example details creating and managing RAID arrays on the Raspberry Pi OS using mdadm. The additions in the traditional ext4-based example shown here in Section 1.8.5 will be done for USB3 thumb drives, but can also be easily extended to other persistent media, such as USB3-mounted external SSD(s), or M.2 NVMe devices, for example.

External Media Additions:
Generally, when you add additional media some significant time after you have installed the operating system on the Raspberry Pi hardware, you will want to partition it. You might even want to create a new partition table on it, create one or more partitions, and format those partitions using a standard file system, such as ext4. We emphasize and encourage the use of the Gparted GUI-based application to do this.

When you add an external USB2 or 3 medium, such as a thumb drive, or other form of persistent storage device, it is generally already formatted to the file system type known as FAT32 (in the case of most popular commercially available USB thumb drives), or to some other format depending on the media. Traditionally, you can then partition the disk using the **fdisk** command, and add a file system to it with the **mkfs** command. We emphasize and encourage the use of **fdisk**, or its newer sister, **gdisk**, to do the partitioning if you choose this traditional operation.

Note that safe removal of USB media can be done manually, via a graphical means, on the Raspberry Pi. For example, on the desktop, left-click on the icon in the upper-right of the menu bar (the icon that looks like an upward-facing arrow with a bar underneath it), choose the available medium, and left-click again on the medium to eject, or unmount it. Unmounting a USB thumb drive, or other USB-bus media, can also be done from the command line with the **umount** command.

When a USB thumb drive, or other external medium, is automatically mounted, the path to it is **/media/your_home_dir/id**, where **your_home_dir** is the name of your home directory on the system, and **id** is the disk id number or identifier of the medium.

For example, when we added a USB thumb drive, and created a single primary partition on it with Gparted, along with an ext4 file system automatically added to that partition at the same time, the newly mounted hard drive was accessed via the path:

/media/bob/04fd2202-8879-46f2-8040-446753ed077c.

1.8.3 Preliminary Considerations When Adding New Media

If you insert a USB thumb drive, or any other USB-mountable media, that you know is functioning properly into your Raspberry Pi, and it is *not* recognized, the chances are that your operating system does *not* have a device driver available to enable communication between the computer and the thumb drive. In that case, it might be very prudent to find an alternative medium.

How do you know if a new disk drive is recognized, and most importantly, is usable on your system?

There are at least three quick and easy ways to know if the new disk drive is recognized.

1) If it is a USB thumb drive, and it is formatted to FAT32, it will automount itself, and an icon for it will open on the desktop (along with a prompt asking you if you want to view of its contents).

2) In a terminal window, you can use the command **systemctl –f** and watch the screen display as you insert the device. It will show that a new device has been added (of course, given that the system has

drivers for it!), even though in the case of a USB thumb drive, it might be formatted to something other than FAT32!

3) Use the before-and-after technique shown in Section 1.8.4 below.

The same is true when you connect another type of USB-mountable external medium properly, but the probability of it *not* being recognized can be lower. The best and easiest thing to do in a case when the medium is not recognized is to use another device. The Raspberry Pi OS has facilities to find and install device drivers on your system for a device, but this process is time consuming, and may not be fruitful for the particular device in question, particularly for the beginner. Also, it is possible to write a driver for your device, which is even more time consuming, and even less fruitful for the beginner. The important thing here is that perhaps the USB thumb drive, for example, is *not* formatted to FAT32, but that a manufacturer hasn't supplied the device drivers, or made them available to Linux kernel developers.

In many instances it is important to know the physical device name, the instance name, and the logical device name of disk drives on your system, but practically speaking, for the Raspberry Pi OS administrator, easily finding out the logical device name of a disk drive is most important.

You may want to add media to your Raspberry Pi system that has been used on another computer operating system previously. In that case, the primary and secondary examples we show can be deployed to repartition and prepare that hard disk for new use with the Raspberry Pi OS.

1.8.4 Five Quick and Easy Ways to Find Out the Logical Device Names of Media

Before attaching a new medium to your Raspberry Pi system, it is important to know how to determine, in a very quick and easy manner, what the currently installed logical device names of the media actually attached and usable on your system are. What we mean by "attached and usable" is that the medium is properly connected and recognized by the system, and has a device driver that the system can use to communicate with it.

Before and after: If you want to find out the logical device name of a newly installed medium, use one of the following methods to see what media are on your system *before* you add the new one, and then use the same method *after* the new one has been added, and note the difference. The different or new logical name that appears will be the logical device name of the new medium.

The five simple methods that follow show how to determine what media are attached, and usable on your system, and what the logical device names of those and any others you might want to add to your system are.

Method 1

Change your current working directory to /dev. Type **ls**. A microSD card, for example, will show up in the **ls** listing as mmcblk*. The full path to the first slice, or partition, on one of these disks is specified as mmcblk0p1. A USB bus device, like a thumb drive, would show up in the **ls** listing as sdb, or whatever letter designation the system has assigned to it, and the full path to the first slice on it would be sdb1. A USB3-mounted SSD will show up as sda, and the first slice to it would be sda1. These are exactly what designations appeared in /dev on our Raspberry pi 4B and Pi 400.

Method 2

Type **df -hT** on the command line, to find out the file system names and paths they are mounted at on your system. On our Raspberry Pi system, when we did this to see if a 32 Gb USB thumb drive was recently successfully attached to the system, this is the output:

```
$ df -hT
```

file system	Type	Size	Used	Avail	Use%	Mounted on
/dev/root	ext4	439G	11G	406G	3%	/
devtmpfs	devtmpfs	1.7G 0	1.7G		0%	/dev
tmpfs	tmpfs	1.9G 0	1.9G		0%	/dev/shm
tmpfs	tmpfs	759M	1.4M	758M	1%	/run
tmpfs	tmpfs	5.0M	4.0K	5.0M	1%	/run/lock
/dev/sda1	vfat	253M	31M	222M	13%	/boot
tmpfs	tmpfs	380M	28K	380M	1%	/run/user/1000
/dev/sdb1	ext4	29G	24K	27G	1%	/media/bob/ 04fd2202-8879- 46f2-8040...

```
$
```

Notice that our root, or system disk(/dev/root) is 439 GB in size. That's because we're running this Raspberry Pi 400 from a USB3-mounted SSD with that capacity, *not* a microSD card. We address more details of the **df** command in Section 1.14.3.

Method 3

Very similar to using the **df** command, use the **lsblk -a** command. When we used this command and option on our Raspberry Pi system, after we had attached the 32 Gb USB thumb drive, we got the following output:

$ lsblk -a

NAME	MAJ:MIN	RM	SIZE	RO	TYPE	MOUNTPOINT
ram0	1:0	0	4M	0	disk	
ram1	1:1	0	4M	0	disk	
Output truncated...						
ram15	1:15	0	4M	0	disk	
loop0	7:0	0	0B	0	loop	
loop1	7:1	0	0B	0	loop	
Output truncated...						
sda	8:0	0	447.1G	0	disk	
├─sda1	8:1	0	256M	0	part	/boot
└─sda2	8:2	0	446.9G	0	part	/
sdb	8:16	1	29.1G	0	disk	
└─sdb1	8:17	1	29.1G	0	part	/media/bob/ 04fd2202-8879-46f2-8040...

$

Method 4

Use the **findmnt** command. When we used this on our Raspberry Pi system, we obtained the following output:

$ findmnt

TARGET	SOURCE	FSTYPE	OPTIONS
/	/dev/sda2	ext4	rw,noatime
└─/dev	devtmpfs	devtmpfs	rw,relatime,size=1677960k, nr_inodes=419490,mode=755
└─/dev/shm	tmpfs	tmpfs	rw,nosuid,nodev
├─/dev/pts	devpts	devpts	rw,nosuid,noexec,relatime,g id=5,mode=620,ptmxmode= 000
└─/dev/mqueue	mqueue	mqueue	rw,nosuid,nodev,noexec, relatime
├─/proc	proc	proc	rw,relatime
└─/proc/sys/fs/binfmt_misc	systemd-1	autofs	rw,relatime,fd=29, pgrp= 1,timeout=0,minproto=5,maxproto=5,
├─/proc/fs/nfsd	nfsd	nfsd	rw,relatime

Output truncated...

| └─/media/bob/04fd2202-8879-46f2-8040-446753ed077c | /dev/sdb1 | ext4 | rw,nosuid,nodev,relatime, errors=remount-ro |

$

Notice that some of the file system types (FSTYPE) are shown as types such as ext4, sysfs, tmpfs, nfsd, proc, etc.

Method 5
You can also very efficiently use the GUI-Based G Partition Editor (Gparted), as shown in Example 1.5 below. With Gparted, you can easily find out the logical device names of disks on your system. In addition, with Gparted you can use graphical editing methods to affect several important characteristics of the media, such as the format and partitioning of the drives.

In-Chapter Exercise

11. Insert a USB thumb drive into your Raspberry Pi, and mount it if necessary. What command would you use to mount it? Use the **findmnt** command to find out its logical device name. What is the logical device name for this thumb drive? Along what path is it mounted on your system? What are the uses and meanings of the other file system types shown, as output to the **findmnt** command? For example, are cgroup, proc, fuse.gvf, and tempfs logical, virtual, or physical file systems, and how exactly do these differ from ext4?

1.8.5 Adding New Media to the System

The following example shows how to add new media to your system, and partition them. We chose to use the GUI-based Gparted partition editor, primarily because it's easy to use, and can be quickly installed on the Raspberry Pi OS. We also choose it, instead of the **gdisk** utility, or the legacy **fdisk** command, because it has a GUI front-end, and GUI is easy to use. For example, with it, you don't have to remember command names, options, or arguments to accomplish what you want. This GUI software not only lets you easily find out what the logical device names of media attached to your Raspberry Pi are, but also allows you to partition newly added media, and put a file system onto them at the same time.

Example 1.5: Adding a New Medium, and Using Gparted to "Slice", or Partition It

Objectives: To practice using the Gparted Partition Editor to place a disk partition, with an ext4 file system on that partition, onto a USB thumb drive mounted on your Raspberry Pi.

Prerequisites: Having a useable USB thumb drive for your system.

Requirements: Do the steps below in the sequence presented to complete the requirements of this example.

1. Install the Gparted Partition Editor software, if it is not already installed on your system. This is most efficiently done using the GUI-based Raspberry Pi menu Preferences > Add/Remove Software. Also, it would be very efficient to place an icon for this software on your desktop.

2. Properly connect the new media to the system, via either the USB2 or USB3 connectors on your Raspberry Pi hardware. USB3 is a faster protocol, and will give you better performance when working with or on the new media.

3. Launch the Gparted Partition Editor, either graphically or from the command line, with the command **gparted**. Enter your password in the window that appears.

4. The Gparted screen opens on screen, as shown in Figure 1.4.

5. The current media attached to the system appear in the pull-down menu bar at the upper right. Make note of all the complete paths to the current disks. For example, the boot or root disk might be designated as /dev/mmcblk0 if you're running your system from a microSD card, or /dev/sda if you're running your system from a USB3-attached and mounted SSD, as seen in Figure 1.4.

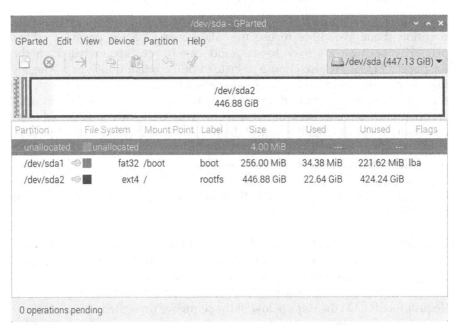

FIGURE 1.4
Gparted Main Window.

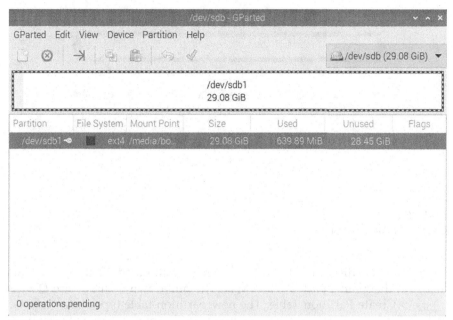

FIGURE 1.5
/dev/sdb Partition 1.

6. Click the down-facing arrow shown in the menu bar in the upper right corner of the Gparted screen. Scroll in that bar until you reach the medium you just added to the system. If the disk drive you just added doesn't appear in the Gparted listing, you can't easily use that disk drive. If it does appear, continue to the next step. On our Raspberry Pi system, the new medium appeared as /dev/sdb.

7. Pick that new medium in the menu bar. It is shown in the main Gparted pane. Click on that disk in the main Gparted pane. You can now partition and format that new disk. In our example it is shown as /dev/sdb, a new disk we inserted at step 2. This is shown in Figure 1.5. Notice in that figure that the disk contains a single partition, /dev/sdb1 that has a fat32 file system on it, and no label.

8. From the pull-down menus at the top of the Gparted window, make the menu choice Partition > Unmount. Then click on the red X in the icon bar. This will delete the partition information on that disk. It is now a pending operation.

9. In order to execute the pending operation, make the pull-down menu choice Edit > Apply All Operations. In the warning window, click Apply. A window appears showing you the progress, and hopefully successful application, of the pending operation. Click close in that window when the operation is complete.

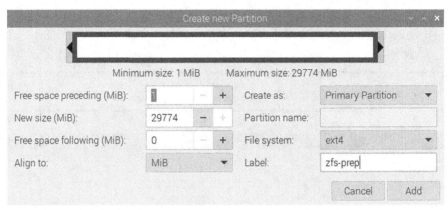

FIGURE 1.6
Create New Partition Window.

10. The new disk should now be shown as unallocated. Click on its listing in the main Gparted pane. Make the pull-down menu choice Device > Create Partition Table. The new partition table type shows msdos. That's good for us. Click Apply in the warning window. Everything on that disk will be erased! When Gparted has created a new partition table, click on that disk again in the main Gparted pane. The Partition and File System appear as unallocated.

11. Make the pull-down menu choice Partition > New. The Create new Partition window appears on screen, as shown in Figure 1.6. The defaults for the new partition, as seen in Figure 1.6, are to take the whole disk up with this partition, create it as a primary partition, and create the file system on it as ext4.

12. Add any label designation of your choice in the Label field, so that you can more readily identify this medium. We have chosen to label this partition as zfs-prep, as seen in Figure 1.6. Leave all of the other defaults in place. Click the Add button. Make the pull-down menu choice Edit > Apply All Operations (it appears as a green check mark in the menu bar at the top of the Gparted window). In the warning window, click Apply. Click the Close button when the Applying pending operations message appears, showing the operation has completed successfully.

13. You now have a created a partition table on, partitioned, and formatted a usable medium on the system. Congratulations! On our system, it is shown in Figure 1.7 as /dev/sdb1 29.08 GB.

14. Quit Gparted, by making the pull-down menu choice Gparted>Quit.

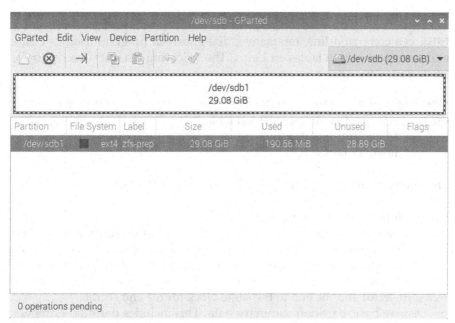

FIGURE 1.7
/dev/sdb1, Partition 1 Modified.

Conclusion: We have added a new hard disk to our Raspberry Pi OS hardware, and partitioned it with Gparted.

1.8.6 Adding Disks Using **fdisk**

A more traditional approach to adding media to the system a significant time after installation is covered in this section. We conform to our recommended storage model, as in the previous section where we implemented it for an additional hard disk added using Gparted. In this section, we use the **fdisk** command to partition another disk. The example in this section uses an externally mounted USB thumb drive, which is more easily added, cheaper, and much more available to the ordinary user as an additional storage medium.

This example can be easily extended to externally mounted USB3 SATA SSDs, or other forms of media. In Section 1.9 below, entitled "Installing ZFS, and **zpool** and **zfs** Command Syntax", we give examples of ZFS-based redundancy, to illustrate a similar backup strategy with ZFS.

1.8.6.1 Partitioning a Disk Using fdisk

fdisk is a command line, interactive, dialog-driven program used to create and manage partition tables on Linux. The following is a brief description of **fdisk** syntax and use:

****

fdisk – Create and manages partition tables
Syntax: fdisk [options] device
         fdisk -l [device...]

Output: New or manipulated partitions on the media **device**.

Common Interactive Commands:

n   Create a new partition. You enter a partition number, starting sector, and an ending sector. Both start and end sectors can be specified in absolute terms as sector numbers. Pressing the Enter key with no input specifies the default value, which is the start of the largest available block for the start sector and the end of the same block for the end sector.

p   Display basic partition summary data. This includes partition numbers, starting and ending sector numbers, partition sizes, fdisk's partition types codes, and partition names.

t   Change a single partition's type code. You enter the type code using a two-byte hexadecimal number.

w   Write data. Use this command to save your changes.

Example:
$ **sudo fdisk /dev/sdb** As superuser, run fdisk on the disk /dev/sdb

****

Example 1.6 Placing a Single Partition on a USB thumb drive using **fdisk**

Objectives: To use the **fdisk** utility to practice placing a disk partition, with an ext4 file system on that partition, on a USB thumb drive mounted on your Raspberry Pi.

Prerequisites: Having a useable USB thumb drive for your system.

Requirements: Do the steps below in the sequence presented to complete the requirements of this example.

1.   Having previously determined that the thumb drive is recognized on your system, and what its logical device name is (ours was /dev/sdb), insert it into a USB port. We used an 8 GB Kingston thumb drive; it's *very* reliable, and always auto-mounts on Raspberry Pi 4B or Pi 400 systems.

On our Raspberry Pi 400, the thumb drive was auto-mounted. Use the following commands to unmount it:

$ **sudo umount /dev/sdb1**

2. Use the **fdisk** command to partition the newly added USB thumb drive, making sure to first delete any partitions that are on it. For our Kingston USB thumb drive, there was only one default partition on it: a fat32 partition, with a msdos partition table.

$ **sudo fdisk /dev/sdb**
Welcome to fdisk (util-linux 2.36.1).
Changes will remain in memory only, until you decide to write them.
Be careful before using the write command.

The device contains 'vfat' signature and it will be removed by a write command. See fdisk (8) man page and --wipe option for more details.

Device does not contain a recognized partition table.
Created a new DOS disklabel with disk identifier 0xa4dcc322.

Command (m for help): **n**
Partition type
  p   primary (0 primary, 0 extended, 4 free)
  e   extended (container for logical partitions)
Select (default p): **p**
Partition number (1-4, default 1): **<Enter>**
First sector (2048-60975103, default 2048): **<Enter>**
Last sector, +/-sectors or +/-size{K,M,G,T,P} (2048-60975103, default 60975103): **<Enter>**

Created a new partition 1 of type 'Linux' and of size 29.1 GiB.

Command (m for help):

Command (m for help): **p**
Disk /dev/sdb1: 29.08 GiB, 31219253248 bytes, 60975104 sectors
Units: sectors of 1 * 512 = 512 bytes
Sector size (logical/physical): 512 bytes / 512 bytes
I/O size (minimum/optimal): 512 bytes / 512 bytes
Disklabel type: dos
Disk identifier: 0xa4dcc322

Device   Boot Start   End   Sectors Size Id Type
/dev/sdb1p1   2048 6 0975103 60973056 29.1G 83 Linux

Command (m for help): **l**

A long list of types and codes is displayed; we want type 83- Linux!

Command (m for help): **t**
Selected partition 1
Hex code or alias (type L to list all): **83**
Changed type of partition 'Linux ' to 'Linux'.

Command (m for help): **p**
Disk /dev/sdb1: 29.08 GiB, 31219253248 bytes, 60975104 sectors
Units: sectors of 1 * 512 = 512 bytes
Sector size (logical/physical): 512 bytes / 512 bytes
I/O size (minimum/optimal): 512 bytes / 512 bytes
Disklabel type: dos
Disk identifier: 0xa4dcc322

Device Boot Start End Sectors Size Id Type
/dev/sdb1p1 2048 60975103 60973056 29.1G 83 Linux

Command (m for help): **w**
The partition table has been altered.
Calling ioctl() to re-read partition table.
Syncing disks.
$

3. In order for this partition to be usable, you must add a file system to
    it. We would like to add an ext4 file system to the partition. To do this,
    use the **mkfs** command as follows:

    $ **sudo mkfs -t ext4 /dev/sdb1**
    mke2fs 1.46.2 (28-Feb-2021)
    Found a dos partition table in /dev/sdb1
    Proceed anyway? (y,N) **y**
    Creating file system with 7621888 4k blocks and 1908736 inodes
    file system UUID: 8946ddbc-b94a-4dc4-9966-66f0a8411b4e
    Superblock backups stored on blocks:
            32768, 98304, 163840, 229376, 294912, 819200, 884736, 1605632,
            2654208, 4096000

Allocating group tables: done
Writing inode tables: done
Creating journal (32768 blocks): done
Writing superblocks and file system accounting information: done
$

Now in order to use this partition for data, you can create directories, and files in those directories.

Conclusion: Using the fdisk utility, and the **mkfs** command, we deleted any existing partitions on a USB thumb drive, and created a Linux partition on it with an ext4 file system.

In-Chapter Exercises

12. Why do you have to remount /*dev*/sdb1 in Example 1.6 in order to add directories and files to the disk, and how do you achieve remounting? What is the designation of this thumb drive on your system, and where is it mounted?

13. Do the steps of Example 1.6 to partition a USB thumb drive with a single primary partition, and then add an ext4 file system to it. Create directories on the thumb drive.

14. Do the steps of Example 1.6 to partition an externally mounted SSD in a USB3 enclosure, placing a single primary partition on it, and then add an ext4 file system to it. Create directories on the hard drive.

1.9 Installing ZFS, and **zpool** and **zfs** Command Syntax

The Zettabyte File System (ZFS) is an advanced journaling file system, and volume manager, developed at Sun Microsystems, and has many useful functions and facilities for maintaining redundancy and security on server-class computers. But it's also useful for an individual user at home, who wants to ensure the same objectives, but on a smaller scale system, such as one using Raspberry Pi hardware. The following are the instructions for installing ZFS, and the general syntax forms for the **zpool** and **zfs** commands, the two premiere ZFS tools. Everything we show in the sections below is done on Ubuntu 23.04, running on a Raspberry Pi 4B, the installation of which is shown in Section 1.2.4 above. For a more complete description of these two important commands, see the man pages for zfs and zpool on an Ubuntu 23.04 system (*after* you have installed ZFS according to the instructions given below in Section 1.9.1).

1.9.1 Installing ZFS on an Ubuntu System Running on Raspberry Pi Hardware

Installing ZFS on Ubuntu is a simple, straight forward operation. Use the following command-

$ **sudo apt install zfsutils-linux -y**
Output truncated...

After a few minutes, the software is installed. Then, use the following commands to verify that ZFS has been installed correctly:

$ **zfs · ·version**
zfs-2.1.9-2ubuntu1
zfs-kmod-2.1.9-2ubuntu1
$ **zpool list**
no pools available
$

1.9.2 The Syntax of the **zpool** and **zfs** Commands

Following are the abbreviated syntax of the **zpool** and **zfs** commands, taken from the man pages on our system:

****

zpool
Syntax:
zpool subcommand [options] [option arguments] [command arguments]

Purpose: To create and manage storage pools of virtual devices, such as disk drives

Commonly used options/features:

zpool create name vdev	Creates a new pool with name on the specified vdev
zpool create –o copies=2 name	Creates a new pool name with the property copies set to 2
zpool destroy name	Destroys, or removes, a pool name
zpool list name	Lists storage space and health of pool name
zpool scrub name	Verifies that the checksums on pool name are correct
zpool status name	Displays the status of pool name

****

****

zfs

Syntax:

zfs subcommand [options] [option arguments] [command arguments]

Purpose: To create and manage datasets or file systems mapped to devices such as disk drives

Commonly used options/features:

zfs create name	Creates a dataset with name
zfs create –o copies=2 name	Creates a dataset name with the property copies set to 2
zfs destroy name	Destroys, or removes, a dataset name
zfs list	Lists all datasets
zfs rollback name	Returns dataset name to a previous snapshot state

****

1.9.3 ZFS Terminology

The following describes the basic terminology used throughout this section, and as it applies to ZFS practice in general as well:

Boot environment: A boot environment is a bootable environment consisting of a ZFS root file system and, optionally, other file systems mounted underneath it. Exactly one boot environment can be active at a time.

*****Warning*****: This warning applies at the time of the writing of this book, and it is important to realize that if you want to create and use ZFS on any system other than for the practice Example 1.7 below, you must have an additional storage device, or devices, attached to your hardware. This could be additional externally mounted SSDs, M.2 NVM.e devices hard drives, or USB2 or USB3 thumb drives. We have found that if you attempt to create zpools on your system or boot disk, this will render that disk *unbootable*!

Checksum: A 256-bit hash of the data in a file system block. The checksum capability can range from the simple and fast fletcher4 (the default) to cryptographically strong hashes such as SHA256.

Clone: A file system whose initial contents are identical to the contents of a ZFS snapshot.

Dataset: A generic name for the following ZFS components: clones, file systems, snapshots, and volumes. Each dataset is identified by a unique name in the ZFS name space. Datasets are identified using the following format:

pool/path[@snapshot]

where:

pool   Identifies the name of the storage pool that contains the dataset
path   A slash-delimited pathname for the dataset component
snapshot An optional component that identifies a snapshot of a dataset

Deduplication: Data deduplication is a method of reducing storage capacity needs by eliminating redundant data. Only one unique instance of the data is actually retained on storage media. Redundant data is replaced with a pointer to the unique data copy.

file system: A ZFS dataset of type file system that is mounted within the standard system namespace and behaves like other file systems.

Mirror: A vdev that stores identical copies of data on two or more disks, in a variety of ways defined by Redundant Array of Independent Disks (RAID) specifications. If any disk in a mirror fails, any other disk in that mirror can provide the same data, according to those RAID specifications.

Pool: A logical group of devices describing the layout and physical characteristics of the available storage. Disk space for datasets is allocated from a pool.

RAIDZ: A virtual device that stores data and parity on multiple disks, using the RAID specifications.

Resilvering: The process of copying data from one device to another device is known as resilvering. For example, if a mirror device is replaced or taken offline, the data from an up-to-date mirror device is copied to the newly restored mirror device. This process is referred to as mirror resynchronization in traditional volume management.

Slice: A disk partition created with partitioning software.

Snapshot: A read-only copy of a file system or volume at a given point in time.

Vdev (virtual device): A whole disk, a disk partition, a file, or a collection of the previous, usually all of the same type. There is no performance penalty for using disk partitions rather than entire disks. The write cache is disabled for partitions, thus incurring a performance penalty. Using files as vdevs is discouraged, except for experimenting and testing purposes as we do in this chapter for beginners! A collection of vdevs is a mirror.

Volume: A dataset that represents a block device. For example, you can create a ZFS volume as a swap device.

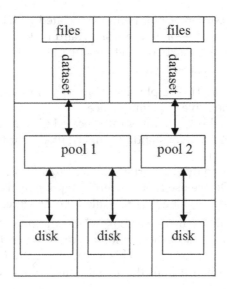

FIGURE 1.8
ZFS Components.

1.9.4 How ZFS Works

The following simplified statement summarizes the operation of ZFS:

**Create zpool mapped to vdev > Create ZFS file system(s) on zpool >
Add files**

So, simply stated, you create a named zpool first, which at the time it is created is mapped or associated with a vdev, such as an external, USB3 medium. Then you create one or more file systems in that zpool; you add files to those file systems. Finally, you manage the files, file systems, pools, and vdevs using the appropriate ZFS commands.

Working with ZFS is a matter of efficiently and easily managing zpools that have vdevs "mapped" to them, and then managing file systems, and their files, in those zpools.

Figure 1.8 shows these relationships between files, datasets (file systems), pools, and disks. **Pool 1** has two disks mapped to it, and a dataset with a number of files in it. **Pool 2** has a single disk mapped to it, and has a dataset in it. This layering of files and datasets, pools, and disks is the basic structure of ZFS.

1.9.5 Important ZFS Concepts

Some very important points have to be made here:

1. Only one zpool can be mapped or associated with any vdev. So if you want to create a zpool on a physical hard disk or one of its slices, no other existing active zpool can be mapped to that vdev!

2. There are six types of vdev in ZFS:

    a. Disk (default): The physical hard drives in your system, usually the whole drive or primary slice.

    b. File: The absolute path of preallocated files/images.

    c. Raidz1/2/3: Nonstandard distributed parity-based software RAID levels.

    d. Spare: Hard drives marked as a *hot spare* for ZFS software RAID.

    e. Cache: Device used for a level-2 adaptive read cache (L2ARC).

    f. Log: A separate log (SLOG) called the ZFS intent log (ZIL).

3. Unlike a traditional file system, where the mount point of the file system begins at a particular logical drive letter, the default mount point for a zpool is root (/). This is how the path to a file named **test. txt** appears when it is in the zpool named **data1** on the file system named **bobs**:

    /data1/bobs/test.txt

    Here's how the path to a file named **test.txt** appears on a traditional file system:

    C:\Users\bob\Desktop\test.txt

    When you want a ZFS file system to expand onto more than one disk, for example, you add more disks to the zpool.

4. A zpool can be enlarged by adding more devices, but it cannot be shrunk (at least not at this time)!

1.9.6 Basic ZFS Example

In this section we present an instructive, introductory example of how to work with ZFS. It is expected that for you to get the full benefit from it, you do it and the attendant In-Chapter Exercises in the order presented.

Example 1.7: The zpool Command: Using Files Instead of Disks as Vdevs
Objective: To introduce the **zpool** command, implemented on files instead of disks, and to show forms of ZFS pool creation and mirroring.
Introduction: A vdev, as defined previously, can be a physical device such as a disk drive, a file, a single slice on a hard disk drive, or a collection of devices. Before beginning to use ZFS on physical

devices, and to practice using ZFS on an existing file system instead of deploying ZFS on actual physical media, we will create and manipulate files with the important ZFS commands.

Also, if you do not have attached USB3 media, you can do this example to gain an appreciation of what ZFS is.

In case you want to use real disks mounted and partitioned in this pre-liminary introductory example, make a note of the full path to their device names (e.g. /dev/sdb1). You will be destroying all the partition information and data on these disks, so be sure they're not needed!

Note If you make a mistake anywhere along the way, you can always start over by executing the cleanup steps shown at the end of the example and begin again.

Prerequisites: Installation of ZFS on an Ubuntu system running on your Raspberry Pi hardware, as shown in Section 1.9.1.

Procedures: Follow the steps in the order shown to complete this example.

1. Become root, and then create four 128 MB files as follows (the files must be a minimum of 64 MB in size):

```
$ sudo -i

root@bob-desktop:~#
root@bob-desktop:~# truncate --size 128m /home/bob/disk1
root@bob-desktop:~# truncate --size 128m /home/bob/disk2
root@bob-desktop:~# truncate --size 128m /home/bob/disk3
root@bob-desktop:~# truncate --size 128m /home/bob/disk4
```

Check the /home/bob directory with the following command:

```
root@bob-desktop:~# ls -lh /home/bob
total 48K
...
-rw-r--r-- 1 root root 128M May 22 18:47 disk1
-rw-r--r-- 1 root root 128M May 22 18:47 disk2
-rw-r--r-- 1 root root 128M May 22 18:47 disk3
-rw-r--r-- 1 root root 128M May 22 18:48 disk4
Output truncated...
```

In this example, we initially create and use files to *simulate* disks on an already existing file system, and we named them **disk1, disk2, disk3**, and **disk4** to enhance that illusion. Also, it is assumed in the example code that the current working directory is **/home/bob** unless otherwise noted.

2. Before creating new pools you should check for existing pools, if there are any, to avoid confusing them with the example pools we create here. You can check what pools exist with the **zpool list** command:

```
root@bob-desktop:~# zpool list
no pools available
root@bob-desktop:~#
```

3. Pools are created using **zpool create**. We can create a single disk pool using a file as follows (you must use the absolute path to the file), and check the zpools that now exist:

```
root@bob-desktop:~# zpool create data /home/bob/disk1
root@bob-desktop:~# zpool list
NAME SIZE ALLOC FREE CKPOINT EXPANDSZ FRAG CAP
DEDUP HEALTH ALTROOT
data   112M 106K   112M  -           -          2%
0%      1.00x      ONLINE -
```

4. Now we will create an actual file in the new pool, check its size, and get a zpool listing of it:

```
root@bob-desktop:~# truncate --size 32m /data/data20file
root@bob-desktop:~# ls -lh /data/data20file
-rw-r--r-- 1 root root 32M May 22 18:54 /data/data20file
root@bob-desktop:~# zpool list
NAME SIZE ALLOC FREE  CKPOINT EXPANDSZ FRAG CAP
DEDUP HEALTH ALTROOT
data   112M 110K   112M  -           -          2%
0%      1.00x      ONLINE -
```

5. We will now destroy the pool data with zpool destroy, and check on zpools now available:

```
root@bob-desktop:~# zpool destroy data
root@bob-desktop:~# zpool list
No pools available
```

6. Creating a Mirrored Pool with Files

   A pool composed of a single disk doesn't offer any redundancy! One way of providing protection against physical disk failure is to use a mirrored pair of disks in a pool:

```
root@bob-desktop:~# zpool create data2 mirror /home/bob/disk1 / \
home/bob/disk2
root@bob-desktop:~# zpool list
```

```
NAME  SIZE  ALLOC  FREE  CKPOINT  EXPANDSZ  FRAG CAP
DEDUP  HEALTH  ALTROOT
data2   112M  105K     112M  -                    -               2%
0%      1.00x      ONLINE -
```

7. To get more information about the pool **data2**, we use **zpool status**:

   ```
   root@bob-desktop:~# zpool status data2
   pool: data2
   state: ONLINE
   config:
   ```

NAME	STATE	READ	WRITE	CKSUM
data2	ONLINE	0	0	0
mirror-0	ONLINE	0	0	0
/home/bob/disk1	ONLINE	0	0	0
/home/bob/disk2	ONLINE	0	0	0

   errors: No known data errors

8. Create a file in the **data2** pool.

   ```
   root@bob-desktop:~# truncate --size 32m /data2/data2file
   ```

Note the change in the pool after we have added a file to it, using the following command:

```
root@bob-desktop:~# zpool list
NAME  SIZE  ALLOC  FREE  CKPOINT  EXPANDSZ  FRAG  CAP
DEDUP  HEALTH  ALTROOT
data2   112M  154K     112M  -                    -               4%     0%
1.00x      ONLINE   -
```

A fraction of the disk has been used, but more importantly the data is now stored redundantly over two disks.

9. Let's test that redundancy by overwriting the first "disk" label with random data. If you are using real media, like a thumb drive, you could physically remove it from the computer to achieve this next operation.

   ```
   root@bob-desktop:~# dd if=/dev/random of=/home/bob/disk1 bs=\
   512 count=1
   1+0 records in
   1+0 records out
   512 bytes copied, 0.00143395 s, 357 kB/s
   ```

10. ZFS automatically checks for errors when it reads/writes files, but we can force a check with the **zfs scrub** command.

    root@bob-desktop:~# **zpool scrub data2**

11. Let's check the status of the pool:

    root@bob-desktop:~# **zpool status**
    pool: data2
    state: DEGRADED
    status: One or more devices could not be used because the label is missing or
             invalid. Sufficient replicas exist for the pool to continue functioning in a degraded state.
    action: Replace the device using 'zpool replace'.
    see: https://openzfs.github.io/openzfs-docs/msg/ZFS-8000-4J
    scan: scrub repaired 0B in 00:00:01 with 0 errors on Tue May 23 05:56:49 2023
    config:

NAME	STATE	READ	WRITE	CKSUM
data2	DEGRADED	0	0	0
mirror-0	EGRADED	0	0	0
/home/bob/disk1	UNAVAIL	0	0	0
				corrupted data
/home/bob/disk2	ONLINE	0	0	0

    errors: No known data errors

12. The disk we used the **dd** command on is showing as UNAVAIL (unavailable) with corrupted data, but no data errors are reported for the pool as a whole, and we can still read and write to the pool as follows:

    root@bob-desktop:~# **truncate --size 32m /data2/data2file2**
    root@bob-desktop:~# **ls -l /data2/**
    total 1
    -rw-r--r-- 1 root root 33554432 May 23 05:52 data2file
    -rw-r--r-- 1 root root 33554432 May 23 06:01 data2file2

13. To maintain redundancy we should replace the broken disk with another. If you are using real media, you can use the **zpool replace** command (the zpool man page provides details of this command). However, in this file-based example we simply remove the disk file from the mirror and recreate it.

Devices can be detached with the **zpool detach** command, as follows:

root@bob-desktop:~# **zpool detach data2 /home/bob/disk1**

14. Let's check the status of the pool:

root@bob-desktop:~# **zpool status data2**
pool: data2
state: ONLINE
scan: scrub repaired 0B in 00:00:01 with 0 errors on Tue May 23 05:56:49 2023
config:

NAME	STATE	READ	WRITE	CKSUM
data2	ONLINE	0	0	0
/home/bob/disk2	ONLINE	0	0	0

errors: No known data errors

15. Let's remove the disk, and then try to replace it, to simulate a failure:

root@bob-desktop:~# **rm /home/bob/disk1**
root@bob-desktop:~# **truncate --size 128m /home/bob/disk1**

16. In order to replace it in the mirror, we need to do the following. To attach another device we specify an existing device in the mirror to attach it to with **zpool attach**:

root@bob-desktop:~# **zpool attach data2 /home/bob/disk2 /home/bob/\ disk1**

17. Check the status of the pool:

root@bob-desktop:~# **zpool status data2**
pool: data2
state: ONLINE
scan: resilvered 206K in 00:00:00 with 0 errors on Tue May 23 06:23:02 2023
config:

NAME	STATE	READ	WRITE	CKSUM
data2	ONLINE	0	0	0
mirror-0	ONLINE	0	0	0
/home/bob/disk2	ONLINE	0	0	0
/home/bob/disk1	ONLINE	0	0	0

errors: No known data errors

18. Adding to a Mirrored Pool

A very critical systems administration procedure accomplished by ZFS is to add media to a pool *without taking it offline*. Let's double the size of our **data2** pool:

root@bob-desktop:~# **zpool list**

NAME SIZE ALLOC FREE CKPOINT EXPANDSZ FRAG CAP DEDUP HEALTH ALTROOT
data2 112M 126K 112M   -   - 5%   0% 1.00x
ONLINE -

19. We can use the **zpool add** command to add disks to the existing pool.

root@bob-desktop:~# **zpool add data2 mirror /home/bob/disk3 /home/\
bob/disk4**
root@bob-desktop:~# **zpool list**

NAME SIZE ALLOC FREE CKPOINT EXPANDSZ FRAG CAP DEDUP HEALTH ALTROOT
data2 224M 184K 224M   -   - 2%   0% 1.00x
ONLINE -

20. The file systems within the pool are always available. If we look at the status now, it shows the pool consists of two mirrors:

root@bob-desktop:~# **zpool status data2**
  pool: data2
  state: ONLINE
  scan: resilvered 206K in 00:00:00 with 0 errors on Tue May 23
06:23:02 2023
config:

NAME	STATE	READ	WRITE	CKSUM
data2	ONLINE	0	0	0
mirror-0	ONLINE	0	0	0
/home/bob/disk2	ONLINE	0	0	0
/home/bob/disk1	ONLINE	0	0	0
mirror-1	ONLINE	0	0	0
/home/bob/disk3	ONLINE	0	0	0
/home/bob/disk4	ONLINE	0	0	0

errors: No known data errors

21. We can see where the data is currently written in our pool using the **zpool iostat -v** command:

```
root@bob-desktop:~# zpool iostat -v data2
```

pool	capacity		operations		bandwidth	
	alloc	free	read	write	read	write
-------------------	-----	-----	-----	-----	-----	-----
data2	141K	224M	0	0	23	360
mirror-0	127K	112M	0	2	1.54K	16.8K
/home/bob/disk2	-	-	0	0	21	151
/home/bob/disk1	-	-	0	1	41	6.27K
mirror-1	14K	112M	0	0	152	14.9K
/home/bob/disk3	-	-	0	0	76	7.47K
/home/bob/disk4	-	-	0	0	76	7.47K
-------------------	-----	-----	-----	-----	-----	-----

22. All the data is currently written on the first mirror pair and none on the second. This is logical, since the second pair of disks was added after the data was written. If we write some new data to the pool, the new mirror will be used:

```
root@bob-desktop:~# truncate --size 64m /data2/data2file3
root@bob-desktop:~# zpool iostat -v data2
```

pool	capacity		operations		bandwidth	
	alloc	free	read	write	read	write
-------------------	-----	-----	-----	-----	-----	-----
data2	142K	224M	0	0	23	363
mirror-0	119K	112M	0	2	1.28K	14.1K
/home/bob/disk2	-	-	0	0	21	152
/home/bob/disk1	-	-	0	0	34	5.29K
mirror-1	23K	112M	0	0	111	11.1K
/home/bob/disk3	-	-	0	0	55	5.53K
/home/bob/disk4	-	-	0	0	55	5.53K
-------------------	-----	-----	-----	-----	-----	-----

23. We see how a little more of the data has been written to the new mirror than to the old: ZFS tries to make the best use of all the resources in the pool. Now do these In-Chapter Exercises, and then continue onto the final "cleanup" steps.

In-Chapter Exercises

15. If you have not already done so, execute all of the steps of Example 1.7 using proper commands and pathnames.

16. In Example 1.7, step 4, what is the pathname to **datafile20**?

17. If you were to use a text editor like emacs to create a text file named **text1.txt** in the file system named **data**, how would you designate the complete pathname to that text file?

18. In Example 1.7, after step 6 was executed correctly, and you created a text file with emacs in the **data2** file system, would the pathnames to the two mirrored versions of that text file be different? In other words, could you edit each one of them separately by designating different pathnames to them?

19. In Example 1.7, step 19, could you add a single disk into the mirrored **data2** zpool, instead of the two disks specified?

20. In Example 1.7, step 20, are the mirrors named **mirror-0** and **mirror-1** mirrors of each other?

24. To clean up after doing our work, let's delete everything we created in this example.

    From the root directory, destroy the **data2** file system and its files.

    root@bob-desktop:~# zfs destroy -r data2

25. Next, destroy the **data2** zpool.

    root@bob-desktop:~# zpool destroy data2

26. Finally, destroy the disk simulation files, and leave root.

    root@bob-desktop:~# rm /home/bob/disk*
    root@bob-desktop:~# exit
    logout
    $

Conclusion: We can use the **zpool** command and its **create** sub-command to associate or map file systems to vdevs, whether the vdev is a file itself or a disk drive.

Example 1.8: Creating a ZFS Pool on a USB thumb drive

Objectives: To create a zpool, and a ZFS dataset in that pool, on a USB thumb drive mounted to an Ubuntu system running on your Raspberry Pi hardware.

Introduction:

Question: Where would this example be most useful?
Answer: In preparation for implementing our recommended storage model on a ZFS zpool, and because you want to learn the basics of ZFS.

The following example uses the most essential command in ZFS, the **zpool** command, with the sub-command **create** applied to a USB thumb drive on an Ubuntu 23.04 system, installed on a Raspberry Pi 4B. The real power of ZFS can be harnessed to common, readily available hardware vdevs that are available on that system, by an ordinary user.

Note
If the only thing you want to do is use a USB thumb drive to transfer files (such as text files, C program source code, LibreOffice documents, and so on) to and from the computer, *you do not have to use the procedures of this example to accomplish that!*
If you make a mistake anywhere along the way, you can always start over by executing the cleanup step shown at the end of the example, and then simply begin again.

Prerequisites:

0. You have installed ZFS on an Ubuntu system, as shown in Section 1.9.1, and are using that system on Raspberry Pi hardware.
1. That you have an expendable USB thumb drive that is usable on that system, and already has only one partition, and no data you want to keep on it. More specifically, if the USB thumb drive is by default formatted to FAT32 (which most commercially-available thumb drives are), then there is a high probability that it will automatically mount and show up as an icon on your desktop in the Ubuntu software system. But for us, it didn't. Go figure.2. That there is no zpool named **test3** already defined on the primary partition of the USB thumb drive, and there is no zpool named **test3** on your Ubuntu system. To find this out, in a terminal window type **zpool list** on the command line, after the USB thumb drive has been inserted and auto-mounts.
3. That you can determine the logical device name and the full path to the thumb drive using any one of the methods in Section 1.8.4 "Five Quick and Easy Ways to Find Out the Logical Device Names of Media". The full path to our USB thumb drive is /dev/sda, and the path to the first partition on it is /dev/sda1. This may not be the same designations as the USB thumb drive on your system, but you can substitute your logical device designations for them.

4. That you have done Examples 1.5 or 1.6, on disk partitioning with Gparted or the **fdisk** command.

Procedure: All commands are shown in **bold** type, and are typed at the command line, followed by pressing the <Enter> key on the keyboard.

1. Plug the thumb drive into a USB port on your Ubuntu system. If it's a fat32-formatted USB thumb drive, it should automatically mount and appear as an icon on your system desktop. Determine the logical device name of the USB thumb drive, as shown in Section 1.8.4. Then, clear any ZFS information off the thumb drive using the following command:

Note
On our Ubuntu 23.04 system, the thumb drive did *not* automount, therefore we couldn't unmount it, for obvious reasons!

$ **sudo zpool labelclear -f /dev/sda1**
$

This step is necessary because, if for some reason, this thumb drive had been used in a ZFS pool before, you need to clear the ZFS meta-data information from the thumb drive so that the old ZFS meta-data information does not conflict with what we are going to do in this example.

2. If it is mounted, unmount the thumb drive using the **umount** command:

$ **sudo umount /dev/sda1**
$

At this point, the desktop icon for the USB thumb drive will disappears on your system, if the thumb drive automounted!

It must still show up in an **ls** listing of /dev to be useable. If the thumb drive is not recognized in /dev after the above step has been done, you need to use another thumb drive!

3. You can now create a zpool named **test3** on the primary partition on the thumb drive you worked on in step 2. To create a zpool on the thumb drive, use the following command:

$ **sudo zpool create -f test3 /dev/sda1**
$

We included the **-f** option on **zpool create** to force creation of a ZFS file system on partition 1 of the thumb drive, effectively eradicating whatever file system was on it.

4. Check that the zpool has been created:

```
$ zpool list
NAME SIZE  ALLOC  FREE  CKPOINT  EXPANDSZ  FRAG
CAP  DEDUP  HEALTH  ALTROOT
test3   29G    108K    29.0G        -            -              0%
0%   1.00x    ONLINE  -
$
```

5. You can now create a file system named **newfile system** on the zpool **test3**, using the following command:

```
$ sudo zfs create test3/newfile system
$
```

6. Obtain a listing of the datasets on your computer, using the following command. Several datasets may be listed. Notice in the listing that the mount point of each dataset is given in the last column. This is the path that you designate leading to the datasets' directory. If you put files in that directory, they are part of that file system.

```
$ sudo zfs list
```

```
NAME                     USED  AVAIL  REFER  MOUNTPOINT
test3                    146K  28.1G  24K    /test3
test3/newfile system     24K   28.1G  24K    /test3/newfile system
$
```

To put files in the ZFS dataset *newfile system*, put them in the directory */test3/newfile system*.

7. If you want to continue using this thumb drive as an additional ZFS drive on your system, stop here. Be aware that if you remove the thumb drive without taking it offline according to ZFS protocols, unexpected results will occur. If you want to use the thumb drive for other purposes, continue.

The following three steps allow you to undo everything you have done in this example (except, of course, the deletion of any data that was on the thumb drive before you began this example!).

8. To begin, first destroy the file system.

```
$ sudo zfs destroy test3/newfile system
```

9. Then destroy the zpool.

   $ **sudo zpool destroy test3**

10. Pull the thumb drive out of the USB port. To reuse the thumb drive for non-ZFS, purely data storage purposes, you will need to use Gparted, or other facilities such as fdisk, to delete the partition on it, and put a new partition table and partition on it. This effectively destroys the ZFS partition we created in this example.

Conclusion: You have created and destroyed a zpool and a ZFS dataset on a USB thumb drive that you attached to a Ubuntu 23.04 system running on Raspberry Pi hardware. If you did *not* destroy the zpool and dataset on it, you can now create additional datasets on it and place files in those datasets.

All of the ZFS commands in this Section 1.9 can be used to manage zpools and datasets on this drive. You can also use this drive as a backup for user data files, and use all of the ZFS functionality to do backups.

1.10 Configuring a Printer

There are fundamental and modern methods for adding and configuring a local printer on a Raspberry Pi, and printing documents on it, using the Common UNIX Printing System (CUPS). We detail these methods *extensively* in Volume 1, Section 1.6, entitled "What the Common Unix Printing System Accomplishes". There we also give some additional details of traditional print commands such as **lpadmin, lpc, lpinfo, lpmove, lpoptions, lpq, lp, lpr, lprm**, and **lpstat**.

We review that section here. You can configure and manage a printer for use on your Raspberry Pi OS, using the three basic methods. These methods are generally applicable to printers that are connected directly to your computer, and this most likely is via a USB connection.

The three basic methods are:

1. A web-based browser CUPS interface,

2. Using the Raspberry Pi OS Menu choice Preferences > Print Settings, and

3. Using the Raspberry Pi OS command line in a terminal.

The configured printer in all three methods is controlled and managed with the Common UNIX Printing System (CUPS).

In method 1, a web-based browser front end to CUPS allows you to manage printers, print jobs, and other configuration settings using intranet connectivity, or over the Internet.

In method 2, the built-in graphical front end to CUPS, accessed via the Raspberry Pi Menu > Preferences > Print Settings, which comes with Raspberry Pi OS, achieves much of the same functionality as method 1.

In method 3, there is a completely text-based interface for controlling and managing printers from the Raspberry Pi OS command line.

1.10.1 What the Common UNIX Printing System (CUPS) Accomplishes

Using CUPS is a standard way of printing in both Linux and Unix. Since it was developed to provide as many printer definitions as possible, it will more than likely enable you to directly connect your model of printer, or connect to a print server on your LAN.

It is basically composed of two parts: a scheduler and a filtering system. The scheduler arranges jobs in print queues and sends them to the filtering system that translates the print data into device driver information for the particular printer you want your documents to print on.

1.10.2 Managing CUPS Locally with systemd

Using systemd, via the **systemctl** command, allows you to start, stop, reload, or restart the CUPS service. This is a higher level of management for your local printers via a system service.

1.10.2.1 Starting CUPS Service Using systemd

In the Raspberry Pi OS, when you attach a new printer via a USB cable to the hardware, it will generally be automatically recognized and attached via CUPS. If the CUPS service has not already been started, it will be automatically started and run in the process of connecting the new printer. But to start the CUPS service without having any printers attached or powered on, do the following:

To start the CUPS service, and check its status, use the following commands:

```
$ sudo systemctl start cups
$ sudo systemctl status cups
```
• cups.service - CUPS Scheduler
  Loaded: loaded (/lib/systemd/system/cups.service; enabled; vendor preset: enabled)
  Active: active (running) since Thu 2022-10-06 00:00:45 PDT; 10h ago

TriggeredBy: • cups.socket
         • cups.path
    Docs: man:cupsd(8)
 Main PID: 11613 (cupsd)
   Status: "Scheduler is running..."
    Tasks: 1 (limit: 4164)
     CPU: 33ms
   CGroup: /system.slice/cups.service
        └─11613 /usr/sbin/cupsd -l

Oct 06 00:00:45 raspberrypi systemd[1]: Starting CUPS Scheduler...
Oct 06 00:00:45 raspberrypi systemd[1]: Started CUPS Scheduler.

We see from the output that CUPS is running.

1.10.2.2 Stopping CUPS Service with systemd

The CUPS service can be stopped using the **systemctl stop cups.service** command, as follows:

$ **sudo systemctl stop cups.service**

When you check the status of the CUPS service after stopping the CUPS service, its status is inactive (dead), but still enabled.

Note
"Enabled" is systemd jargon that means it will persistently start every time the system is rebooted.

1.10.2.3 Restarting, Enabling, or Disabling the CUPS Service with systemd

Restarting a service means that a service is stopped and then started again. If the service was not currently running, restarting it simply starts the service. Use the following command to restart the CUPS service:

$ **sudo systemctl restart cups.service**

You can also perform a conditional restart of a service using systemctl. A conditional restart only restarts a service if it is currently running. Any service in an inactive state is not started.

$ **sudo systemctl condrestart cups.service**

In the above command example, the CUPS service was in an inactive state before the command was executed. When the conditional restart is accomplished, no error messages appear. The cups daemon was not started because conditional restarts only affect active services.

It is always a good practice to check the status of a service, after stopping, starting, or conditionally restarting it.

1.10.2.4 Configuring CUPS as a Persistent Service Using systemd

You can use the **systemctl** command to enable or disable the CUPS services on your Raspberry Pi OS server, whether that is local or remote.

Using the **enable** option on the **systemctl** command sets a service to always start at boot (be persistent). The following shows exactly how to accomplish this:

```
$ sudo systemctl enable cups.service
```

1.10.2.5 Disabling a Service with systemd

You can use the disable option of the **systemctl** command to keep a service from starting at boot. However, it does not immediately stop the service. You need to use the **stop** command shown above to achieve stopping the service. The following command example shows how to disable a currently enabled service:

```
$ sudo systemctl disable cups.service
```

1.11 File System Backup and Recovery

The general necessity of backing up user and system files on a single-user Raspberry Pi system, as a part of an ordinary user's routine operations, should be obvious, even to the beginner. Also, for complex, multi-machine, multi-user systems, it's an absolutely necessary procedure for anyone responsible for the administration of those class of systems.

According to Linux system administration professionals, there is an easy-to-remember and important set of considerations you must make when backing up the system, as the system administrator. This set of considerations can be posed in simple question form as:

How, What, Why, When, Where, and Who?

Some of the answers to these simple questions can be dovetailed together, and we provide a selected list of example answers as follows:

"How" means most importantly using specific commands, utilities, applications, or combinations of hardware and software to accomplish the backup and archival process. These facilities are described in the sub-sections below. It also means incrementally, in a rolling fashion, or across the entire file system structure totally, using various strategies.

"What" means just some of the user files and user account files, all of them, only certain kinds of documents, the whole microSD card or other storage media, multiple media, system files, either all or a selected subset of the system files, etc.

"Why" means deciding on the relative importance of *"What"* you are backing up.

"When" means hourly, once a day, once a week, once a month, every time you save a particular file, and at what time exactly, like 3 A.M.

"Where" means on a local medium, like automatically to an externally mounted USB3 SSD, to Dropbox/Google/Amazon cloud storage, to a USB thumb drive manually, to another computer or NAS on your home network via NFSv4, automatically by cron, to another kind of attached medium manually, totally, incrementally, to RAID of various levels using ZFS, or any variant and combination of the previous.

"Who" means by the only user on the system, by the initiator or executor, such as by cron automatically, by the designated system administrator, either manually or semi-automatically, or by an automated process running at Dropbox, Google, or Amazon, for example.

1.11.1 A Strategic Synopsis and Overview of File Backup Facilities

There are several strategies that a single user, or system administrator, can use in confidently and efficiently backing up the file components of a Raspberry Pi system. Table 1.7 and its included Descriptions, give a basic overview of those strategies, and the facilities that implement them on the Raspberry Pi OS. In the sections that follow the table, we briefly give details of these facilities. The man pages on your system give more complete descriptions, along with command options, arguments, and option arguments for all of the Raspberry Pi OS commands listed in the Table 1.7.

1.11.2 Linux GNU tar

A Linux operating system, such as the Raspberry Pi OS, has several utilities that allow you to archive your files and directories in a single file, and the **tar** command is the most popular, widely used, and traditional method that allows you to do this.

TABLE 1.7

Raspberry Pi OS File Backup Facilities

Backup Facility	Description
tar	Command and options to pack a file or a directory hierarchy as an ordinary disk file for backup, archiving, or moving to another location or system. **gtar** is the GNU version
cpio	Less popular than tar, but with much of the same functionality
rsync	A disk space-efficient command to copy files and directories
dd	A simple and abbreviated backup utility
zfs snapshot	Built-in commands and options in ZFS that offer a variety of backup modes
SD Card Copier	The built-in backup facility of the Raspberry Pi OS
git & Github	Online facility, and command repertoire, to archive code, etc.
Script files	Administrator or user-written shell scripts or other programming language backup systems, that can use all of the above commands in them
3rd party software	Many products, both local and online. Obe very useful example that is most significant for ordinary use is FileZilla

Note

Contemporary **tar** on Linux *is* the GNU version.

The **tar** (short for *tape archive*) utility was originally designed to save file systems on tape as a backup, so that files could be recovered in the event of a system crash. It is primarily used now to pack a directory hierarchy as an ordinary disk file. That disk file can then be either saved for system backup purposes locally or remotely, or transmitted to someone via the Internet. It is also used commonly with a compression utility, such as **gzip**, via a command line option. Doing so saves disk space and transmission time. The saving in disk space results primarily from the fact that empty space within a cluster is not wasted. A brief description of the **tar** utility follows.

The GNU version of **tar** has some important functional features, and incorporates a more friendly syntax, than traditional UNIX **tar**. Therefore, for beginners we only show the "long form" of the GNU-style syntax because it's more intuitive, and easy to understand. Once you get more familiar with **tar**, you may switch to the UNIX-style short form at your discretion.

System administrators normally use a cost-effective archival medium for archiving complete file system structures as backups, so that when a system crashes for some reason, files can be recovered. Linux-based computer systems normally crash for reasons beyond the operating system's control, such as a microSD card failure, or failure of the processor itself. The Raspberry Pi OS rarely causes a system to crash, because it's a well-designed, coded, and tested operating system. In a typical commercial installation, backup is done every day during off hours (late night or early morning) when the system is not normally in use, with appreciable demand placed on it.

The general syntax of the **tar** command, shown with GNU-style syntax as opposed to traditional UNIX-style syntax, is as follows:

****

tar

Syntax: tar [operation mode] [operation mode options] [FILE...]

Purpose: Archive (copy in a particular format) files to or, restore files from, an archival medium (which can be an ordinary file). Directories are by default archived and restored recursively.

Output: Archived or restored files or directory structures.

Main Operations and Operation Options in GNU-Style Usage:

--append	Append files to the end of an archive.
--concatenate	Append an archive to the end of another archive.
--compare	Find differences between archive and file system.
--create	Create a new tape and record archive files on it
--delete	Delete from the archive.
--extract	Extract files from an archive.
--help	Display a short option summary.
--list	List the contents of an archive.
--show-defaults	Show built-in defaults for options.
--test-label	Test the archive volume label and then exit.
--update	Append files which are newer than the versions in an archive.
--usage	Display a list of available options.
--version	Display program version and copyright information.

Common Options:

--preserve-permissions	Extract information about traditional file permissions.
--acls	Enable POSIX.1e ACL support.
--gzip	Filter the archive through gzip.
--verbose	Verbosely list files processed.
--file ARCHIVE.tar	Send archive to file named ARCHIVE.tar.

Command Arguments:

FILE... Target, either an archive file, or file object to be archived.

****

1.11.2.1 Archiving and Restoring Files Using **tar**

A normal Raspberry Pi OS user can archive their own work if they want to. They would normally need to do this with file objects related to a project, so that they can transfer them to someone via e-mail, ssh, or via mobile secondary storage media (USB thumb drive, for example). Or perhaps they would want to retain their own file system objects as backups via the same methods.

The primary reason for making an archive is the convenience of dealing with (sending or receiving) a single file instead of a complete directory hierarchy. Without an archive, the sender might have to send several files and directories (a file structure) that the receiver would have to restore in their correct hierarchical structure. Without an archiving facility such as **tar**, depending on the size of the files and directory structure, the task of sending, receiving, and reconstructing the file structure can be very time consuming.

There are other file compression facilities, such as the **bzip2, gzip, gunzip, gzexe, xz, zcat**, and **zmore** commands, and we must point out that compression saves disk space and transmission time. But compressing small files normally does not result in much compression, and storage space. Also, compressing files of one cluster in size (the minimum unit of disk storage, i.e. one or more sectors) or less does not help save storage media space, even if compression does result in smaller files, because the system ends up using one cluster to save the compressed file anyway. But if compression does result in a smaller file, you do save time in transmitting the compressed version. If the disk block size is 512 bytes and a cluster consists of more than two blocks, you can use the **tar** command to pack files together in one file, with a 512-byte tar header at the beginning of each file, as shown in Figure 1.9.

FIGURE 1.9
tar-Packed File.

1.11.2.2 *Eight Easy* tars

In this section, we show eight of the simplest uses of the **tar** command.

1. Creating an archive:

   This is the simplest command to create an archive file from a directory.

   $ **tar --create --verbose --file archive_name.tar directory_name**

   where:
--create	is the operation to create a new archive
--verbose	is the operation to list the files being processed
--file	is the operation that specifies that the file **archive_**
name.tar	is the name of the archive file, and
directory_name	is the directory you want to archive.

2. Creating an archive and preserving its ACL permissions:
   A simple variation on creating an archive is using an option to preserve ACLs that the directory has. ACLs are detailed fully in Volume 1, both the POSIX.1e and NFSv4 varieties.

   $ **tar --acls --create --verbose --file archive_name.tar directory_name**

   where:
--acls	is the option to preserve the ACLs that the directory has
--create	is the operation to create a new archive
--verbose	is the operation to list the files being processed
--file	is the operation that specifies that the file **archive_**
name.tar	is the name of the archive file, and
directory_name	is the directory you want to archive.

3. Extracting an archive:
   This is the simplest command to extract a directory from an archive file an archive file.

   $ **tar --extract --verbose --file archive_name.tar**

   where:
--extract	is the operation to extract a **directory_name** from an archive file
--verbose	is the operation to list the files being processed
--file	is the operation that specifies that the file **archive_name.tar** is the name of the archive file.

In this simplest form, the directory which will be created from the archived file will have the same name as the archive file, minus the .tar extension.

4. Extracting an archive and restoring its ACL entries
   A simple variation on extracting an archive is using an option to restore the preserved ACLs that the archive file has (if any).

   $ **tar --acls --extract --verbose --file archive_name.tar**

   where:
   --acls   is the option to restore the preserved the ACLs that the archived file has
   --extract   is the operation to extract the archived file
   --verbose is the operation to list the files being processed
   --file   is the operation that specifies that the file **archive_name.tar** is the name of the archive file

In this simplest form variation, the directory which will be created from the archived file will have the same name as the archive file, minus the .tar extension.

5. Listing the contents of an archive
   This procedure allows you to view the contents of an archive file without extracting anything from it

   $ **tar --list --verbose --file archive_name.tar**

   where:
   --list   is the operation that lists the contents of the archive file
   --verbose is the operation to list the files being processed
   --file   is the operation that specifies that the file **archive_name.tar** is the name of the archive file

6. Extracting a single file from an archive file
   The following command extracts only a specific file from an archive file.

   $ **tar --extract --verbose --file archive_file.tar file_pathname**

   where:
   --extract   is the operation to extract the single file
   --verbose   is the operation to list the files being processed
   --file   is the operation that specifies that the file **archive_name.tar** is the name of the archive file you are extracting from, and
   file_pathname is the complete pathname specification to the file you want to extract inside the archive.

7. Extracting a single directory from an archive file
   A variation on extracting just a single file from an archive, to extract a
   single directory, along with recursively extracting any of it's subdirectories and files, specify the directory name that you want to extract as
   follows:

   $ **tar --extract --verbose --filef archive_file.tar directory_pathname**

   where:
   --extract is the operation to extract the single file
   --verbose is the operation to list the files being processed
   --file is the operation that specifies that the file **archive_name.tar** is the
   name of the archive file you are extracting from, and
   directory_pathname is the complete pathname specification to the directory you want to extract inside the archive.

8. Adding a file or directory to an existing archive using **--append** option
   To add files to an existing archive, do the following:

   $ **tar --append --verbose --file archive_name.tar file_or_directory_name**

   where:

--append	is the operation to add the single file or direc-tory to the archive
--verbose	is the operation to list the files or directories being processed
--file	is the operation that specifies that the file **archive_name.tar** is the name of the archive file you are adding files or directories to, and
file_or_directory_name	is the complete pathname specification to the file or directory you want to add inside the archive.

In-Chapter Exercise

21.
   a. Referring to the abbreviated man page shown above, or to the
      man page for **tar** on your Raspberry Pi system, give a command
      that would create a gzipped archive of a directory named
      ziptest.
   b. Give a command that would extract the gzipped archive into
      another directory named ziptest2.

1.12 Other Raspberry Pi OS Archiving and Backup Facilities

In addition to the traditional **tar** facility briefly shown in the previous section, there are several other facilities and methods a system administrator can use to archive and backup individual user accounts, files, file systems, and the entire system itself. As stated above, to get a more complete listing of the capabilities and options available for the command line facilities shown in this, and all other sections, consult the man pages on your system for these commands. We briefly describe and give simple examples of some of the more modern and useful of these facilities and methods below.

1.12.1 rsync

The **rsync** command is a very modern and space-efficient way to backup files and directories, particularly from one machine to another, using **ssh** across a network. Its operation can also be automated, via the use of systemd scheduling.

Its most important and defining feature is the data transfer "quick check" algorithm it uses, which reduces the amount of data transmitted. This is done by sending only the differences between the source files, and the same existing destination files (if any). If files need to be transferred, because there is a difference between source and destination, they are copied, or "synced", using this algorithm. The algorithm looks for files that have changed in size or modification time. Changes in the other possible preserved file object attributes (such as permissions, or ACLs) are made on the destination file directly when the quick check indicates that the destination file needs to be updated in that way.

An abbreviated summary of the **rsync** man page is as follows:

```
************************************************************************
```
rsync
Syntax:
Local: rsync [OPTION...] SRC... [DEST]
Remote:
    via remote shell:
    Pull mode: rsync [OPTION...] [USER@]HOST:SRC... [DEST]
    Push mode: rsync [OPTION...] SRC... [USER@]HOST:DEST

    via rsync daemon:
    Pull mode: rsync [OPTION...] [USER@]HOST::SRC... [DEST]
        rsync [OPTION...] rsync://[USER@]HOST[:PORT]/SRC... [DEST]
    Push mode: rsync [OPTION...] SRC... [USER@]HOST::DEST
        rsync [OPTION...] SRC... rsync://[USER@]HOST[:PORT]/DEST

Purpose: To transfer files locally or remotely using an efficient and fast data transfer algorithm. To copy locally, to/from (push/pull) another host over any remote shell, or to/from (push/pull) a remote rsync daemon.

Output: Transferred files, either locally or remotely.

Common Options:

-a, --archive	archive mode
-A, --acls	preserve ACLs (implies -p)
--delete	delete extraneous files from destination dirs
-e, --rsh=COMMAND	specify the remote shell to use
--existing	skip creating new files on receiver
-h, --human-readable	output numbers in a human-readable format
-H, --hard-links	preserve hard links
-k, --copy-dirlinks	transform symlink to dir into referent dir
-K, --keep-dirlinks	treat symlinked dir on receiver as dir
-n, --dry-run	perform a trial run with no changes made
-p, --perms	preserve permissions
-q, --quiet	suppress non-error messages
-r, --recursive	recursively descend into directories
--remove-source-files	sender removes synchronized files (non-directory)
-v, --verbose	increase verbosity
-z, --compress	compress file data during the transfer

Command Arguments:

SRC   the source file or directory
DEST   the destination path

****

1.12.1.1 rsync Examples

One of the basic assumptions we are making in the following set of examples is that the source is generally a file object that is changing over time, such as a directory where you are modifying files by adding or deleting them from it, or from its sub-directories. Also, the destination is a file object that is unchanging, or fixed over time, such as when you do an archival backup. This is usually the case when you are using an archiving utility, although as you have seen above with the **tar** command, the archive (or destination) can be added to, or extracted from in various ways.

Note

We do not cover more complex, or advanced uses of **rsync**.

We have organized the **rsync** examples below based upon whether they apply where both source and destination are on a local machine, or where either the source or destination is on a remote machine. The examples may also be divided into those that deal with files exclusively, or those that deal with directories and files.

Local Examples:

1. Using **rsync** to copy a single file named **rsynctest** from the source current working directory to the local destination directory **/home/ bob/USBint**. The files are transferred in "archive" mode, done using the **-a** option of the command.

    This ensures that symbolic links, devices, attributes, permissions, ownerships, etc. are preserved.

    `$ rsync -av rsynctest /home/bob/USBint`

2. Copying a single local file in compressed form, with the operation feedback presented in human-readable form, from the source **backup. tar** (in the current working directory) to the destination directory **/ home/bob/backup1** which you have permissions on.

    `$ rsync -zvh backup.tar /home/bob/backup1`

3. Using **rsync** to copy an entire source directory contents from the directory named **syncdir** locally to a destination directory locally named **/usr/home/bob/USBint**. The slash at the end the designated source means "copy the contents of this directory", *not* "copy the directory by name".

    `$ rsync -av syncdir/ /usr/home/bob/USBint`

4. Copying a single source directory **/home/bob/backups** in compressed form, with the operation feedback presented in human-readable form, to the destination directory **/home/remote/backups** which you have permissions on.

    `$ rsync -avzh /home/bob/backups /home/remote/backups/`

5. Copying a single source directory **/home/bob/backups**, and its files and sub-directory structure, in compressed form, to the destination directory **/home/remote/backups** which you have permissions on.

    `$ rsync -zvr /home/bob/backups /home/remote/backups`

6. Doing a dry-run, where you remove the source files and compress the transmitted file object.

   $ **rsync --dry-run --remove-source-files -zvh backup.tar /tmp/backups/\
   backup.tar**

   Remote Examples:

7. Copying a single directory, named **Music**, from the local machine to a remote machine at **192.168.1.8** into bob's home.

   $ **rsync -avz Music bob@192.168.1.8:/home/bob/**

8. Copying an entire local directory, named **syncdir2**, using ssh, to a remote machine at **192.168.0.7** and into the OS X-style directory /Users/b/Linux3e.

   $ **rsync -av -e ssh syncdir2 bob@192.168.0.7:/Users/b/Linux3e**

9. Copying a remote directory to a local directory.

   $ **rsync -avzh root@192.168.0.100:/home/bob/backups /home/bob/\
   temp**

10. Copying just the contents of the remote directory **/home/bob/Linux2e**, updating (sometimes called "syncing") with the **--existing** option, only the existing files at the destination. If the source has new files, which are not on the destination, these new files are not put on the destination. The destination is signified by the .(period) at the end of the command, which translates to the current working directory.

    $ **rsync -avz --existing bob@192.168.1.2:/home/bob/Linux2e/**

11. Copying a single local file, named **backup.tar**, using ssh, to a remote machine at **192.168.0.8**

    $ **rsync -avzhe ssh backup.tar bob@192.168.0.8:/home/bob/backups/**

12. Copying a single remote file to the current working directory using ssh.

    $ **rsync -avzhe ssh bob@192.168.0.100:/usr/home/bob/systemctl.log**

13. Copying only the local files in **/home/bob/files** to a remote machine with an IP address of **192.168.0.8** With the **--delete** option present, extraneous files on the destination that no longer exist in the source

directory, are deleted. The **-v** option ensures that what is being trans-ferred is output. **rsync** using ssh on an ephemeral port 32000.

$ **rsync-av--delete-e'ssh-p32000'/home/bob/files/bob@192.168.0.8:/\ home/bob/files/**

In-Chapter Exercises

22. What is the basic assumption in all of the examples above where you copy to a remote host?
23. Do all of the above 13 examples locally on your system, and remotely on your LAN, substituting file names, directories, account names, and IP addresses as necessary.

1.12.2 Script Files for Backup and Recovery

User-written script files can be deployed by a Raspberry Pi OS administrator to quickly and efficiently do backup and archiving. Whether they are coded in Python (or some other scripting language), or in a shell programming language that embeds any of the above command line facilities that we've shown, they can be used to expedite, facilitate, and automate the backup, recovery, and archiving of files, directories, or entire file systems.

Additionally, there are several on-line sources for commercially available backup and archiving script files available, but there's no need for us to jus-tify the utility for planning, coding, or maintaining your own script file code base, versus using an on-line, ready-made program.

Following is an example of a Bash shell script files, using a legacy applica-tion of **tar**.

Example 1.9 Simple Bash Shell Example for Automating **tar** Backups

Objective: The following Bash shell script will backup a directory, /home/ bob/bashtest, to another directory previously created named simple_backup, in a compressed format.

Procedures: Do the following steps, in the order presented, to complete the requirements of this example.

1. Create a sub-directory of your home directory named **bashtest**.
2. Create another sub-directory of your home directory named **simple_ backup**.
3. Copy some files into the directory **bashtest**.
4. Use an editor of your choice, such as nano, to create the following file in your home directory, and name that file **backup.bash**. Be sure to substitute your username for bob in the body of the script file!

```
#!/bin/bash
# To backup additional directories, put more pathnames in the
following command,
# separated by spaces, such as /home/bob, /home/bill, etc.
backup_source=/home/bob/bashtest
backup_destination=/home/bob/simple_backup
filename=back1.tgz
echo "Backing up your bashtest directory"
tar --create --verbose --gzip --file $backup_destination/$filename
$backup_source
echo "Backup Complete"
```

5. Give yourself execute privilege on the file **backup.bash** with the following command:

    ```
    $ chmod u+x backup.bash
    $
    ```

6. Execute the Bash script with the following command:

    ```
    $ ./backup.bash
    ```
    "Backing up your bashtest directory"
    tar: Removing leading `/' from member names
    /home/bob/bashtest/
    /home/bob/bashtest/nfs_client.txt
    "Backup Complete"
    $

7. Check that the backup was achieved with the following two commands:

    ```
    $ cd simple_backup
    $ ls -la
    total 12
    drwxr-xr-x    2  bob bob  4096  May 24 11:46   .
    drwxr-xr-x   27  bob bob  4096  May 24 11:42   ..
    -rw-r--r--    1  bob bob   808  May 24 11:46   back1.tgz
    $
    ```

In-Chapter Exercises

24. Give the commands necessary to automate the above script file using systemd, to run the backup.bash script at 3:00 AM every day of the week. Feel free to modify time, days, and source and destination directories and files, so that you can use the script file to backup information important to you on your Raspberry Pi system.

25. How would you "decompress" the file you created with backup.bash in another directory?

1.12.3 Software for Backup and Recovery: Filezilla, SD Card Copier, and git

There are many commercial software and hardware packages that can be deployed to backup and archive your system. One very easy-to-use commercial product that allows you to clone entire hard disks in a "broadcast" fashion over a network, from a server to one or more machines, is Norton Ghost.

But the most readily available, useful, and free software facility, available through the Pi Menu choice > Preferences > Add/Remove Software on the Raspberry Pi OS, that can do a variety of file system backup and recovery, disk recovery, and disk cloning operations is FileZilla. We have introduced that software application in Volume 1.

Additionally, the Raspberry Pi menu choice Accessories > SD Card Copier allows you to clone the entire microSD card, thus replicating whatever is on your system/boot disk at the time you do the copy. Admittedly a brute force approach to backup for recovery, it is effective even for copying the microSD card to a USB2 or 3-mounted SSD, or other suitable USB medium.

You can also use the **git** command, and Github.com, to effectively backup user files. We give a verbose description of the **git** command in Volume 3.

Of course, if you adhere to our recommended storage strategy of keeping user files on media other than the boot/system medium, then whatever strategies you use to back those media up, for recovery or archival purposes, apply. You can mix and match any of the techniques and facilities we show in the following three sections, to suit your requirements, and the specific needs of your selected data storage model.

1.12.3.1 FileZilla

FileZilla is nominally a graphics-based ftp client and server program that can use ssh as the tunnel, or conduit between systems. It has a number of useful functions and menu choices that allow the system administrator to successfully, confidentially, and efficiently backup and restore single files or directories, via a network, locally or globally. It is most useful for backing up and restoring single-user files and directories. It is not a replacement or substitute for the command line facilities shown in the preceding sections.

Figure 1.10 illustrates the screen display and menus available in the "client" version of FileZilla.

Both client and server, in our case a local machine running the Raspberry Pi OS, and a remote Linux machine, must have ssh communications protocol enabled between them. You can have login access to an account on the remote server, or you can anonymously login as well if that is enabled.

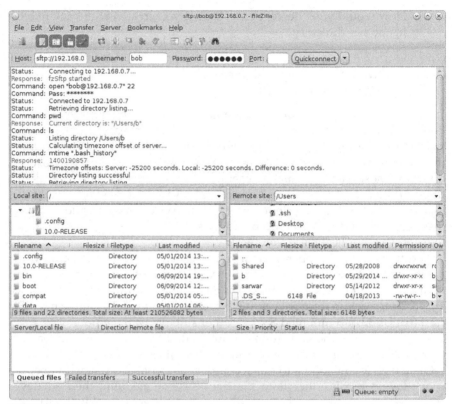

FIGURE 1.10
FileZilla Main Window.

After launching FileZilla on the client, to login to a remote host server you need to supply the IP address of the server, the login name and password, and the port number (22 for ssh). Once you have successfully logged in by making the Quickconnect menu choice, the local machine's directory and file structure is shown on the left side of the figure. The remote machine's directory structure is shown on the right side of the figure. To transfer files or directories between machines, you simply drag and drop between the appropriate panes on the left or right. If you are overwriting previously transferred files or directories, the FileZilla default is to give you the chance to overwrite or rename the files being transferred.

There are a number of other menu choices at the top of the FileZilla screen that allow you to affect preferences, set bookmarks, etc. For example, via the menu choice Manage Bookmarks and the Site Manager, you can automatically make multiple local directories and remote directories available for ssh transfer as soon as you log in to the remote server sites.

There are some limitations to using Filezilla, however. It's primarily designed as an ftp client and server software, rather than as a dedicated backup tool. While it can be used to transfer files between systems, it lacks built-in functionality for automated backups. However, you can achieve automatic file backups by utilizing external tools in conjunction with FileZilla. Here's a general approach you can consider:

1. Set up a backup tool: Choose a backup software or script that suits your needs. There are numerous options available, such as **rsync** triggered by systemd systemctl timers. *Ensure that your chosen tool supports automatic scheduling.*

2. Configure the backup software: Set up the backup software to include the specific files and folders you want to back up. Configure the backup destination (e.g., local storage, network drive, cloud storage) and establish the backup schedule (e.g., hourly, daily, weekly).

3. Integrate FileZilla: Use FileZilla to transfer the files to the designated backup location. You can manually initiate the transfers, or create a bash script file as we show in Example 1.9, for example, that executes the transfers automatically. FileZilla Pro and FileZilla Pro CLI provide a command-line interface (CLI) that allows you to do script file transfers, *but they're not free!*

4. Schedule the backup process: Depending on the backup tool you've chosen, use its scheduling capabilities to automatically trigger the backup process at regular intervals. This ensures that the specified files are backed up periodically.

By combining a backup tool with FileZilla, and scheduling functionality, you can create an automated backup system for your specific files. Remember to consult the documentation and resources of your chosen backup software for detailed instructions on configuration and automation.

1.12.3.2 SD Card Copier

There's system cloning software built right into the Raspberry Pi OS!

If you deployed the system installation technique shown back in Section 1.2.3, entitled "How to Boot from and Run a Raspberry Pi OS from a USB3-mounted SSD", you can use a hybrid form of that method to archive your entire operating system, including the boot partition. If the system/boot disk is a microSD card, then you can simply add another blank (or not) microSD card into a suitable microSD-to-USB adapter, mount it in one of the USB ports on your Raspberry Pi hardware, and then use the Pi Menu choice Accessories > SD Card Copier menu choice to clone the current system/boot disk to the blank one.

And if you followed the technique in Section 1.2.3, and your boot/system medium is an externally mounted USB2 or 3 device, like an SSD, you can use the SD Card Copier to clone that original SSD onto another one of at least the same, or greater, capacity than the original.

A couple of words of caution are in order here.

First, when using the SD Card Copier, make sure you specify the "Copy from Device", and the "Copy to Device" **correctly**. The "Copy from Device" must be the original boot/system medium, and the "Copy to Device" can be another equal-or-larger capacity medium that is mounted inside of an enclosure, and connected via another USB port on the Raspberry Pi hardware. Don't confuse the two media, or else you'll end up with no usable clone, and no bootable system! When we cloned a boot/system SSD, the original and the clone were the exact same 128 GB SSDs, made by Silicon Power, mounted in Orico USB3 External Hard Drive enclosures. And we were very careful to specify them correctly to the SD Card Copier!

Second, some manufacturer's products, even though they're nominally the same capacity, are in fact different. So you should try to ensure this ahead of time.

The drawback to using this approach is of course that the cloning takes a snapshot of the entire system as it exists at *one particular moment in time*. This is unlike using the **rsync** command, automated by either cron, or a systemctl timer, where the snapshots can be taken *regularly*, and automatically, according to some timed schedule.

1.12.3.3 Using git and github to Backup File Systems

The **git** command and github.com are useful, efficient, and powerful means you can use to create a distributed version-control system for your software projects. They can also be used as a cloud-based storage and archiving facility, particularly if you follow the storage model we recommend in this chapter. That is, if your Raspberry Pi OS is installed on one medium, and all of your user data files are stored on another persistent medium, such as an additional USB3-mounted SSD.

Of course, using a private github.com repository for backup and archiving is not free. In addition, there are limits to the amount of data that you can store on github. Therefore, this method of backup and archiving works best for an ordinary user, in a *public* repository at github, with small user data storage requirements. Also, if you use another data storage model than what we recommend, the mechanics of doing github archiving and backup would be dependent on that data storage model.

1.13 Software Updates and Operating System Upgrades

Question: Why would the two most-significant, post-installation tasks, that an ordinary user on a single-user Raspberry Pi system need to perform, be as follows?

a) The addition, removal, or update of software applications as packages on the system.

b) The upgrade of the operating system itself to a newer, currently stable release

Answer:

a) The standard installation of the operating system does *not* include software that the user needs, given the use-cases she puts the system to. And also, changing conditions in use-cases require removal of software packages as well. Finally, as newer and improved versions of installed packages become available, there must be a quick and easy way to update the packages to incorporate those improvements.

b) Purely from a performance and *security viewpoint*, upgrades of the system happen very regularly, and even an ordinary user should take advantage of these improvements via upgrades.

Question: What is the difference between "updating" and " upgrading" a Raspberry Pi system?

Answer: Generally in the literature, the two terms are often confused with one another. But from our perspective in this section (and throughout this chapter), we define the two terms as follows:

Updating is the process of adding or replacing application software packages. For example, bringing the nginx web server application from an earlier-installed version to the latest stable release of it.

Upgrading is the process of replacing the entire operating system with a newer, hopefully stable release. The upgrade can be to a newer minor release, or to a new major release. For example, upgrading from what was named Raspbian to the Raspberry Pi OS, an upgrade which was not just a naming convention change. Additionally, a change in the kernel from an earlier release to a later release constitutes a major upgrade of the operating system.

In this section we show the basics of how these two fundamental tasks can be done on our representative Raspberry Pi OS.

For software application addition, removal, or updates, we limit the discussion to covering the Advanced Packaging Tool (APT), because that's the default package manager on the Raspberry Pi OS. APT can be used very effectively in a text-based, CUI environment. That's how we approach it in this book. That doesn't preclude use of GUI-based front ends to package managers, available via the Raspberry Pi menu Preferences > Add/Remove Software.

Additionally, we offer some information about Snaps here in this section. The Snap package manager is a software package management system developed by Canonical, the company supporting Ubuntu Linux. It is designed to work across different Linux distributions, and provides a way to package and distribute software in a self-contained format called "Snaps".

Snaps are containerized software packages that include all the necessary dependencies and libraries required for the application to run, making them more isolated and secure. They aim to simplify software installation and updates by providing a consistent experience across different Linux distributions.

As for the Raspberry Pi OS, the Snap package manager is *not* installed by default. However, it is possible to install Snap on Raspberry Pi OS if desired. Canonical provides a version of the Snap package manager, that is compatible with ARM-based systems like the Raspberry Pi OS. Instructions for installing Snap on Raspberry Pi OS can be found on the official Snapcraft website, or through community resources.

Snap can be installed on a Raspberry Pi running the latest version of the Raspberry Pi OS by opening a terminal, and typing the following commands.

```
$ sudo apt update
$ sudo apt install snapd
Output truncated...
$
```

You will need to then reboot your system.

```
$ sudo reboot
```

Then install the core snap so you can get the latest snapd.

```
$ sudo snap install core
Output truncated...
core 16-2.45.2 from Canonical✓ installed
$
```

For upgrading the operating system itself, we show you a basic set of procedures in Section 1.13.4 that suits the variable conditions of upgrading an operating system.

In-Chapter Exercise

26. In light of what we have said about updating and upgrading your Raspberry Pi system, list applications that you want to install, given the use case(s) you undertake on your system. Then, as you go through the rest of this section, use the APT package manager to install these.

The best way for you to get more basic help on the package management commands we show in this section is to read the man pages available for them on your system.

1.13.1 Preliminary Storage Model Suggestions

We previously provided an ordinary user with a suggested storage model, where the operating system is on a single medium (which we call the "boot/system disk"), and the user data is on one or more other media. One of the most useful and practical advantages this model gives an ordinary user is the ability to add or update software applications, and upgrade the operating system itself in a very reliable and time-efficient way. The software applications and operating system, since they exist on the boot/system disk, can be incrementally updated or upgraded independently of the user data. So, for example, if you want to go from an earlier major release of the operating system to the latest release, you can detach and unmount the user data media, do a clean install of the new release onto the old, or even new, boot/system disk, and then simply reattach the user data to it. We have found that this storage model, and this method of update/upgrade is safest and most reliable, even for an ordinary user, i.e. it doesn't break the system, and lose user data.

If you choose to keep the older major release of the operating system, and just want to incrementally update software and upgrade the operating system, the sections below will give you a basic overview of how to do that.

There is a very wide selection of software programs available via the use of the facilities we show here. These programs are found in software archives known as "repositories". The repositories contain collections of "packages", and each package contains bundled-together software and dependencies that can all be automatically installed together. When downloaded and installed on your system by package management facilities such as APT or Snap (the two package management systems we mentioned earlier), that software becomes available to a user without the need to do anything else.

1.13.1.1 Default Repositories

The default repositories for Raspberry Pi OS are usually specified in the file /etc/apt/sources.list. This file contains a list of package repositories that are used by the APT package manager to install and update software.

By default, the Raspberry Pi OS sources.list file on our Raspberry Pi400, at the time this book was written, contained the following lines:

deb http://deb.debia n.org/debian bullseye main contrib non-free
deb http://security.debian.org/debian-security bullseye-security main contrib non-free
deb http://deb.debian.org/debian bullseye-updates main contrib non-free
 # Uncomment deb-src lines below then 'apt-get update' to enable 'apt-get source'
#deb-src http://deb.debian.org/debian bullseye main contrib non-free
#deb-src http://security.debian.org/debian-security bullseye-security main contrib non-free
#deb-src http://deb.debian.org/debian bullseye-updates main contrib non-free

In the above example listing, the repository URL is specified as http://deb. debian.org/debian*. This URL points to the official Raspberry Pi OS repository server.

The repositories are divided into three components:

main: This component contains the core software packages officially supported by the Raspberry Pi OS team.

contrib: This component contains packages that are not part of the core distribution but are still provided by the Raspberry Pi OS team. These packages depend on software from the main component.

non-free: This component contains packages that are not free software and may have licensing restrictions. These packages depend on software from the main component.

Note
The contents of the sources.list file may change with updates to Raspberry Pi OS, so it's always a good idea to check the file on your specific installation, or consult the official Raspberry Pi OS documentation for the most up-to-date information.

For software that provides a system service, such as sshd, or a web server like nginx, the package manager not only downloads and installs all necessary components and their dependencies, but also uses systemd facilities to start the service, and ensure it automatically starts at every subsequent system boot.

In-Chapter Exercise

27. Determine exactly how your Raspberry Pi system deploys a storage model. For example, what are the paths to a user's home directory? How is the file system structure segregated on the storage media, if it is? How is this different from the storage model we suggest? How can you migrate the storage model that now exists on your Raspberry Pi system, so that it conforms to our suggested model?

1.13.2 Using the Advanced Packaging Tool (APT)

For beginners, a CUI approach to package management at first might not seem to be the quickest and easiest way to accomplish one of the most significant post-installation tasks a system administrator must do. GUI approaches have some tremendous advantages, and not only in terms of saving time. But we feel the explicit control you get by using APT, on the command line, outweighs the initial advantages of a GUI. Of all of the tools available for APT, the **apt-get** command is the most useful for a beginner.

1.13.2.1 Using **apt-get**

The Advanced Packaging Tool (APT) is used for all aspects of managing packages. The most used (and useful) of its package management utilities is the CUI **apt-get** tool. Following is an abbreviated man page description of **apt-get**, taken from the man page for it on our Raspberry Pi system:

****

apt-get - APT package handling utility – CUI version

Syntax:
apt-get [-asqdyfmubV] [-o=config_string] [-c=config_file]
      [-t=target_release] [-a=architecture] {update | upgrade |
      dselect-upgrade | dist-upgrade |
      install pkg [{=pkg_version_number | /target_release}]... |
      remove pkg... | purge pkg... |
      source pkg [{=pkg_version_number | /target_release}]... |
      build-dep pkg [{=pkg_version_number | /target_release}]... |
      download pkg [{=pkg_version_number | /target_release}]... |
      check | clean | autoclean | autoremove | {-v | --version} |
      {-h | --help}}

Purpose: **apt-get** is the command-line tool for handling packages, and may be considered the user's "back-end" to other tools using the APT library. Several "front-end" interfaces exist.

Output: Added, removed, or updated software packages on the system.

Common Options and Commands:
Note: Unless the -h, or --help option is given, one of the commands below must be present.
Options:
-d, --download-only
> Download only; package files are only retrieved, not unpacked or installed. Configuration Item: APT::Get::Download-Only.

--only-upgrade
> Do not install new packages; when used in conjunction with install, only-upgrade will install upgrades for already installed packages only and ignore requests to install new packages.

-q, --quiet
> Quiet; produces output suitable for logging, omitting progress indicators.

-y, --yes, --assume-yes
> Automatic yes to prompts; assume "yes" as answer to all prompts and run non-interactively.

Commands:
install
> install is followed by one or more packages desired for installation or upgrading. The /etc/apt/sources.list file is used to locate the desired packages.

remove
> remove is identical to install except that packages are removed instead of installed. Removing a package leaves its configuration files on the system.

update
> update is used to resynchronize the package index files from their sources. The indexes of available packages are fetched from the location(s) specified in /etc/apt/sources.list.

upgrade
> upgrade is used to install the newest versions of all packages currently installed on the system from the sources enumerated in /etc/apt/sources.list.

****

We cover the following functions in APT for the Raspberry Pi OS:

Installing, reinstalling, removing, and searching for packages.
Upgrading and updating packages.

In the Operations below, when we refer to **package_name**, this represents any specific named package.

Operation 1

To use the apt-cache package query function to list available packages on your system, use the following command:

root@raspberrypi:~# **apt-cache pkgnames**

Although this listing can be quite long, it is useful to find out if a package has been installed on your system. For example, in the nginx example we show below, before you try to install a package named "nginx", it is a good idea to see if it has already been installed!

Operation 2

To install a package, use the following command:

root@raspberrypi:~# **apt-get install package_name**

Operation 3

To remove a package, or the package and its configuration files, use the following commands:

root@raspberrypi:~# **apt-get remove package_name**
root@raspberrypi:~# **apt-get purge package_name**

Operation 4

To update the package index files from the local sources.list directories (the metadata for packages), or upgrade all Debian packages to their latest versions, use the following commands:

root@raspberrypi:~# **apt-get update**
root@raspberrypi:~# **apt-get upgrade**

Operation 5

To individually update an installed package, by removing it and then reinstalling it use the following command:

root@raspberrypi:~# **apt-get --reinstall install package_name**

Operation 6

To show metadata associated with an installed package on the system, use the following command:

root@raspberrypi:~# **apt-cache show package_name**

For example, on our Raspberry Pi system, the output of this command shows the nginx metadata information-

root@raspberrypi:~# **apt-cache show nginx**
Package: nginx
Version: 1.18.0-6.1+deb11u3
Installed-Size: 102
Maintainer: Debian Nginx Maintainers <pkg-nginx-maintainers@alioth-lists.debian.net>
Architecture: all
Depends: nginx-core (<< 1.18.0-6.1+deb11u3.1~) | nginx-full (<< 1.18.0-6.1+deb11u3.1~) | nginx-light (<< 1.18.0-6.1+deb11u3.1~) | nginx-extras (<< 1.18.0-6.1+deb11u3.1~), nginx-core (>= 1.18.0-6.1+deb11u3) | nginx-full (>= 1.18.0-6.1+deb11u3) | nginx-light (>= 1.18.0-6.1+deb11u3) | nginx-extras (>= 1.18.0-6.1+deb11u3)
Description-en: small, powerful, scalable web/proxy server
Nginx ("engine X") is a high-performance web and reverse proxy server created by Igor Sysoev. It can be used both as a standalone web server and as a proxy to reduce the load on back-end HTTP or mail servers.

Output truncated...

In-Chapter Exercises

28. First, install a single package on your system from the list you compiled in answer to In-Chapter Exercise 26. above, and as detailed in this section. Then, if they haven't already been installed by yourself, or a system administrator, use APT on your Raspberry Pi system to install the following application packages: gnome-disk-utility 3.38.2, GIMP, openssh-server, nginx, and vsftpd. Finally, test each of these applications. Do these applications restart after a system reboot? How can you know if they would do that, without actually rebooting the system?

29. Use APT on your Raspberry Pi system to install application packages that fit your particular use-case(s). Go back to your answer to In-Chapter Exercise 26 for a preliminary listing of these.

1.13.3 Upgrading the Operating System

Similar to our recommendations for the exact, specific details of initially installing your system, the minor or major release upgrades of the system itself are very dependent on:

1. The specific system you are dealing with.
2. The versions of that system you are trying to upgrade between.

Although the Raspberry Pi OS uses APT, there is enough variability due to 2, that presenting the exact, specific details of upgrading the system is best left to consulting relevant online sources at the time you want to do the upgrades. When we wrote this book, the upgrade procedure using APT, could be summarized as follows:

1. The following APT commands worked for minor release upgrades:

    root@raspberrypi:~# **apt update**

    root@raspberrypi:~# **apt upgrade**

    root@raspberrypi:~# **apt dist-upgrade**

2. The major upgrade procedure is best done by consulting the online documentation at the time you want to do the upgrade, and of course is constrained by 1 above.

In-Chapter Exercise

30. Create a document which details exactly what steps you must take to upgrade your Raspberry Pi system, serving for both minor releases and major releases of the software. The scheduling of your procedural steps should reflect, for example, a weekly or monthly basis for minor release changes, or at some unspecified interval for major release changes. Then, implement the procedures that your document specifies.

1.14 System and Software Performance Monitoring and Adjustment

The most important considerations a Raspberry Pi OS administrator (and the ordinary, single user on her own computer) has to make, when dealing with system performance, revolves around CPU process management, memory management, disk usage/management, and network performance. Table 1.8 lists the controlling facilities and functions the Raspberry Pi OS provides for system tuning and performance monitoring, most notably with the kernel-loadable ZFS component added, if that ever is the stable, and easily implemented case.

The commands that implement and affect some of the functions from Table 1.8 are shown in bold type below. We also include commands that allow you to monitor these functions as well. We cover some of these commands in

TABLE 1.8

Performance Tuning Functions

System Component	Control Facility
CPU	Nice numbers
	Process priorities
	Cgroup management
	Batch queues
	Scheduler parameters
Memory	Process resource limits
	Cgroup management
	Memory management parameters
	Paging space
ZFS vdevs, zpools and I/O (if installed)	ZFS pool and file system organization
	ZFS deduplication, efficiency, optimization
	I/O parameters
	Zvol creation and administration
Network I/O	Network memory buffers
	Network-related parameters
	Network infrastructure

the following sections. The systemd-specific commands are covered in detail in Volume 1, Chapter 2.

df, du, free, journalctl, nice, pgrep, ps, renice, systemctl, systemd-cgls, systemd-run, top

1.14.1 Application-Level Process/Thread Resource Management

The basic reason for monitoring system resources, such as process CPU usage and system memory, in terms of how the system is performing given its designed for and intended use-case(s), is to allow you to observe, assess, and then gain control, at the application level, of how programs important to you are effectively using major components of system resources.

For example, if a particular standard application (such as a web server which you have installed from an on-line repository,) or even a user-written program's processes, are consuming too much of CPU or memory resources, according to criteria you determine given the use case(s) your system is designed or intended for, you can scale back that task's operation to better serve your user base. On the other hand, if those same processes are being under-served, or starved for resources, for whatever reason, you can scale up that task's operation as well. There may be some situations where under-service may be caused by hardware malfunctions, or illegal intrusion, but we do not cover those situations in this section.

A classic case of this, within the context of systemd control, is scaling back from the graphical.target state to the multi-user.target state. This is akin to using a server class install, rather than a full-blown desktop installation. We cover this change of system state, using the **isolate** command, in depth in Volume 1.

The key is to be able to observe and assess the usage of system resources in a contemporary way on your Raspberry Pi, and then take some actions based on those observations and assessments. Those actions are of course guided by how you have strategically designed and implemented your administrative plan, given the use case(s) of your system.

Another way of assessing process activity, for example, in terms of scheduling processes and process groups through the CPU, is to examine the proc file system.

1.14.1.1 Traditional Process Control

Traditionally, the most important, complete, and readily available display of system process activity is given by the **ps** and **top** (or **htop**) commands, which allow you to monitor running processes.

1.14.1.2 systemd Cgroups, Affecting the Limits of CPU Scheduling

With the adoption of systemd into the Linux kernel in all major branches of Linux, including Debian and its downstream distro, the Raspberry Pi OS, several new and many updated features have been introduced. These features completely change the startup phase of booting the system, for example. But most importantly, they radically modify how both system and applications services (such as sshd), and even common userland processes, are managed. One of these radically modified and updated features, known as Control Groups (cgroups), is completely reorganized with respect to service and process/thread management. Processes and threads, as well as system services, are grouped together in a unified manner. This moves system resource management, such as what percentage of CPU time a process, thread, or service is allocated, from the process level up to the application level. This is achieved by mapping cgroup structure to the systemd "unit tree". We sketch systemd cgroups impact on the performance scheduling of processes and threads through the CPU in this section. In the next section, we focus on how cgroups impact memory management to affect system performance.

cgroups are a mechanism for organizing services and processes/threads in a hierarchic tree, or "unit tree", of numbered groups to facilitate resource management. The structure of this tree is graphically illustrated using the **systemd-cgls** command. We show how the **systemd-cgls** command can be used to view and assess the cgroups strucure. Then, control is exercised on these numbered groups to affect resources like CPU usage, memory management, network bandwidth, and other system service-related activities. This control can be done on a transient, or temporary, basis using the **systemd-run** command. Or it can be done on a persistent, or permanent basis, by making critical changes to the systemd units file that all permanent, start-at-boot-time services have. We organize our presentation in this section around these two bases.

Before the introduction of cgroups and systemd in the Linux kernel, all processes received similar amounts of system resources that the administrator could modify to enhance performance (per the use-case(s) the system operated under by design) with process *nice* values. The drawback of this legacy approach was that, for an application, such as a webserver or database management program, which may have a large number of sub-processes or threads running at the same time, there was an inadequate mechanism available to give priority to these groups of tasks. Another task or set of tasks that was more use-case, mission-critical, but had a much smaller number of sub-tasks, had to share resources equally with the webserver or database management program.

systemd cgroups have a tremendous advantage over the legacy approach. For example, using systemd cgroups, all the processes started by the nginx webserver will have their own cgroup numbers. This allows you to control nginx at the application level, and all of its "worker children", with the systemd **systemctl** command. We completely detail the **systemctl** command in Volume 1, Chapter 2.

We give a more in-depth explanation of the hierarchic cgroups unit tree in Volume 1, Chapter 2, Section 2.7.1. In that section we also show the utility of the **systemd-cgls** command, and how it depicts, in an easy-to-read, graphical tree format, all of the cgroups and their hierarchic structuring on your Raspberry Pi system.

The key takeaway here, and something that is often misunderstood, is that if you run some task, and nothing else of higher "priority" (in terms of cgroup-levied resource controls) is running at the same time, that task gets 100% of the resources (or nearly so, since the system needs to have a small chunk of resources to keep itself running!).

1.14.1.2.1 Creating a Transient or Persistent Control Group

As we detailed in Volume 1, Chapter 2, Section 2.7.1, the place where cgroup resources are managed is the systemd "unit" file. Placing this management resource facility at the level of unit files allows their operations to be managed with systemd's command-line utilities. Depending on the kind of unit file, your resource management settings can be *transient* or *persistent*.

To create a **transient cgroup** for a service via its unit file, start the service with the **systemd-run** command. A brief description of the **systemd-run** command, taken from the man page for it, is as follows:

****

systemd-run - Run programs in transient scope units, service units, or path-, socket-, or timer-triggered service units

Syntax:
  systemd-run [OPTIONS...] COMMAND [ARGS...]

  systemd-run [OPTIONS...] [PATH OPTIONS...] {COMMAND} [ARGS...]

  systemd-run [OPTIONS...] [SOCKET OPTIONS...] {COMMAND} [ARGS...]

  systemd-run [OPTIONS...] [TIMER OPTIONS...] {COMMAND} [ARGS...]

Purpose:
  systemd-run may be used to create and start a transient .service or .scope unit and run the specified COMMAND in it. It may also be used to create and start a transient .path, .socket, or .timer unit, that activates a .service unit when elapsing.

Common Options:

env	Logs environment variables given by systemd to services.
-p BlockIOWeight=10 updatedb	Limits resources available to a command.
--on-active=30	Runs commands at a specific time.
-t --send-sighup /bin/bash	Allows access to a tty using bash in this case.
--scope --user screen	Starts a screen as a user service.

****

You can then modify resources on an application according to the design of your system use case(s). It is worth noting here that system programming applications can create transient cgroups by using cgroup API calls to **systemd**. A transient unit is removed from the system as soon as the service is stopped using the **systemctl stop** command, or the system is rebooted (since there is no permanent unit file created for the service using **systemd-run**.)

To create a **persistent cgroup** for a service, you must create or edit its unit configuration file. The configuration can be preserved after system reboot, so it can be used to manage services that are started automatically by systemd.

We present Examples 1.10 and 1.11 below, with relevant background information, on these two methods of service creation.

Creating a Transient cgroup with systemd-run and Changing its CPUShare
To create a transient cgroup, and run a command in that cgroup, the **systemd-run** command is used. The general form of the **systemd-run** command, with some specific options, is as follows:

$ **systemd-run --unit=*name* --slice=*slice_name* --property *prop_name=val command*** where:

name is your name for the unit. If **--unit** is not specified, a non-descriptive unit name will be chosen automatically. It is highly recommended to always include this option, and choose some descriptive name you can easily recognize.

slice_name is one of the standard, existing slices on your system you want the unit to operate under. You can list slices on your system using the **systemctl -t slice** command. Or you can even create a new slice by designating a new, unique name. By default, services and scopes are created in the **system.slice**.

prop_name is an allowed property you want to initially set for the unit, and Val is the value you want to assign to that property. In this section, we use a separate **systemctl** command to do this in order to change a unit's CPUShares. But it can also be done using this option of the **systemd-run** command.

command is the Linux command, and its valid options, option arguments, and command arguments that will execute in the service unit, when it is started. The command should always be at the end of the **systemd-run** command, to avoid confusing **systemd-run** options with the command you want to run in the unit!

   See the **systemd-run** man page on your system for more information on options and their arguments.

   In order to set a property, such as the **% share** of the CPU that a service gets, you use the **systemctl** command. The general syntax for setting a property of a service with **systemctl** is:

$ systemctl set-property service_name property=property_value

where:

service_name	is the name of the service you want to modify the property of,
property	is the valid name of a property, and
property_value	is an allowable value of the given property.

See the man page for **systemctl** on your Raspberry Pi system for more information.

Example 1.10 Starting a New Service with **systemd-run** and Allocating CPU Resources

Objectives: The following example allows you to start three transient services in the user.slice, and allocate a larger percentage of the CPU to one of them. Therefore, one of them will get more time in the CPU. The program that will be running in each of the services will be the **top** command, with the **-b** batch option.

Prerequisites: That you have superuser privilege on the system.

Requirements: Do the following steps, in the order presented below.

1. Execute the following **systemd-run** command, with the arguments shown:

    root@raspberrypi:~# **systemd-run --unit=test --slice=user.slice top -b**
    Running as unit: test.service.
    root@raspberrypi:~#

2. Check the status of the service.

    root@raspberrypi:~# **systemctl status test.service**
      Loaded: loaded (/run/systemd/transient/test.service; transient)
     Transient: yes
      Active: active (running) since Sat 2023-05-27 14:28:26 PDT; 56s ago
     Main PID: 51751 (top)
      Tasks: 1 (limit: 3932)
    CPU: 574ms
    CGroup: /user.slice/test.service
       └─51751 /usr/bin/top -b

    May 27 14:29:21 raspberrypi top[51751]: 51645 root 20 0 ...
    Output truncated...
    root@raspberrypi:~#

3. Run two more similar transient units, to provide a comparison test for the relative setting of CPUShares.

    root@raspberrypi:~# **systemd-run --unit=test2 --slice=user.slice top -b**
    Running as unit: test2.service
    root@raspberrypi:~# **systemd-run --unit=test3 --slice=user.slice top -b**
    Running as unit: test3.service
    root@raspberrypi:~#

4. Use the **systemctl** command, and the **set-property** sub-command, to give the user.slice and test.service a higher CPU share. Then reload the systemd daemon.

    root@raspberrypi:~# **systemctl set-property user.slice CPUShares=3000**
    root@raspberrypi:~# **systemctl set-property test.service CPUShares=3000**
    root@raspberrypi:~# **systemctl daemon-reload**
    root@raspberrypi:~#

In-Chapter Exercises

31. Use the **top** command on your system to verify that test.service is actually receiving more of a percentage of the CPU time than both services test2, test3, and other user.slice services. How much more % time on every cycle through the top command output?

32. If the default CPU allocation number for a process is 1024, what do numbers like 3000 (shown in the above **systemctl set-property** command) or 100, mean, in terms of relative percentage utilization of the CPU? Correlate your answer to this last question to the output of the **top** command. Why did we set the CPUShares of user.slice to 3000 also?

5. Finally, to stop the three transient services started above, use the following commands:

```
root@raspberrypi:~# systemctl stop test.service
root@raspberrypi:~# systemctl stop test2.service
root@raspberrypi:~# systemctl stop test3.service
root@raspberrypi:~#
```

Conclusion: We used **systemd-run** to execute a set of three transient services, then gave one of those services a higher CPU priority. We had to use the **systemctl daemon-reload** command to basically reload the systemd manager configuration, reload all service unit files and other units, and redo the systemd dependency tree. This forces the CPUShares changes we made to take effect.

1.14.1.2.2 Persistent Cgroups and Setting Their Resources

Example 1.11 Creating Persistent Cgroups and Modifying Their CPUShare and CPUQuota

Objectives: To create a persistent, or permanent, cgroup, by constructing a service unit file for it in the /etc/systemd/system directory. This is the standard location for user-installed and user-defined services in systemd, as shown in Volume 1, Chapter 2. The basic objectives of the following example will be to create a simple, user-defined service, and balance its CPU usage with the same **systemctl set-property** command we have shown for transient services in Example 1.10.

Prerequisites: Completion of Example 1.10, and having superuser privilege on the system.

Requirements: Do the following steps, in the order presented below.

1. Use your favorite text editor (such as nano) as the root, or superuser, to create and save the following text file, named **test4.service**, exactly as shown, in /etc/systemd/system:

   [Unit]
   Description=A test service that uses the sha256sum command.
   After=remote-fs.target nss-lookup.target

   [Service]
   ExecStart=/usr/bin/sha256sum /dev/zero
   ExecStop=/bin/kill -WINCH ${MAINPID}

   [Install]
   WantedBy=multi-user.target

   The structure and components of the above file are detailed completely in Volume 1, Chapter 2.

2. Now we can start this service, and make it persistent, using the **systemctl** command, and its **unit** sub-command. We can also use the **ps** and **systemctl** commands, and the unit sub-command **systemctl status**, to monitor valuable information about test4.service:

   root@raspberrypi:~# **systemctl start test4.service**

   root@raspberrypi:~# **systemctl enable test4.service**
   Created symlink /etc/systemd/system/multi-user.target.wants... .
   Output truncated...
   root@raspberrypi:~# **systemctl status test4.service**
   ● test4.service - A test service that uses the sha256sum command.
      Loaded: loaded (/etc/systemd/system/test4.service; enabled;
      vendor preset: enabled)
      Active: active (running) since Sun 2023-05-28 06:39:18 PDT; 1min
      14s ago
     Main PID: 62874 (sha256sum)
      Tasks: 1 (limit: 3932)
       CPU: 1min 13.874s
     CGroup: /system.slice/test4.service
             └─62874 /usr/bin/sha256sum /dev/zero

   May 28 06:39:18 raspberrypi systemd[1]: Started A test service that
   uses the sha256sum command.

   root@raspberrypi:~#
   root@raspberrypi:~# **ps -p 62874 -o pid,comm,cputime,%cpu**

```
PID    COMMAND       TIME      %CPU
62874  sha256sum     00:03:35  99.5
root@raspberrypi:~# systemctl status 62874 | grep CGroup
    CGroup: /system.slice/test4.service

root@raspberrypi:~#
```

The valuable information we can see from the **systemctl status** and **ps** commands is that this service is consuming 99.5% of the CPU resource on our Raspberry Pi 400 system. Also, that its pid is 62874, it is running the command **sha256sum**, and it is in the system.slice cgroup.

3. There are two approaches we can take to "throttle" back the amount of CPU resource test4.service consumes. First, we can decrease the CPUShare for test4.service, to "throttle" it back to a more acceptable value. This change will be persistent across system reboots. We can set the value of CPUShares for test4.service to 100 (the value we will set in the command below), which will be effective upon all subsequent restarts of that service. Second, we can set a maximum quota on CPU consumption for test4.service, by changing its CPUQuota property to some lower percentage value.

To make a change in CPUShares or CPUQuota for test4.service that is transient, or temporary (non-persistent across restarts or reboots,) add the **--runtime** option to the following **systemctl set-property** commands.
To throttle back test4.service using CPUShares, use the following command:

```
root@raspberrypi:~# systemctl set-property test4.service CPUShares=100
```

To throttle back test4.service using CPUQuota, use the following command:

```
root@raspberrypi:~# systemctl set-property test4.service CPUQuota=20%
```

To make these changes effective, use the following commands:

```
root@raspberrypi:~# systemctl daemon-reload
root@raspberrypi:~# systemctl restart test4.service
```

In-Chapter Exercises

33. Use the **top** command to verify the CPU % usage of test4.service after just limiting its CPUShare to 100. What is the CPUShare on your system, and why? Is this percentage in agreement with the **ps** command percentage shown in the above session? What does the **top**

command reveal about %CPU usage for test4.service after you have throttled it back with the CPUQuota property value of 20% that we show. Do both methods yield similar results? Why, or why not?

34. Create and start another system.slice service with the **systemd-run** command, named test5.service, that executes the md5sum command. Start it, and make it persistent. Then use the **top** command to verify the % CPU of both test4.service and test5.service. What are their relative % CPU usages on your system, and why?

35. How do you stop test4.service and test5.service from running?

4. To cleanup your system to stop and remove the test4.service (and test5.service), use the following commands:

```
root@raspberrypi:~# systemctl stop test4.service
root@raspberrypi:~# systemctl stop test5.service
root@raspberrypi:~# rm -r /etc/systemd/system/test4.service
root@raspberrypi:~# rm -r /etc/systemd/system/test5.service
root@raspberrypi:~#
```

Conclusion: We have successfully created a simple, yet persistent, user-defined service, and balanced its CPU usage with the **systemctl** command, and its options.

1.14.2 Managing Memory

systemd allows you to easily control and set limits on a unit's memory usage. This can be critical in cases where there is a smaller amount of installed memory on your Raspberry Pi hardware. To see what percentage of memory a unit is consuming, use the **top** command, and examine the column output for %MEM. Given the use-case(s) your system has been designed for, if an application or service is consuming too much memory, there are two ways you can limit its memory usage.

The limit specifies how much process and kernel memory can be used by tasks in this unit. The limit is a memory size in bytes. If the numerical value is followed by K, M, G or T, the specified memory size is parsed as Kilobytes, Megabytes, Gigabytes, or Terabytes (with the base 1024), respectively. The special value "infinity" means that no memory limit is to be applied.

The simplest way to achieve this is to put the following directive in the [Service] section of the unit's configuration file:

MemoryLimit=value

Replace value with a limit on maximum memory usage of the processes executed in the cgroup. Use suffixes K, M, G, or T to identify Kilobyte,

Megabyte, Gigabyte, or Terabyte as the unit of measurement. Also, the MemoryAccounting parameter has to be enabled for the unit.

The MemoryLimit parameter controls the memory.limit_in_bytes control group parameter.

To assign a 500 Megabyte memory limit to the test4 service, add a MemoryLimit setting in the /etc/systemd/system/test4.service file to include the following:

[Service]
MemoryLimit=500M

To apply the changes in either of the two ways, reload systemd's configuration and restart The service.

```
$ sudo systemctl daemon-reload
$ sudo systemctl restart test4.service
```

In-Chapter Exercises

36. Set the MemoryLimit value for selected services on your Raspberry Pi system, either higher, or lower, depending upon specific use-case requirements.

37. Use the **free** command on your system, and its options, to gauge the distribution of system memory. Do the quantities you get agree with the amount of installed system memory you have?

    From the output of the **free** commands, what can you infer about the installed memory quantity on your system, in GB? See the man page for the **free** command on your system to get more information about its usage and options.

1.14.3 Assessment of System Disk Usage

Along with CPU usage and memory management, the ability to look at, then assess and possibly modify the resources of persistent storage media, particularly of a limited-capacity microSD card, is critical to a system administrator's task. Even for an ordinary user, storage space is a precious commodity, regardless of the availability and lower costs of terabyte-capacity externally mounted media. Consider a Raspberry Pi system that can only physically support a smaller capacity microSD card, for whatever reason. Or a system where an ordinary user is storing large files, such as video or other types of media file.

Traditionally, the **du** command allowed you to get a text-based summary of disk usage for files and directories, in a variety of formats. An administrator could then take action to trim storage usage according to the use case of the system. For more information on the **du** command, see the man page for **du** on your Raspberry Pi system.

The **df** command (df is an abbreviation for disk free) allows you to display the amount of available storage space for file systems on which the invoking user has read access. **df** is typically invoked using the **-h** and **T** option, which gives a human-readable output format, which includes the file system types. For example, on our Raspberry Pi 400 system whose boot/system medium is an externally mounted USB3 SSD, the following command gives information about storage and file system layout:

```
$ df -hT
```

file system	Type	Size	Used	Avail	Use%	Mounted on
/dev/root	ext4	439G	15G	403G	4%	/
devtmpfs	devtmpfs	1.7G	0	1.7G	0%	/dev
tmpfs	tmpfs	1.9G	0	1.9G	0%	/dev/shm
tmpfs	tmpfs	759M	1.5M	758M	1%	/run
tmpfs	tmpfs	5.0M	4.0K	5.0M	1%	/run/lock
/dev/sda1	vfat	253M	31M	222M	13%	/boot
tmpfs	tmpfs	380M	32K	3 80M	1%	/run/user/1000

```
$
```

More contemporary graphical methods can be used to view and assess disk usage on Raspberry Pi systems. For example, you can use the gnome disk usage analyzer, named "Baobab". It displays either a bar or sector chart representation of relative disk usage, for any attached persistent medium. This tool is very useful when you want to get a picture of where, and what, your disks are being used for. Figure 1.11 shows a typical disk capacity display of the root directory on the same Raspberry Pi 400 system. Similar tools are found on all Linux systems. Another useful summary tool, similar to Gparted, is the gnome-disk-utility, launched from the Preferences Menu.

1.14.4 Network Configuration with the **ip** Command

The most important and useful command for the system administrator when doing a post-install network configuration is the **ip** command. The following sections illustrate the basic usage of this command, and give a use case example that illustrates how to assign more than one IP address to a Raspberry Pi network interface.

With the new toolkit, it is as easy as with the old to add new ip addresses, as follows:

```
$ ip addr add 192.168.1.1/24 dev eth0
```

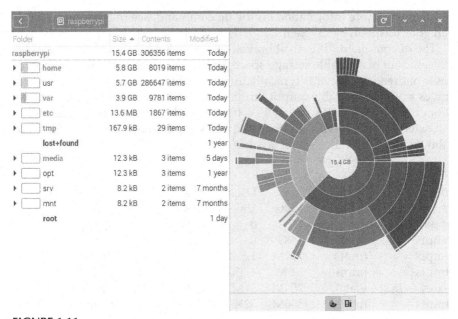

FIGURE 1.11
Disk Usage Analyzer Display of the Root Directory.

1.14.4.1 Basic ip Command Syntax, Options, and Operations

An abbreviated version of the man page for the **ip** command is as follows:

****

ip

Syntax: ip [Options] Object {Command | help}
**   ip [-force] -batch filename**
where
    Object {link | addr | addrlabel | route | rule | neigh | ntable | tunnel
       | tuntap | mad-dress | mroute | mrule | monitor | xfrm | netns |
       l2tp | tcp_metrics}
    Options {-V[ersion] | -h[uman-readable] | -s[tatistics] | -r[esolve] | -
       f[amily] {inet | inet6 | ipx | dnet | link} | -o[neline] | -n[etns] name
       | -a[ll] | -c[olor]}

Command
Specifies the action to perform on the object. The set of possible actions
depends on the object type.

For most objects, the commands possible are **add**, **delete**, and **show**. Some objects do not allow all of these operations, or have some additional commands. The help command is available for all objects. It prints out a list of available commands and argument syntax conventions.
If no command is given, usually the **show** command is the default, if that option can be applied to the objects specified.

Purpose: Show or manipulate routing, devices, policy routing and tunnels.
Output: Output or modified routing, devices, policy routing, or tunnels.
Common Options, Objects, and Commands:
addr   IP address

To view an abbreviated syntax display of help on the ip route command, type the following:

$ **ip addr help**
Usage: ip address {add | change | replace} IFADDR dev IFNAME [LIFETIME]
                  [CONFFLAG-LIST]
       ip address del IFADDR dev IFNAME [mngtmpaddr]
       ip address {show | save | flush} [dev IFNAME] [scope SCOPE-ID]
               [to PREFIX] [FLAG-LIST] [label LABEL] [up]
       ip address {showdump | restore}
IFADDR:= PREFIX | ADDR peer PREFIX
     [broadcast ADDR] [anycast ADDR]
     [label IFNAME] [scope SCOPE-ID]
Output truncated...

****

From the above abbreviated listing, you can see the Commands available to work on the Object route, i.e. add, change, replace, del(ete), show, save, flush, and showdump.
    To see the status of the specific network interface named eth0 for example, type the following:

$ **ip addr show eth0**
2: eth0: <BROADCAST,MULTICAST,UP,LOWER_UP> mtu 1500 qdisc mq state UP group default qlen 1000
    link/ether e4:11:5b:12:c2:77 brd ff:ff:ff:ff:ff:ff
    inet 192.168.1.26/24 brd 192.168.1.255 scope global dynamic noprefixroute eth0
       valid_lft 14608sec preferred_lft 3808sec
    inet6 fe80::9ef2:8f7f:e4c4:7ea2/64 scope link
       valid_lft forever preferred_lft forever

To see the status of the all network interfaces attached to, or defined on, the system, type the following:

$ **ip addr show**
1: lo: <LOOPBACK,UP,LOWER_UP> mtu 65536 qdisc noqueue state
UNKNOWN group default qlen 1000
    link/loopback 00:00:00:00:00:00 brd 00:00:00:00:00:00
    inet 127.0.0.1/8 scope host lo
    valid_lft forever preferred_lft forever
    inet6::1/128 scope host
      valid_lft forever preferred_lft forever
2: eth0: <BROADCAST,MULTICAST,UP,LOWER_UP> mtu 1500 qdisc mq
state UP group default qlen 1000
    link/ether e4:11:5b:12:c2:77 brd ff:ff:ff:ff:ff:ff
    inet 192.168.1.26/24 brd 192.168.1.255 scope global dynamic
    noprefixroute eth0
      valid_lft 14227sec preferred_lft 3427sec
    inet6 fe80::9ef2:8f7f:e4c4:7ea2/64 scope link
      valid_lft forever preferred_lft forever

To display link characteristics of eth0, type the following:

$ **ip link show dev eth0**
2: eth0: <BROADCAST,MULTICAST,UP,LOWER_UP> mtu 1500 qdisc mq
state UP mode DEFAULT group default qlen 1000
link/ether e4:11:5b:12:c2:77 brd ff:ff:ff:ff:ff:ff
$

1.14.4.2 Use Case Example: Assigning Multiple IP Addresses to a Raspberry Pi

This section, and its example, show how to assign multiple IP addresses to your system, without using the deprecated **ifconfig** command, or its obsolete "alias" notation.

Question: Why would you want to do this?

Answer: You want to have your favorite web server, nginx, listen on several IP addresses on your LAN. You proceed with the following commands, and then modify the nginx configuration to do so. We do not show the nginx configuration changes here.

Example 1.12 Assigning Several IP Addresses to a Network Interface

    Objectives: To use the **ip** command to assign several IP addresses to your system's network interface.

Prerequisites: Having superuser privileges on your system.

Requirements: Do the following steps, in the order presented.

1. If you need an additional IP address temporarily, you can add it to any
    network interface by using the following general format command:

    $ **sudo ip address add <ip-address>/<netmask> dev <interface>**

An actual example would be as follows:

$ **sudo ip address add 192.168.1.100/24 dev eth0**
[sudo] password for bob: **QQQ**
$

The above command would add an additional IP address to the network
interface, using a 24 bit netmask, to whatever current IP addresses are already
assigned to the nic eth0.

You can check the result with the following command. Notice that the
address 192.168.1.26 has already been assigned via the DHCP server on the
network, by default:

$ **ip address show eth0**
2: eth0: <BROADCAST,MULTICAST,UP,LOWER_UP> mtu 1500 qdisc mq
state UP group default qlen 1000
  link/ether e4:11:5b:12:c2:77 brd ff:ff:ff:ff:ff:ff
  inet 192.168.1.26/24 brd 192.168.1.255 scope global dynamic
  noprefixroute eth0
    valid_lft 14015sec preferred_lft 3215sec
  inet 192.168.1.100/24 scope global secondary eth0
    valid_lft forever preferred_lft forever
  inet6 fe80::9ef2:8f7f:e4c4:7ea2/64 scope link
    valid_lft forever preferred_lft forever

You can delete this address again using the following command:

$ **sudo ip address del 192.168.1.100/24 dev eth0**

These changes are lost when you reboot your machine.

2. To make the additional IP address permanent, as superuser you can
    edit the file /etc/network/interfaces, and add the above IP address at
    the bottom of the existing entries, while retaining the defaults found in
    that file. This is what the interfaces file must look like with the above
    assignment added to that file:

```
# interfaces(5) file used by ifup(8) and ifdown(8)
auto lo
iface lo inet loopback
## The primary network interface, the default which must be included in
    this file!
auto eth0
iface eth0 inet dhcp
# The address added to the default
iface eth0 inet static
address 192.168.1.100/24
```

The above file contents shows you **must** explicitly retain the default settings for network interfaces, and add additional ones. If, in the above /*etc*/network/ interfaces file the primary network interface is *not* specified (the one assigned, in our case, by DHCP), you must specify it as a DHCP-assigned address.

Note

In fact, that was the case for us in our default /*etc*/network/interface file on our Raspberry Pi.

Save the file, and reboot to make the new network settings permanent.

To return to the default network interface settings for eth0, simply edit the /etc/network/interfaces file again and remove the add IP address lines.

In-Chapter Exercises

38. How would you delete the assignment of the address 192.168.1.100 to eth0 during this session?

39. How would you ensure that the deletion persisted between system boots, after you have completed step 2?

40. How would you add more than just one new assignment of an ip address?

Conclusion: We assigned several IP addresses on our LAN for our Raspberry Pi system.

1.15 System Security

There are two meaninghs of the word "security" relevant here, when referring to computers such as the Raspberry Pi. We will consider only one of them.

The first meaning denotes reliability. In other words, the files and data on the disks can be relied upon to be persistent over time. That is the objective of not only having persistent media, but also of backing up the operating system itself, and the user files and data. For example, if the operating system crashes and cannot be brought back to the exact state it was before the crash, the user files and data are archived, secure, and can be recovered in total.

The second meaning denotes free from malicious intrusion by agents (such as robotic cracker programs) or objects (such as the processes that are the basis of program execution) that do *not* have the authority to access a specific part of the system, or any of its components, files, or data. The reasons for implementing system security in this second sense, both for an ordinary, single-user system, and in a multi-user environment, should be very obvious to the beginner. Especially in the light of contemporary privacy issues, and the widespread hacking and system penetration forces prevalent on the Internet currently.

Since we've already dealt with the issues of persistent media in the previous sections, here in this section we deal primarily with the second meaning of computer security.

Fundamentally, according to this second meaning, there are at least four places where you can situate system security measures as we show them in this section. They are as follows:

1. At the Process Level: The process model of the Raspberry Pi OS makes this site most important. This model dictates security implemented on processes, via authentication and credentialing techniques. Processes that are the basis for program execution, and that bridge kernel and user spaces. Examples of these measures are:

    * Setting traditional UNIX permission bits (rwx), the special permission bits SUID, SGID, and the sticky bit. The setting of permission bits implies that the processes that shell commands create, are the real objects that the permission bits files possess are aimed at, or applied to. This is true of everything that creates processes in the Raspberry Pi OS, which means user-written programs, and all other applications programs and system programs as well.

    * Deployment of ACLs, either extended POSIX1.e ACLs or NFSv4 ACLs, as detailed in Volume 1.

    * Use of Linux-specific "capabilities" applied to processes, as detailed in the sections below.

    * Namespace isolation of processes, using the Linux kernel namespace API, and the six major implementations of it.

2. At the Physical Level: When someone sits directly in front of the Raspberry Pi and tries to log in and use it. One of the ways that can be accomplished is through the use of password protection into user accounts. On a public computer system (which is kind of rare as far as we know for a Raspberry Pi!), this is the most valuable way to maintain general access security, and user/account security. There are also many security techniques in this place that limit physical access to

the hardware of the system, such as locking the door to the room you keep the machine in, or having protocols in place for limiting physical access to the machine.

3. At the Network Level: By placing safeguards on the computer's network connection. This is accomplished using various forms of not only monitoring with systemd journalctl, and using the many forms of intrusion detection, but also with the intrusion prevention systems we illustrate below.

4. At the Persistent Media Level: On the persistent media attached, either physically or virtually, to the computer itself. These techniques are applied to the boot/system medium, and other attached media such as user data disks, or mounted network file systems (NFS). Examples of this are the use of virtualized "sandboxed" machines on traditional volumes, or on ZFS volumes, and the various domains of disk data encryption shown below.

Furthermore, the above sites use the following specific techniques. We will describe some of the important ones in the sections below. A further elaboration of some of these techniques is given in Section 1.15.2, entitled "Access Control Credentials: Discretionary (DAC), Mandatory (MAC), and Role-Based (RBAC)".

* Password-based authentication
* Access control, either discretionary (DAC), mandatory (MAC), or role-based (RBAC)
* The **sudo** command
* Setting POSIX1.e ACLs and extended ACLs, and NFSv4 ACLs for files and directories
* Intrusion Detection and Intrusion Prevention
* Security Software
* ufw System Firewall
* Process Credentialing
* User namespace process isolation
* Whole disk, partition, directory, or file-level data encryption

1.15.1 Password-Based Authentication

The first line of defense in system security, and the technique employed almost universally across many types of computer system, is password-based authentication. The Raspberry Pi OS compares a user-entered password at login for a user's ID, compares the password to a previously established and stored one held in a password file for that user, and based on the comparison, either authenticates the user, or denies access. The ID not only determines whether the user can gain access to the system itself, but also determines what privileges the user has. For example, superuser privilege. Also, the ID is used in Discretionary Access Control (DAC), as shown in Section 1.15.2. The password file and a hash/salt scheme using a SHA256 hashing algorithm for encrypting the password, work together to authenticate a user's ID. The password file on the system, in /etc/passwd, holds user information and works in conjunction with the /etc/shadow file to authenticate a user ID.

In-Chapter Exercise

41. Examine the contents of the /etc/passwd file on your Raspberry Pi system. With reference to your username entry in that file, how many colon-delimited fields are there, and what are the meanings of those colon-delimited fields?

1.15.2 Access Control Credentials: Discretionary (DAC), Mandatory (MAC), and Role-Based (RBAC)

The terms we use in this section are important if you want to understand the different types of access control. When we talk about access control via security checks, here are the important terms:

Objects: A fundamental component of an executing kernel is the programs and processes it maintains. Objects are the entities that are targeted, or worked on, by the processes of a program. For example, processes themselves can be objects, or the processes that are generated by executing instances of a program.

Files/inodes are another form of object, particularly the executable form of file objects, and the data structure(s) holding their information. You shouldn't mix this up with file system objects, which we have referred to as either ordinary or directory.

Object Ownership: Indicates the owning, user, and group.

Object Context: Security checks done when objects are acted on.

Subjects: An object that is acted upon by another object. Processes are active subjects, such as those processes that are created by an **exec()** or **fork()** system call from some originating process.

Subject Context: Security checks done when an active subject performs its operations.

Action: What a subject does to an object. This includes reading, writing, creating, and deleting files or forking and signaling.

Permissions: Security checks when a subject acts upon an object. Taking the subject context, the object context, and the action, and searching one or more sets of permissions to see whether the subject is granted, or denied permission to act in the intended way on the object, given those contexts. In simple terms, match subject and object permissions, and let the subject act, or not, on the object.

There are three basic "classes" of permissions. These are:

1.   Discretionary Access Control (DAC):

Sometimes the object will include sets of rules as part of its description. This is an "Access Control List" or "ACL". A file may supply more than one ACL. A traditional Linux file, for example, includes a permissions mask that is an abbreviated ACL with three fixed classes of subject ("user", "group", and "other"), each of which may be granted certain privileges ("read", "write" and "execute"—or whatever those map to for the object in question). Linux file permissions do not allow the arbitrary specification of subjects, however, and so are of limited use.

A Linux file might also support a POSIX1e ACL, or an NFSv4 ACL. This is a list of rules that grants various permissions to arbitrary subjects.

2.   Mandatory Access Control (MAC):

The system as a whole may have one or more sets of permissions that get applied to all subjects and objects, regardless of their source. Security Extended Linux (SELinux) is an example of this.

3.   Role-Based Access Control (RBAC):

Rather than use the user ID to find out what access rights users and groups have on the system, the Role-Based Access Control (RBAC) model gives access based on the role, or roles that a user assumes. The classic RBAC example is the use of the **su** or **sudo** commands to grant an unprivileged user root privileges, in a transient way. Another example can be found in ZFS, when you execute the **zfs** command, and your action is checked to see that the subject issuing the command has the role privilege, *even if the user is root.*

These classes of access control policies determine what action is allowed on what object, under what circumstances (DAC, MAC, or Role-Based Access Control [RBAC]), and by what subject.

A permission in the traditional UNIX/Linux sense, for example, is read, write, or execute privilege. A subject, for example, can be thought of as an executing process. Most importantly, an object can be thought of as a Linux process, since everything done on files and the data in them, is done through active processes on the system.

In-Chapter Exercises

42. What major apparatus controls the execution of processes in the Raspberry Pi OS?
43. Give other examples of DAC, MAC, and RBAC.

On the command line, an ordinary user, or the system administrator, is able to implement resource use restrictions and privileges by controlling process credential assignments, levied on subject executable image files, via the **chmod** command. An ordinary unprivileged user can be given the required privileged role with the **su** or **sudo** command. Then, as root, she can issue a privileged **chmod**, **chown**, and **chgrp** to grant, or modify file and directory access permissions, and use the DAC, MAC, or RBAC methods.

1.15.2.1 Types of Credentials

We are concerned with the three basic types of credentials that the Linux kernel supports. These are as follows.

Traditional UNIX Credentials

1. Real User ID
2. Real Group ID

UID and GID are assigned to most objects. These mostly define the object context of that object, with processes included in this assignment.

3. Effective (EUID), Saved (SUID), and FS (FSID) User ID
4. Effective (EGID), Saved (SGID), and FS (FSGID) Group ID
5. Supplementary groups

The additional credentials used by processes are EUID/EGID/GROUPS, and are used as the subject context, and real UID/GID will be used as the object context.

1.15.2.2 ACLs (Access Control Lists)

ACLs provide the ordinary, unprivileged user with the ability to set finer access controls on directories and files than the traditional permissions, whether they are used on ext4, or ZFS file systems. Two different basic types of ACL apply to files and directories. An ACL that defines the current access permissions of files and directories is called an *access* ACL. An ACL, which can only logically be set on a directory, and that defines the permissions that a directory object inherits from its parent directory at the time of its creation, is called a *default* ACL. Additional basic types of ACL are *minimal* and *extended* ACLs. ACL permissions that that can be equivalent to the traditional file mode permissions are called *minimal ACLs*. Minimal ACLs have three entries, which can be the same as the traditional file permissions. ACLs with more than the three entries are called extended ACLs. Extended ACLs also contain a mask entry and may contain any number of named user and named group entries.

Unfortunately, at the time of the writing of this book, the Raspberry Pi OS and the POSIX.1e ACL model that it supports, do not easily allow for the interoperability, in terms of Network File System, version 4 (NFSv4) ACLs, between Linux and non-Linux servers and clients.

For example, if a Linux user were to mount an NFSv4 ACL-compliant file system as an NFS shared resource, the default POSIX.1e implementation on Linux would not be able to take advantage of the NFSv4 ACL model of that file system. As noted above, that restriction is true even if a user were to install a special tool, nfs4-acl-tools, in addition to enabling NFS server facilities on the remote system, and client facilities on her Linux system. That is necessarily a more advanced application of ACLs.

Another very practical limitation in this respect is virtualization with LXC/LXD containers. If you create LXC/LXD containers, on the Linux host for those containers, the NFSv4 ACLs could not be used on LXD container file objects.

Additionally, ACLs are *not* retained by the **tar** command.

See Volume 1 for more information about POSIX.1e and NFSV4 ACLs.

1.15.2.3 Capabilities

Sets of capabilities are as follows:

1.   Set of permitted capabilities
2.   Set of inheritable capabilities
3.   Set of effective capabilities
4.   Capability bounding set

These are most pertinent when they apply to processes, which are the active element in system operation. They are privileged permissions exercised in a "finer-grained" context. Finer-grained is used here to mean a more specific, targeted privilege. These are applied to a process, or processes, that ordinarily, via the traditional model, could only be granted a blanket, all-or-nothing scheme of privileges. Putting a user in the sudoers file is an example of this traditional model's application.

Capabilities are controlled by changes in the traditional **rwx** permissions, but can also be set more finely and viewed directly by the **capset** and **getcap** system calls.

See the man page for capabilities on your system for further information about capabilities.

In-Chapter Exercise

44. How (and why) do you apply Linux capabilities on the command line? Provide an example of this, that you have implemented and tested on your Raspberry Pi system.

1.15.3 sudo

On the Raspberry Pi OS, programs, commands, and files are accessed through user and group permissions. Each user has a unique identifier, given as a username, or UID. Users belong to unique groups, given either as a group name, or a GID. Specific users and groups have permission to access available programs, commands, and files.

The **sudo** program, or command, allows a single command to be run as the root user, or superuser, *or even as some other user*. Only the system administrator, or root user, can utilize a policy listing file (named *sudoers*) that contains commands that each user can execute. So the administrator controls what users have what privileges on the system. When any user needs to run a command that requires root permissions, that user types **sudo command** in a terminal window or console, allowing them to run **command** with root privilege. Then, **sudo** consults its permissions list in the policy listing file. If the user has permission to run that command, it runs the command. If the user does not have permission to run the command, **sudo** denies execution. Running **sudo** does not require knowing root's password, but by default requires entry of the user's own password to execute successfully.

An example of the use of the sudo command on our Raspberry Pi system is as follows:

```
bob@raspberrypi:~ $ sudo -i
root@raspberrypi:~#
root@raspberrypi:~# exit
bob@raspberrypi:~ $
```

For a more detailed description of the **sudo** command, see Volume 1.

The **su** command (an abbreviation for "switch user") allows a user to switch roles and become the superuser on the system without logging off from their own account. You must know the password of the root account if you want to assume the role of root. On a Raspberry Pi system, this command is restricted, and you are encouraged to include users that need to have higher levels of privilege on the system in the sudoers file. That way they can only execute privileged operations on a per-command basis.

In-Chapter Exercises

45. Are you included in the sudoers group and file on your Raspberry Pi system? How did you find out if you are?

46. Enter some unprivileged user on your Linux system into the sudoers file. Then have them test the **sudo** command and its operation, as we have shown it in the above section.

47. Is the **su** command available for your use on your Raspberry Pi system? Why or why not?

1.15.4 Intrusion Detection and Prevention Systems

A conceptual layout of how malicious activity from outside of the Raspberry Pi OS interfaces through the components of a system is given in Figure 1.12. It is important to realize that this figure does not specify the multitude of types of attack that can intrude upon your system from a LAN or the Internet, but does show the arrangement of system components that these attacks can

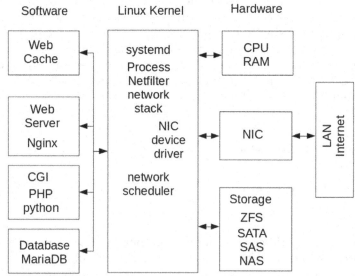

FIGURE 1.12
Routes of Attack and System Components.

target. It also does not show where in the software, kernel, or hardware any defensive or preventative mechanisms are placed.

In-Chapter Exercises

48. Where would a Russian bot be situated in Figure 1.12?
49. What is the Red Team Field Manual (RTFM)? What is the Blue Team Field Manual (BTFM)? What is Pen testing? Why would you need either or both of these manuals in the context of Pen testing?

An intrusion detection system (IDS) is a software application that monitors a network, or a single system, for unauthorized activity, or user protocol violations. It is situated on a software-specific interface, and its output is seen using log file monitoring. A wide variety of free or commercial IDS, from antivirus software to hierarchical systems that monitor the traffic of a backbone network, are available. They can be classified as Network Intrusion Detection Systems (NIDS) or Host Intrusion Detection Systems (HIDS). An IDS that monitors operating system files is an example of a HIDS. An IDS that analyzes incoming network traffic is an example of a NIDS. Also, IDS can be classified by detection strategy. The most well-known types of detection strategies are signature-based detection (recognizing bad patterns, such as malware), and anomaly-based detection (detecting deviations from a predefined model of "good" traffic, which uses a form of Artificial Intelligence (AI). IDS that have some pre-determined and structured response protocol are referred to as Intrusion Prevention Systems (IPS).

A typical network intrusion detection system tries to detect malicious activity, such as a brute force attack, a denial of service attack, port scans, or attempts to crack into computers by monitoring network traffic.

Following is a partial listing of some free IDS available for installation, but not installed by default, on our Raspberry Pi system:

* AIDE is a HIDS that can monitor and analyse the internals of the operating system.
* Snort is a NIDS which performs packet logging and real-time traffic analysis on IP networks.
* fail2ban is an example of an IPS. One of the configurations it takes is based upon malicious activity coming into your system from a LAN, or the Internet, and locks out IP addresses that attempt to login via ssh more than five times with the wrong password. This prevents brute force attacks through port 22.

These three IDS are available via APT, or the Raspberry Pi Menu Preferences > Add/Remove Software. The best way to find out more about the particulars of installing and configuring them is by reading their online documentation and tutorials.

In-Chapter Exercises

50. Install one or all of the above IDS packages on your system, using the package management system available. How do you deploy fail2ban, and how do you control its environment? For example, how do you "unblock" an IP address using fail2ban? Test this on your Raspberry Pi system.

51. What are the capabilities and uses of Wireshark? Give a description of it in terms of the IDSs we describe above, and then install Wireshark and use it on your system.

1.15.5 Linux Security Software

All larger Linux computer server systems, as well as individual Raspberry Pi desktop systems used by an ordinary user, can have several types of network-based and host-based security software available to detect malicious activity, protect systems and data, support intrusion detection, and the responses to them. They can be organized into the following categories:

* Intrusion Detection and Intrusion Prevention Systems
* Remote Access Software
* Web Proxies
* Vulnerability Management Software
* Authentication Servers
* Routers
* Firewalls
* Network Quarantine Servers

We covered some of the details of intrusion detection, and also give a more complete description of firewalls in the next section.

1.15.5.1 System Firewall

A firewall is a facility that prevents unauthorized access to or from a private network or a computer. Firewalls can be implemented in either hardware, software, or both. Firewalls are mainly used to halt unauthorized access to a private network or intranet, from the Internet. All traffic entering or leaving a single computer, or intranet, passes through the firewall, which can look at each message packet stream, and block those that do not meet specific security requirements set by the system administrator. These requirements are codified in what are known as *firewall rules*.

In addition to limiting access to your computer and network, a firewall is also useful for allowing remote access to a private network through secure authentication certificates and logins. A common practice is to let a stand-alone computer serve as a single hardware firewall to a private network. Hardware firewalls can be purchased as a stand-alone product. They can also be found integral to broadband routers. Most hardware firewalls will have a minimum of four network connectors to link them to other computers, but for larger networks, there are business networking firewall solutions.

The Raspberry Pi OS uses Uncomplicated Firewall, or **ufw**, to protect the system. The default configuration file for its rules is located in /etc/ufw/ufw. conf. The easiest way for you to find out more about text-based modifications to firewall rules is to see the **ufw** man page on your system. We provide an extensive section giving the basic details of using the command-line method of modifying firewall rules in Volume 1, Section 1.16, entitled "ufw and Netfilter Interface in the Raspberry Pi OS".

It is not absolutely necessary to change the ufw firewall rules, unless your security model, and its impact on your particular use case, warrants firewall rule customization. We provide a general overview of ufw in the next section.

In the Raspberry Pi OS, if the firewall is *active* (enabled, or running), incoming traffic from the network is usually *blocked* until you specify a TCP or UDP port that traffic is allowed to come in on. Also, usually all out-going traffic on all ports is allowed. In the next sections we describe the Uncomplicated FireWall (**ufw**).

To determine whether the firewall is active, use the following systemd command on your Raspberry Pi system:

```
$ systemctl status ufw
• ufw.service - Uncomplicated firewall
   Loaded: loaded (/lib/systemd/system/ufw.service; enabled; vendor
   preset: enabled)
   Active: active (exited) since Wed 2023-05-24 15:47:42 PDT; 6 days ago
     Docs: man:ufw(8)
 Main PID: 157 (code=exited, status=0/SUCCESS)
    Tasks: 0 (limit: 3932)
      CPU: 0
   CGroup: /system.slice/ufw.service
```

Warning: journal has been rotated since unit was started, output may be incomplete.
$

Note
Be very careful when adding custom rules or modifying the firewall, it may endanger your system's security!

In-Chapter Exercise

52. Is ufw active on your system? Are there any firewall rules in effect by default, and what are they? How did you find this out?

1.15.5.2 *Linux Uncomplicated Firewall* (**ufw**)

Unlike other firewall rules-based systems, such as the **iptables** firewall configuration utility, **ufw** is a much easier way to create an IPv4 or IPv6 host-based firewall. A "rules-based system" means that you create syntactically correct rules to control network connection access to your system. **ufw**'s most basic application is to allow or deny access on ports, or deny them from specific IP addresses that you know are problematic security risks.

ufw is based upon the Netfilter interface to the Linux kernel, and particularly the filter table operations and protocols found in that interface. The rule format is also similar to the Packet Filter (PF) syntax in OpenBSD UNIX.

1.15.5.2.1 **ufw** *Defaults*

The default firewall configuration utility for the Raspberry Pi OS is **ufw**. Unlike the iptables firewall configuration utility, **ufw** is a much easier way to create an IPv4 or IPv6 host-based firewall. It is a rule-based system, which means that you create rules to control network connection access to your system. By default, **ufw** is disabled for example. But once enabled, it has a minimal set of rules, as part of its profile, that go into effect. **ufw**'s most basic application is to allow or deny access on ports or from specific IP addresses.

There is a GUI front end for **ufw**, known as gufw. It was installed by default on our Raspberry Pi OS, and can be found in the Raspberry Pi Menu > Preferences > Firewall Configuration.

1.15.5.2.2 **ufw** *Basic Syntax*

An abbreviated listing of the **ufw** man page is as follows:

```
**********************************************************************
```
ufw
Purpose:
> **ufw** is used to manage a Linux firewall, and provides an easy to use interfacefor the creation of firewall rules. The rules use a basic syntax as shown below.

Syntax:
> **ufw [option[s]] [command] [rule[s]]**

Output: New, modified, or deleted firewall rules to/from ports/IP addresses, or devices.

Common Options:

--version	show program's version number and exit
-h, --help	show help message and exit
--dry-run	don't modify anything, just show the changes

Common Commands:

enable	reloads firewall and enables firewall on boot
disable	unloads firewall and disables firewall on boot
reload	reloads firewall rules
default	change the default connection policy
logging	toggle and affect logging to journalctl
reset	disables and resets firewall to defaults
status	show status of firewall and rules
allow	add a valid allow rule
deny	add a valid deny rule
reject	add a valid reject rule
limit	add a valid limit rule
delete	deletes a valid by specification
insert	inserts a valid rule as a numbered rule

Common Rules:

ufw allow 22	allow tcp and udp port 22 to any IP address on a valid NIC
ufw deny proto tcp to any port 80	deny all connectons to tcp port 80
ufw allow in on enp2s0 to 192.168.0.6 proto tcp	allow tcp connections through enp2s0 nic to IP address 192.168.0.6
ufw limit ssh/tcp	allow rate limiting on ssh to prevent brute-force attacks
ufw delete deny 80/tcp	delete the rule denying tcp connections on port 80
ufw delete 3	delete rule 3, number determined with the status command

****

We give several **ufw** use case and rules examples in Volume 1, Section 1.16.2.

1.15.6 Persistent Media Security

There are two basic strategies a system administrator can take to secure the persistent media, such as SSD, USB3-mounted media, and also to harden the file system structure on those media. The actual techniques of these two strategies overlap considerably with the other system administration tasks we have shown in the other Sections of this chapter.

An example of an overlapping technique is found in the adding of additional media to the system, perhaps using ZFS to provide redundancy on these disks per the recommended storage model that we have shown. This allows a system administrator to segregate the user files and other components of the system. That segregation provides a way of isolating those resources, and therefore allows them to be more securely accessed. And adding additional media addresses the administrator's responsibility to backup important data, most critically user data files.

The first strategy involves providing additional physical media, or additional partitions on existing media, to accommodate user data files, or other components of your Raspberry Pi OS file system.

The second strategy involves designing and implementing file and directory access permissions on those additional partitions or media, so that process authentication through the various forms of process credentialing can be achieved.

1.15.6.1 Persistent Media Allocations For /home

According to the recommended user data storage model we provided above, you should put the /home subdirectories, where all of your user directories are located, on its own physical medium. That is a traditional system administration technique of designing your file system structure. When you add mount options to a single formatted partition on this medium, you can do the following:

* Set the nosuid option to prevent SUID and SGID permission-enabled executable programs running from there. Programs that need SUID and SGID permissions should not be stored in /home, as a preventative measure.

* Set the nodev option so no device file located there will be recognized. *Device files should be stored in /dev, not in /home.*

* Optionally set the noexec option, so no executable programs which are stored in /home can be run.

In-Chapter Exercise

53. You are tasked by your boss to migrate all of the *home directories of all users on your system off their default location on a microSD-based* /boot/ system medium, to a multi-media installation on the same Raspberry Pi. Sketch a detailed plan of exactly how you would do this, using the migration of a single user as an example. Show all commands you would use to achieve the migration, and successfully delete the old / home directory for that user's account.

1.15.6.2 Securing the File System

Another important part of securing your Raspberry Pi system is setting proper file system security. We covered POSIX1e ACL's in detail in Volume 1, Section 1.14, entitled "Raspberry Pi OS POSIX.1e Access Control Lists (ACLs)".

1.15.7 Process Credentials

The multi-programming model requires that processes, whether they are generated by shell built-ins, external commands, user-written programs, or by any system programs that use the **fork**, **exec**, or **execve** system calls, have their credentials authenticated before they can make use of objects such as system resources, other processes, sockets, or files/inodes.

Linux systems assign credentials to processes, which associate the process with a specific user and a specific group. These credentials are essential in a multi-user and multi-programming system because they determine what each process can or cannot do in user space and in kernel space, maintaining the autonomy and the security of each user's personal data, and by extension the stability of the system.

The use of credentials is applied in the process data structure, and in the shared resources the processes are trying to access. This is similar to a key and a set of tumblers in a lock. Files are the critical resource on the system. Thus, in the default ext4 file system, each file is owned by a specific user and belongs to a group of users. The owner of a file determines what kind of operations are allowed on that file, distinguishing among herself, the file's user group, and all other users on the system. When a process tries to make use of a file, the Linux Virtual File System (VFS) always validates whether the access is allowed or not, according to the permissions established by the file owner and the process credentials. Process credentials and file access permissions are integrated and inseparable. This authentication coupling is based upon the forms of file permissions we have detailed so far. We have shown that the **chmod** command is the instrument for granting these permissions to files and directories.

1.15.7.1 File Permission-Based Mechanisms

In file-based permission mechanisms, those forms involve managing the basic permission bits on files and directories, and the SetUID (SUID), the SetGID (SGID), and sticky bit permissions. Examples include setting permissions using DAC on the **/usr/bin/passwd**, and **/usr/bin/sudo** commands. Each of these files should maintain their SUID permissions, as shown in the following output:

```
$ sudo ls -la /usr/bin/passwd
-rwsr-xr-x 1 root root 63744 Feb 7 2020 /usr/bin/passwd
$ sudo ls -la /usr/bin/sudo
-rwsr-xr-x 1 root root 178432 Jan 14 05:29 /usr/bin/sudo
$
```

The commands **passwd** and **sudo** are SUID-capable programs. Even though those commands are ostensibly run with root user privilege, a non-privileged user can only change their own password with the **passwd** command, and can only assume root privileges with **sudo**. That is if they are given privilege to do so in the /etc/sudoers file!

The **find** command allows you to search your system to see if there are any hidden or otherwise inappropriate SUID and SGID commands on your system. The following is an example:

```
$ sudo find / -perm /6000 -ls
15205524   40    -rwsr-xr-x 1  root  root      39768     May 10   2022
/usr/sbin/mount.cifs
15205509   36    -rwxr-sr-x 1  root  shadow 34744       Jun 8    2022
/usr/sbin/unix_chkpwd
15205491   1368 -rwsr-xr-x 1  root  root      1400384   Jul 13   2021
/usr/sbin/exim4
15205701   112  -rwsr-xr-x 1  root  root      114648    Jun 28   2021
/usr/sbin/mount.nfs
Output truncated...
```

The **find** command reveals SetUID and SetGID commands that unprivileged users can run to assume the privileged role.

In-Chapter Exercise

    54. Use the find command to list any hidden or inappropriate SUID and SGID commands on your Raspberry Pi system.

1.15.8 Disk Encryption

When the ordinary user wants to do disk encryption for security purposes, the most critical thing is the scope of encryption she wants to implement. For example, she can encrypt the entire boot/system medium she is installing Linux on at the time she installs the system. Or she can do a post-installation encryption of the entire microSD card, selected partitions on it, selected directories, or individual files. What governs the scope of encryption depends a great deal on the particular use case. It is critical to know why you want to do encryption when considering all of the possible strategies of encrypting your persistent media.

In Volume 1, Section 1.17, entitled "Encrypting Directories and Files Using **tar** and **gpg**", we detail a large-scope encryption strategy. In that section, and its sub-sections, we also show how to deploy a smaller-scope encryption strategy of encrypting a directory, and a particular important file in your home directory, as well as the files on a USB thumb drive.

1.15.8.1 The Meaning of Encryption

Encryption uses a very developed science, known as *cryptography*, to implement data hiding. Cryptography is used on a Raspberry Pi system to encode data to hide it from unprivileged users, and then decrypt, or decode the data for privileged users. On the Raspberry Pi OS, the following are some of the objects that can be possible targets for encryption:

Individual files

Volumes or individual partitions

Web page connections

Network connections

Backup file objects on additional hard disks or other media

Compressed directories or files

Encryption/decryption basically uses a variety of mathematical algorithms to treat the above targets. These algorithms are called *cryptographic ciphers*. The important terms to know when dealing with cryptography are *plain text* and *cypher text*. Plain text is the unencrypted, or decrypted format, and cypher text is the encrypted format.

The details of encryption algorithms, their mathematics and complexity, are not as useful to the ordinary user as knowing where and when to apply them. That is, at the system, whole disk, partition, directory, or individual file levels. And also knowing why you want to use them, and carefully reasoning and designing your strategies for implementing these algorithms with the common command-line tools.

In-Chapter Exercise

55. Which of the encryption strategies, entire disk, selected partitions, selected directories, or individual files, would you deploy on your Raspberry Pi system, and for what specific reasons? After deciding upon one, or even multiple encryption strategies on your system that you would want to use, implement those strategies.

1.16 Virtualization Methodologies

As stated earlier, the three governing functions that the Linux kernel performs in order to maintain the system in a steady state are Virtualization, Concurrency, and Persistence. At a certain level of abstraction, the kernel itself, and its global resources, are virtualized by systemd. In this section, we introduce namespaces and LXC/LXD, which also do forms of "virtualizing".

Historically speaking, to perform the kernel functions of Virtualization and Concurrency, the multiprogramming paradigm was established. Multiprogramming is a computer system model where the computer hardware and software would be shared by several programs (and users) running and working on the system simultaneously. This led to the need for autonomy and sharing among programs. The needs of multiprogramming are closely tied to the concept of "virtual memory" in computers as well. In turn, this virtualization of memory is directly related to the virtualization of the entire operating system itself, as we describe it in this chapter.

Computer hardware virtualization is the simulation, to various degrees, of hardware platforms, parts of them, or only the functionality required to run one or more operating systems ("OSs"). It abstracts and effectively "hides" the physical characteristics of the hardware from the users. Traditionally, the software that controlled virtualized machines was known as the hypervisor. Currently, the hypervisor is often called a Virtual Machine Monitor (VMM).

Platform virtualization is accomplished on any given hardware by host software (the hypervisor), which creates a simulated computer environment, a VM, for its guest software. The guest software can be as small as a single user application, or even as large as a complete OS. The guest software executes as if it were running directly on the physical hardware.

Virtualization comes with some performance disadvantages, both in resources required to run the hypervisor and in reduced performance on the VM guest compared with running applications on a non-virtualized host physical machine. A VM can be more easily controlled and inspected from outside than a physical one, and its configuration is more flexible. This is very useful in kernel development and for teaching OS courses. A new VM can be implemented as needed without the need for an up-front hardware purchase. A VM can easily be moved from one physical machine to another as needed. An unrecoverable fault inside a VM guest does not harm the host system, so there is no risk of crashing the host OS.

Examples of virtualization implementations are as follows:

* Running one or more applications that are not supported by the host OS: A VM running the required guest OS could allow the desired applications to be run, without altering the host OS.

* Evaluating an alternate OS: The new OS could be run within a VM, without altering the host OS.

* Server virtualization: Multiple virtual servers, in what are often referred to as "containers", could be run on a single physical server, to utilize more fully the hardware resources of the physical server. A cloud computing example of this is Amazon Web Services Elastic Cloud Computing (AWS EC2) virtual servers.

* Duplicating specific environments: A VM could, depending on the virtualization software used, be duplicated and installed on multiple hosts, or restored to a previously backed-up system state.

* Creating a protected environment: If a guest OS running on a VM becomes damaged in a way that is difficult to repair, such as may occur when testing, the VM can be discarded without harm to the host system, and a clean copy used next time.

Primary actual contemporary virtualization techniques are as follows:

* Full virtualization: In full virtualization, the VM simulates enough hardware to allow a complete "guest" OS, one designed for the same processor instruction set architecture (ISA) to be run in isolation. Examples for Linux systems running on X86 ISAs or ARM architectures include VirtualBox, Parallels Workstation, Oracle VM, Virtual Server, Hyper-V, VMware Workstation, and VMware.

* Hardware-assisted virtualization: In hardware-assisted virtualization, the hardware provides architectural support that facilitates building a VMM and allows guest OSs to be run in isolation. Examples of virtualization platforms adapted to such hardware include KVM, VMware Workstation, VMware Fusion, Hyper-V, Xen, Oracle VM server for SPARC, and VirtualBox.

* Partial virtualization: In partial virtualization, including address space virtualization, the VM simulates multiple instances of much of an underlying hardware environment, particularly address spaces.

* Paravirtualization: In paravirtualization, the VM does not necessarily simulate hardware, but instead (or in addition) offers a special application programmer's interface (API) that can only be used by modifying the "guest" OS. For this to be possible, the "guest" OS's source code must be available.

* OS-level virtualization: In OS-level virtualization, a physical server is virtualized at the OS level, enabling multiple isolated and secure virtualized servers to run on a single physical server. The "guest" OS environments share the same running instance of the OS as the host system. Thus, the same OS kernel is also used to implement the "guest" environments, and applications running in a given "guest" environment

view it as a stand-alone system. In Linux, examples include LXC and LXD, and their derivative management system, Docker. Similar proprietary derived techniques are used by AWS EC2, Google Cloud, and iCloud.

A virtual environment for a computer program, and for an operating system, can be simply thought of as a shell within which the program functions autonomously. And as we have shown earlier, one of the parts of looking at an operating system at a certain level of abstraction, is the ability of the operating system to present the illusion of virtual environments. A multi-tasking, multi-programming operating system, where all users are presented with this illusion that each individual user is working autonomously on her own discreet computer (when in fact many people might also working on the same hardware platform), is a basic underlying aspect of operating system virtualization. In many respects, and at some other level of abstraction, systemd can be thought of as a virtualizing program. It virtualizes the Linux kernel, and gives you the illusion that you are working directly with it, when in fact you are working in the systemd environment. That way of looking at the systemd "super kernel", and the Linux kernel itself, most importantly assumes that the function of these two programs is to help maintain the steady state of the hardware and software as the power is turned on, the system is running, or it becomes necessary to have the power turned off. In Volume 1, Chapter 2, we give a complete and detailed description of systemd and its operation.

In LXC/LXD containers, any number of different kernels can be running simultaneously on one host machine. That means that for LXC/LXD containers, you can be running many different distributions of operating systems at the same time on one machine.

There are other similar virtualization facilities available for the Raspberry Pi OS. Docker is another container application suite that allows you to "spin up" container instances that are lightweight, in terms of the disk space size they occupy. A typical example of one of these lightweight Docker container instances is the web server software nginx. In terms of disk space occupied in general, the lightest weight facility is a Docker container, the middleweight is an LXC/LXD container, and the heavyweight is a VirtualBox guest.

Both LXC/LXD and Docker rely upon the namespaces system programming API, and the clone(2) system call. We briefly mentioned namespaces above.

1.16.1 Virtualization Applications

The important application of LXC/LXD containers, in the context of system administration, is to provide a measure of system security. For example, it is possible, using LXC containers, to isolate a system service or application program in a guest operating environment, completely autonomous from the host operating system. A service like an SSH server can be run inside of an

LXC/LXD container instance, and anything that intrudes upon that server and its system space does not intrude upon the host operating system space. If LAN or Internet traffic to and from the server is compromised in any way, the server can be stopped, restarted, or even deleted, without affecting the host operating system. Another example would be if a faulty, bug-ridden application program were run in an LXC/LXD container instance, it could bring the guest operating system kernel to a halt without in any way affecting the host operating system. Those two example cases are probably the most useful aspects of maintaining a virtual environment, but there are others.

In addition, another application of these methodologies is to allow you to use and experiment with different operating systems on a single piece of hardware. You can play with these other operating systems in a "sandbox" which is isolated from your host system, and can access that host system *simultaneously* with the virtualized environments.

In-Chapter Exercise

56. What is KVM, and how does it compare to the virtualization applications we describe in this section? Which cloud-based system deploys KVM? Answer this question in terms of type of virtualization, size of a virtual machine instances, ease of use, and speed of execution of virtual machine instances. Compare these KVM criteria to LXC/LXD containers, and Google Cloud and Amazon EC2 instances.

1.17 Summary

In this chapter, we use a "learning-by-doing" approach to accomplish the following common system administration tasks on the Raspberry Pi OS:

1. Do various kinds of installation of a 64-bit version onto desktop systems, and do a preliminary configuration of those hardware systems and the OS.

2. Illustrate booting strategies, and how to gracefully bring the system down.

3. Detail the basics of using systemd to manage system services.

4. Add additional users and groups to the system, and show how to design and maintain user accounts.

5. Add persistent media to the system, in particular externally mounted USB3 types. We also established a framework for connecting and maintaining the file system on that media, which classified the file system as either existing on a physical medium (physically connected

to the computer), a virtual medium (NFSv4, iSCSI), or as a specialized pseudo-file system that was not on a medium at all (cgroups, proc).

6. Provide strategies using traditional and generic commands, to backup and archive the system files and user files.

7. Update and maintain the operating system, and add/upgrade/remove user application package repository software to both increase functionality and upgrade existing packages.

8. Monitor the performance of the system and tune it for optimal performance characteristics.

9. Provide strategies for system security to harden the individual desktop computer.

10. Provide network connectivity strategies, both on a LAN and the Internet.

11. Give an overview of system virtualization, using LXD/LXC.

2

Python3

DOI: 10.1201/b23421-3

2.0 Objectives

* To give a quick start into programming with Python3 using Thonny on the Raspberry Pi OS
* To give an overview of the Python3 programming language
* To cover the basic syntax of Python3
* To show how to install and run Python3 on a Raspberry Pi system
* To provide several basic practical examples of using Python3
* To cover the commands and primitives: python3, Thonny

2.1 Introduction

In this chapter, we give a broad introduction to the Python programming language, using Python version 3. For the beginner Python3 programmer, we illustrate all of its important programming capabilities and syntactic structures, in the context of the three predominant computer programming paradigms: virtualization, concurrency, and persistence. We first give a brief introduction to Thonny, the Python3 Integrated Development Environment (IDE), and then use it throughout the rest of the chapter. We show the details of doing an installation of the latest version of Python3.X on a Raspberry Pi system, instead of utilizing the default installation that comes with the Raspberry Pi OS. We show all of Python3's critical and basic syntax, including numbers and expressions, variables, statements, getting input from the user, functions, OOP in Python, modules, saving and executing Python scripts, string and sequence operations, and error handling. We also give many basic and practical examples, such as another way of writing shell script files, such as rewriting Bash and tcsh scripts, basic user file maintenance, backing up files, remote copying with the **rsync** command, and graphics using tkinter.

Finally, we show how thread execution is achieved in Python3, and how OOP can be deployed to accomplish it.

The major component sections of this chapter are as follows:

2.2 A Quick start into Python3 with the Thonny Integrated Development Environment

2.3 An Overview of the Python3 Language

2.4 Python3 Syntax

2.5 Practical Examples

2.2 A Quick start into Python3 with the Thonny Integrated Development Environment

The easiest, and quickest, way to use Python3 on the Raspberry Pi is to deploy the Thonny Integrated Development Environment (IDE) to interact with Python and construct and run program code. This IDE comes pre-installed on the Raspberry Pi OS, as does the latest version of Python3 that accompanies your version of the Raspberry Pi OS. Thonny is a graphical front end to Python, and as such allows the use of toolbar icons, to execute many useful operations expediently, and very effectively. This is a somewhat different way of interacting with the Raspberry Pi than what we've shown previously in Volumes 1 and 2 of this series of books. By and large, we've used text-based, command line interface operations to perform our system administration tasks. Which is *not* to say that in developing Python3 program code with Thonny, you don't use text! The Python language implementation has a highly structured text syntax and grammar, as you shall see in the sections below.

Everything we do in this chapter is either done with Thonny, or done on the Bash command line. But in most of our work below, we only show the areas of the Thonny window known as the "Script Area" and the "Shell Area". And be aware that Thonny has two modes, Regular and Simple. Since our work here is for beginners, we show the Simple Mode of operation. That's the default when you launch Thonny. If you want to switch to "Regular Mode", there's a text link on the right side of the Thonny window (hidden in Figure 2.1 because we're using Simple Mode, and our window display is too narrow to show it in that figure) that would allow you to change Thonny to a necessarily more complex display, with more pull-down menu choices that go beyond what the Simple Mode gives you.

If you want to change to a necessarily more complex, but verbose, way of interacting with Python3 via Thonny Regular Mode, we give step-by-step instructions in Section 2.3.8.2 that show how to do that.

There are other IDEs available on the Raspberry Pi OS that you can use with Python3. From the Raspberry Pi menu, Programming > Geany is one of them. We've found that the Geany IDE is necessarily more complex, and useful for the development of C++ programs, and other program systems, but feel free to experiment with it for Python3 scripts and program code development. We don't show Geany here, but do illustrate its use for C++ and Python3 in Volume 3.

2.2.1 Launching Thonny, and the Thonny Window

To launch Thonny, from the Raspberry Pi menu, make the choice Programming > Thonny. The Thonny window opens onscreen, as shown in Figure 2.1.

At the top of the window is a row of *Toolbar Area* icons, that allow you to do various operations, such as debug or test, load, save, and execute Python program code.

Next, below the row of toolbar icons, is the *Script Area*, where you can type in multiple lines of Python code, or input an already completed program from a file. Notice that line numbers for your program are illustrated in

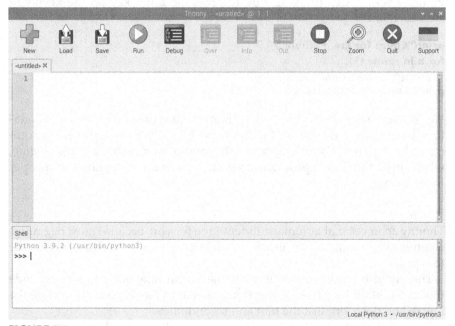

FIGURE 2.1
Thonny Window.

the left margin of the Script Area, and above that area in the upper left is a tab naming the current program being worked on. In Figure 2.1, it reads <untitled>.

And finally, below that is the *Python Shell Area*, where the command line prompt >>> from Python is found. Here, you can type in one line of Python code, and have it executed when you press the Enter key on the keyboard of the Raspberry Pi. Also, error messages, or other feedback from Python, are displayed in this area. In Figure 2.1, it shows we're running Python 3.9.2, found in /*usr*/bin/python3. This version of Python, and Thonny as well, is dependent upon what release of the Raspberry Pi OS you've installed on your system. These versions of Python3, and Thonny, are the defaults on the Raspberry Pi OS we're using.

Note

We have also tested all of the Python3 shown in this chapter in the latest release of Python available at the time this book was written, Python 3.11.3.

2.2.2 Creating and Running a Simple Python3 Program from within Thonny

Let's create and execute a simple Python3 program, that has a determinate repetition structure in it, and prints some output to the Python3 Shell Area. Launch Thonny on your Raspberry Pi, and type the following lines into the Python3 Script Area (making sure to press the Enter key on the keyboard after each line.):

```
print("Count for me, Python!")
for n in range (5):
    print("I'm counting!", n)
print("I'm done counting!")
```

Notice that after the second line, Thonny *automatically* inserts a mandatory four-space indentation for the third line! That mechanism, of automatic indentation, is critical to the technique of *structured programming*, where flow-of-control programming structures are delineated by proper indentation.

Note

Thonny achieves that automatic indentation for you, because most beginners commit either indentation errors in their programs, or syntax errors due to typos.

Thonny also automatically indents the fourth line, but you can override this indentation by pressing the Delete key on your keyboard, to type the fourth line flush left, like the first and second lines.

Now click on the Run Toolbar icon in the Toolbar Area. In the Shell Area, the following should be displayed:

Count for me, Python!
I'm counting! 0
I'm counting! 1
I'm counting! 2
I'm counting! 3
I'm counting! 4
I'm done counting!
>>>

How come the count started at zero(0)? That's because Python is a zero-indexed system, where counts start at 0, not 1.

Now click on the Save icon in the Toolbar Area. In the Save dialog window that appears, name this Python3 program **looper.py**, making sure to add the file extension **.py** as shown, and designate a folder on your system where you want the program to be saved. Then click Save. Once the save is completed, notice that the title bar of the Thonny window shows the path to and name of this program you just saved, and that the tab at the top of the Script Area now shows the name looper.py.

Note
If you want to run that program in "Interactive Mode", outside of the Thonny IDE, you can by launching Python3 as we show in a few places below in this chapter.

In-Chapter Exercises

1. How can you make Python count from 1 to 5, using the above program structure?

2. How can you clear the program from the Script area?

You're done! In the sections below, we'll cover much more of the syntax and structure of a Python3 program. But for now, play around with Thonny and this program, and then you can click on the Quit Toolbar icon. The next time you run Thonny, this same program will be loaded, unless of course you cleared it according to your answer to In-Chapter Exercise 2!

2.3 An Overview of the Python3 Language

Computer programs execute and accomplish their objectives in a particular order, from start to finish. They may "branch" within that order, perhaps to only execute some of their instructions, based on certain logical tests or conditions. They may also repeat segments of their operation, either for some predetermined number of times, or indeterminately, based on changing conditions. Python conforms to this model, and operates using the following scheme of levels:

Level 1. *Everything* in Python3 programs, or scripts, is composed of modular components.

Level 2. These modular components contain syntactically correct Python statements.

Level 3. These statements contain expressions.

Level 4. The expressions create and manipulate objects.

The Python3 code development process starts by formulating syntactically correct elements at Level 1, and proceeds downwards through the levels sequentially until Level 4 is achieved.

In the Raspberry Pi OS environment, if you are presented with a task that requires you to do either script writing or programming, the first thing you have to decide is what programming model you are going to adopt to accomplish the task. In simple terms, this means using any of the three predominant programming models: the procedural/imperative programming model, the Object Oriented Programming (OOP) model, or the logic programming model. Of course, how well you accomplish the task depends on how much script writing or programming experience you have using any, or all, of those models. And perhaps, if you are doing this task with a group of people, their experiences and preferences count for a great deal as well. But, how you formulate the task in terms of any of the models is related, most importantly, to your experience in using these models. There are no simple guidelines for applying any of the models to the vast number of possible script writing or programming tasks that exist in the realm of computer programming.

However, the bottom line in the accomplishment of your task is how familiar you are with the syntax of the languages that implement the model you choose.

That's why we explain Python3 syntax in detail in this chapter. Python3 can utilize all of these programming models, and can, in fact, mix the techniques used in the models. We make some commentary on this here, and illustrate some simple uses of the models in the next few Sections.

Python3 is a *high-level, structured* (in this case, meaning built of regular structured components, like determinate or indeterminate repetition, for example), and *interpreted* programming (or scripting) language, as opposed to a low-level, compiled language like C, or Java. As stated, it is also a *multi-paradigm* programming language, which allows you to use data abstractions

from the three predominant paradigms. For our purposes, "scripting" and "programming" can be thought of as the same thing.
So why use a "pure" OOP approach?

Instead of totally defining the most fundamental aspects and parts of OOP (which you can find descriptions of easily in the extensive literature), we choose to contrast and compare it to the more traditional procedural programming method, to give you a more intuitive feel for the approach OOP uses.

Procedural/imperative, non-OOP programs, as we have noted, can run through their structured, flow-of-control operation using the Python3 syntax we show in the sections below. Non-trivial programs can possibly be made up of groupings of flow-of-control operations, known as procedures, modules, or subroutines. This way of using Python3 syntax, since the language "accommodates" the procedural/imperative model, can put together a program that emphasizes more traditional algorithms and Abstract Data Types (ADT). Simple examples of these two things are the algorithm (or mathematical plan) for computing the greatest common factor of two integers, or the definition of integers themselves as a certain kind of numerical value, along with the prescribed set of possible operations on them.

One of the biggest problems with this approach is that if variables take on a global scope, in a global namespace outside of the "container" they are defined in, the assignment of values to these can be conflicting and cause errors. That is, in part, why using namespaces, as we show in Chapter 1, to essentially isolate processes, is so effective. Variables (which are active in any particular process namespace) are exclusively, and locally, defined and used.

In Python3 OOP, this is basically done using what is known as "encapsulation". The idea is that the data, and the functions that manipulate the data, *are one entity*. This keeps both objects safe from unwanted changes to them from any environment outside the entity. This fundamental component of OOP, that combines data with a set of *methods* for accessing and managing the data, is called an object. Its data treatment model is completely different from the procedural/imperative program model previously described.

Of course, it is possible, with the rich set of syntax available in Python3, to combine both non-OOP and OOP styles in one program. Python does not faithfully implement the functional, or logic, programming structure known as *tail recursion*, as does a language such as MIT scheme. But it is capable of recursion, as we also show below.

2.3.1 Objects and Classes

If you haven't discovered this yet, our coverage of topics here revolves around a little bit of "Why?", and a lot more "How?" It would be prudent to now cover, in an introductory fashion, the "How?" aspect of the data model (and also the "Why?") that Python3 programming uses. In particular, as that applies to OOP. OOP is a programming model that represents concepts as *objects* that have fields (which are basically attributes that describe the object) and associated processes, or if you will, functions, known as *methods*, which are basically known as "messaging" operations on those attributes. Objects, which are established as instances of what are known as "classes", are constructed to interact with one another using the messaging system, to design applications and computer programs. Some examples of modern OOP languages are Smalltalk, C++, C#, Java. Perl, Ruby, PHP, and Python.

Below are some common terms used in OOP:

Class: A user-defined model for an object that defines characteristics of any object in that class. The characteristics are data members (class variables and instance variables) and methods, accessed via what's called dot(.) notation.

Class variable: A variable that is shared by all instances of a class. Class variables are defined within a class, but outside any of the class's methods.

Data member: A class variable or instance variable that holds data associated with a class and its objects.

Instance variable: A variable that is defined inside a method and belongs only to the current instance of a class.

Inheritance: The transfer of the characteristics of a class to other classes that are derived from it.

Instance: An individual object of a certain class. An object that belongs to a class named Circle, for example, is an instance of the class Circle.

Instantiation: The creation of an instance of a class.

Method: A special kind of function that is defined in a class definition.

Object: A unique instance of a data structure defined by its class. An object can comprise both data members (class variables and instance variables) and methods.

The general form of a class definition is:

```
class ClassName:
'Optional class documentation string'
class_suite
```

The class has a documentation string, which can be accessed via **ClassName._ _doc_** .

The **class_suite** consists of all the component statements defining class members, data attributes, and methods.

The following lines of interactive code very simply illustrate the inheritance model of OOP classes, and in particular, its hierarchic nature. Launch Thonny on your Raspberry Pi system, and execute the code below in the Thonny Shell Area. Be sure to press the **<Enter>** key at the end of Line 2 of the code (There is no need to type in the comment line numbers, which we provide here for reference only.)

```
>>> class tab: pass          #Line 1
...                          #These ellipses appear on Line 2
>>> tab.name = 'Bob Koretsky'   #Line 3
>>> tab.age = 85             #Line 4
>>> print (tab.name,tab.age)  #Line 5
Bob Koretsky 85
>>> x = tab()                #Line 6
>>> y = tab()                #Line 7
>>> x.name                   #Line 8
Bob Koretsky
>>> y.name = 'Alan Turing'    #Line 9
>>> tab.name, x.name, y.name  #Line 10
('Bob Koretsky', 'Bob Koretsky', 'Alan Turing')
>>>
```

For beginners, a line-by-line analysis and description of this code is as follows:

Line 1: Starting with the keyword **class**, you name a class **tab**. You use the keyword **pass** to assign the class to an empty namespace object, that is, *it has no class members, attributes or methods yet*. A class is a model of an object!

Line 2: Continue by pressing **<Enter>**.

Line 3: You now add an attribute called **name** to the class named **tab**. The class **tab** has no instances yet!

Line 4: You assign another attribute called **age** to the class tab.

Line 5: You print out the attributes of **tab**.

Line 6: You now assign an instance, named **x**, to the class **tab**, which is now an empty instance.

Line 7: You now assign another instance, named **y**, to the class **tab**, which is another empty instance.

Line 8: The instance **x** inherits the attribute **name** from **tab**. You use the dot (.) operator to connect or refer to the instance **x** with **name** "Bob Koretsky" in the class **tab**.

Line 9: You now explicitly assign the instance **y**, with an attribute **name**, the value "Alan Turing". You use the dot (.) operator to connect the instance **y** with **name** "Alan Turing".

Line 10: You print out the name in **tab**, the name referred to in **x** inherited from **tab**, and the explicitly assigned name in **y**. Attribute references work through the mechanisms of inheritance, and attribute assignments work on the objects to which the assignment is done.

The following is a more involved example of creating a class, and then using some methods to manipulate the objects in that class. Type the following code into a file named **firstclass.py** using your favorite text editor, and save it in the directory that is Thonny's current working directory:

Example 2.1

```
#!/usr/bin/python3
class Structure:
    'Common base class for all Python Structures'
    StrucCount = 0

    def __init__(s, name, number):
        s.name = name
        s.number= number
        Structure.StrucCount += 1

    def displayCount(s):
        print ("Total Structures %d" % Structure.StrucCount)

    def displayStructure(s):
        print ("Name: ", s.name, ", Number: ", s.number)
```

Then, in Thonny, use Way 3 (Import Script mode), which we define more fully below, to run **firstclass.py**.

In the Thonny Shell Area, type the following (you can leave out the comments):

```
>>> import firstclass
>>> Stru1 = firstclass.Structure("Arithmetic Operators", 17)   #creates the
                                                                first object
>>> Stru2 = firstclass.Structure("Logical Operators", 10)   #creates the
                                                             second object
>>> Stru1.displayStructure()
Name: Arithmetic Operators, Number: 17      #displays the first object
>>> Stru2.displayStructure()                #displays the second object
Name: Logical Operators,, Number: 10
>>> print ("Total Structures %d" % firstclass.Structure.StrucCount)
                                            #prints total structures
Total Structures 2
>>> Stru1.inst = 7                          #creates a new attribute of Stru1
>>> hasattr(Stru1, 'inst')                  #checks object for attribute
True
```

```
>>> getattr(Stru1, 'inst')                    #gets the value of the attribute
7
>>> getattr(Stru1, 'name')                    #gets the value of the attribute
'Arithmetic Operators'
>>>
```

There are three important things to notice about this OOP Example:

1. The variable **StrucCount** is a class variable whose value is shared among all instances of this class. This variable can be accessed as **Structure.StrucCount** from inside the class or as **firstclass.Structure.StrucCount** outside the class.

2. The first class method, **__init__()**, is a special method, which is called a *class constructor* or *initialization* method. Python3 calls this method when you create a new instance of this class.

3. You declare other class methods like normal Python functions, with the exception that the first argument to each method is **s**. Python3 adds the **s** argument to the list for you; you do *not* need to include it when you call, or invoke the methods.

2.3.2 Python3 Program Data Model

Following are some statements about the Python3 model of data that might help you organize your concepts and thoughts about what the "nuts and bolts" of Python3 are:

1. Even though Python3 incorporates many of the features of a multi-paradigm programming ensemble, its actual, and fundamental basis is the following:

   Everything in the Python3 program can be referred to as an *object*, with the same exact meaning of the word *object* used in OOP. These objects have three parts: an *identifier*, a *type*, and a *value*.

For example, when you assign x = 62.25 interactively in the Python3 interpreter, or in a Python3 module, script file, or library of modules, a real number object type is created; it has a value of 62.25, and it is identified as an object with a pointer to its location in memory. x is the identifier that refers to its specific location in memory. The equal sign (=) is essentially the reference between an identifier and a value.

2. In OOP languages such as Python3 and Javascript, the type that an object assumes gives it membership in a particular set, called its *class*. The class of the object limits, and also defines, what are known as the *methods*, or operations, which can be performed on or with it.

3. When a particular object of some type is created, that particular object is called an *instance* of that type. In general, an object's identity and type cannot be changed. They are known as *immutable*. If an object's value can be modified, the object is said to be *mutable*. An object that refers to other objects to obtain value and type is known as a *container*.

4. Objects can also define their own *attributes*, or characteristics, of the data they are comprised of, and even the *methods* used on them. An attribute is a property, or value associated with an object. A method is a function internal to a class of objects that performs some sort of operation on those objects when the method is used or invoked.

5. Attributes and methods are accessed using the dot(.) operator, as shown in the following examples:

x = 2 + 4j creates a complex number x.
A = a.real uses a method known as real to extract the real part (an attribute) of a.
c = [1, 2, 3] creates an instance of type list identified as c of the integers 1, −2, and −3.
c.append(7) adds a new element to c using the append method.

2.3.3 Python References and Releases

Before you begin this section, and as you proceed through the rest of this chapter, it would be helpful for you to reference, and read for understanding in a "top-down" manner, the following references (the versions and editions of which were available at the time this book was written). The Python3 online documentation, and a printed book we used, are as follows:

The Python Language Reference—https://docs.python.org/3/reference/
For the latest version of Python, at the time this book was written, the following tutorials and printed books:

https://docs.python.org/3/tutorial/index.html

Learning Python, 5th Edition, by Mark Lutz,
O'Reilly Media, 2013.

Use the latest versions and editions of the above references, and if necessary, have a printed form of them. Whatever top-down principles you can carry with you from these references throughout your Python3 programming experience, both in this chapter and beyond, are very important, and will enable you to see the complex details in a much larger context.

At the time this book was written, Python 3.11.3 was the latest stable version of the Python language available for the Raspberry Pi OS. As you can see from Figure 2.1, for our release of the Raspberry Pi OS on our Raspberry Pi 4B and 400, Python 3.9.2 is used here.

We also provide an abbreviated Python3 command syntax reference at the end of this chapter in Appendix 2A. You can refer to this whenever you need a handy reference for syntactic components of the language. In addition to the command syntax reference, we present a glossary of Python3 terms at the end of the chapter as well.

2.3.4 Python3 Standard Type Hierarchy

The *type* of an object describes the Python data structure representation of the object as well as the methods and operations that can be carried out on that object. Table 2.1 is a listing of the type categories, and following it is a brief description of some of the categories in the table.

The None type has a single value that contains a null object (an object with no value). Its truth value is False.

Numeric types: Booleans, integers, long integers, floating point numbers, and complex numbers.

Sequence types: *Sequences* represent ordered sets of objects indexed by nonnegative integers and include strings, Unicode strings, lists, and tuples.

Mapping types: A *mapping object* represents an arbitrary collection of objects that are indexed by another collection of nearly arbitrary key values. Unlike a sequence, a mapping object is unordered and can be indexed by numbers, strings, and other objects. *Dictionaries* are the only built-in mapping type, and are similar to a *hash*.

Set types: A *set* is an unordered collection of unique items. Unlike sequences, sets provide no indexing or slicing operations. They are also unlike dictionaries in that there are no key values associated with the objects. In addition, the items placed into a set must be immutable.

Callable types: These represent objects that support the function call operation. There are several kinds of objects with this property, including user-defined functions, built-in functions, instance methods, and classes.

Classes and types: When you define a class, the class definition normally produces an object of type *type*.

Modules: The *module* type is a container that holds objects loaded with the **import** statement.

TABLE 2.1

Python3 Type Categories

Category	Name	Description
None	None	Null object
Numbers	int	Plain integer
	Long	Arbitrary-precision integer
	Float	Floating point number
	Complex	Complex number
	Bool	Boolean (True or False)
Sequences (immutable)	str	Character string
	Unicode	Unicode character string
	tuple	Tuple
Sequences (mutable)	list	List
	bytearray	Returned by bytearray()
Mapping	dict	Dictionary
Sets	set	Mutable set
	Frozenset	Immutable set
Callable	BuiltinFunctionType	Built-in functions
	BuiltinMethodType	Built-in methods
	type	Type of built-in types and classes
	object	Ancestor of all types and classes
	FunctionType	User-defined function
	InstanceType	Class object instance
	MethodType	Bound class method
	UnboundMethodType	Unbound class method
" Modules	ModuleType	Module
" Classes	object	Ancestor of all types and classes
" Types	type	Type of built-in types and classes
" Files	file	File
" Internal	CodeType	Byte-compiled code
	FrameType	Execution frame
	GeneratorType	Generator object
	TracebackType	Stacks traceback of an exception
	Slice	Generated by extended slices
	Ellipsis	Used in extended slices
" Classic	Classes ClassType	Legacy class definition
	InstanceType	Legacy class instance

Files: The *file* object represents an open file and is returned by the built-in **open()** function.

Internal types: Objects used by the interpreter are exposed to the user, such as *traceback objects, code objects, frame objects, generator objects, slice objects*, and the *ellipsis object*.

Code objects: These represent raw byte-compiled executable code, or *bytecode*, and are typically returned by the built-in *compile()* function.

Frame objects: These are used to represent execution frames and most frequently occur in traceback objects.

Traceback objects: These are created when an exception occurs and contains *stack trace information*.

Generator objects: These are created when a *generator* function is invoked. A generator function is defined whenever a function makes use of the special yield keyword.

Slice objects: These are used to represent slices given in extended slice syntax, such as:

a[i:j:stride], a[i:j, n:m], or a[..., i:j].

Ellipsis object: The ellipsis object is used to indicate the presence of an ellipsis (...) in a slice. There is a single object of this type, accessed through the built-in name Ellipsis. It has no attributes and evaluates as True.

Classic classes: In versions of Python prior to version 2.2, classes and objects were implemented using an entirely different mechanism, that is now deprecated. For backward compatibility, however, these classes, called *classic classes* or *old-style classes*, are still supported.

2.3.5 Basic Assumptions We Make

The four basic and important assumptions we make in this chapter are:

1. You have the default Python3.X installed on your Raspberry Pi system. Python 3.9.2, for example, was already installed as part of the installation of our Raspberry Pi OS itself.

If you type in the following command (as we did on our Raspberry Pi system), you will see where Python and its components (and what versions) are installed on your system:

```
$ whereis python
```

python: /usr/bin/python2.7 /usr/bin/python3.9 /usr/bin/python3.9-config /usr/bin/python /usr/lib/python2.7 /usr/lib/python3.9 /etc/python2.7 /etc/python3.9 /usr/local/lib/python2.7 /usr/local/lib/python3.9 /usr/include/python3.9 /usr/include/python3.9m /usr/share/python /usr/share/man/man1/python.1.gz

From the above output, both Python 2.7 and 3.9, are installed on our Raspberry Pi system.

2. The path of execution to the Python program and the path of execution to all the Python scripts you create in this chapter include the current working directory that you want to do Python in!

If you don't know, given the particular shell you are using (we use the Bash shell, with the $ prompt), what your path of execution is set to, examine your path and set it properly. For example, in the Bash shell, you can see your path of execution by typing **echo $PATH** at the shell prompt. On our Raspberry Pi system, Python 2.7.X and Python 3.9.X are installed by default in /usr/bin, as seen from the **whereis python** command output of 1. above.

3. You are doing Python3 in the Thonny IDE.

The basic procedures you'll follow in this chapter, to execute either single Python3 interactive commands, or multi-line programs, are as follows:

a. You execute single line Python3 commands interactively, by typing them carefully, and faithfully into the Thonny Shell Area. We call this *"Way 1 (Interactive Mode)"*, and give an illustrative example of it in Section 2.3.6 below.
b. You carefully, and faithfully, type short, or even long, multi-line Python3 scripts that are presented below into the Thonny Script Area, click the Run Toolbar icon, and observe the results. You then save those scripts for later use in a convenient directory on your Raspberry Pi, if necessary. We call this *"Way 2 (Script Mode Mode)"*, and give an illustrative example of it in Section 2.3.6 below.

Note
Of course, since all of the code for the examples below can be found at the book website, as specified in the Preface above, you can download them to a convenient location on your Raspberry Pi, and then use the Thonny Load Toolbar icon to bring them into Thonny and Run them. But we encourage you in the beginning at least to type in the commands shown in the examples, to get practice producing syntactically correct code!

c. You create a multi-line Python3 script in your favorite text editor (such as nano), and import that file into Thonny's Script Area using the **import** Python command. We call this *"Way 3 (Import Script Mode)"*, and give an illustrative example of it in Section 2.3.6 below.

d. Alternately, you type **python3** on the command line of a Raspberry Pi terminal window, which launches and then allows you to use Python version 3.X interactively in the terminal window. We don't deploy this method very frequently, but you need to know about it as an interactive interpreter mode of doing Python. Remember, Python is basically an interpretive language, and it's running an interpreter, rather than a compiler, to execute your code.

4. In general, whenever we want you to type something on the Python interactive command line, or in the Thonny Script Area, we will indicate what is to be typed in **bold** text. In addition, output from Python will be shown in unbolded text.

2.3.6 Running Python3 Using Our Standard Ways

The following subsection illustrates the ways that we use Thonny to run Python3 on our Raspberry Pi systems.

Way 1 (Interactive Mode)
In the Shell Area of Thonny, you type a single line of Python code on the Python command line (>>>), or maybe multiple lines of Python3, and see the results immediately. A good reason to use this mode is that you can test small fragments of Python3 code, one line, or a couple of lines, at a time, directly in the current Python interpreter which is either the default Python3 interpreter, or another one that you've installed and selected. A simple example of this (seen in the Thonny Shell Area) would be as follows:

```
>>>print ("How about some more?")
How about some more?
>>>
```

Remember, to submit a line of Python code to its interpreter, at the end of the line, press **<Enter>** on the keyboard.

Way 2 (Script Mode)
You type possibly multiple, properly formatted, and syntactically correct Python3 commands into the Thonny Script Area. This is traditionally called a *script file* (perhaps saved and named **first.py**). Then you click on the Thonny Run Toolbar icon, and the results of the execution of the Python3 commands are seen. Generally, those results scroll by in the Shell Area of Thonny.

A good reason to use this mode is if you have scripts with more than a few lines of code in them, and you do *not* want to type that code in every time you want to run it. A simple example of this would be as follows:

Example 2.2

```
print("Count for me, Python!")
for n in range (5):
    print("I'm counting!", n)
print("I'm done counting!")
```

>>> %Run -c $EDITOR_CONTENT
Count for me, Python!
I' m counting! 0
I' m counting! 1
I' m counting! 2
I' m counting! 3
I' m counting! 4
I' m done counting!
>>>

If the commands contain any output directed to the screen, such as using print statements as shown in Example 2.2, the shell prompt will immediately reappear at the termination of execution, *if the script file terminates without error!*

Of course, if you use the Thonny Toolbar Save icon, you can save the multiline Python3 code into a file in Python3's current working directory, and then at some later time, use Thonny's Load Toolbar icon to bring that file back into the Script Area.

Way 3 (Import Script Mode)
Similarly to Way 2 (Script Mode), you use a text editor of your choice to create and save multiple Python commands in a script file, perhaps named **first.py**, in the current working directory that has been set in Thonny.

In the Thonny Shell Area, and at the Python3 command prompt there, you bring the script file into Python with the Python3 **import** command. A good reason to use this mode is if your script files contain function definitions. A simple example of this is as follows:
Example 2.3

>>>**import first**
Count for me, Python!
I'm counting! 0
I'm counting! 1
I'm counting! 2
I'm counting! 3
I'm counting! 4

I'm done counting!
>>>

where **first** is the file without the **.py** extension. It should contain syntactically correct Python3 commands, and be in the current working directory. Now, the objects, statements, expressions, and modules (like Python functions) in **first.py** are available to you in Thonny. A good reason to use this mode is to bring those structures and functions into the current interactive Thonny Python session environment, or namespace.

Note
Once you leave Thonny by clicking on the Toolbar icon Quit, the current interactive session is ended, and the environment you have created in Python is lost.

How do you know what the Thonny current working directory is?
It's set to a default, and can be changed to any directory you want in the filesystem of your Raspberry Pi OS, to retrieve, or save, Python3 script files from or to. To find out, and be able to reset the current working directory in Thonny, in the Thonny Shell Area, type the following commands:

```
>>> import os
>>> os.getcwd()
'/home/bob/Public'
>>>
```

We see from the above output that the current working directory, where Thonny retrieves and saves script files to/from the Script Area is */home/*bob/Public.

To change that current working directory to */home/*bob/Documents, for example, type the following command on the command line in the Thonny Shell Area, after you've typed in the previous two commands:

```
>>>os.chdir("/home/bob/Documents")
```

Way 4 (Bash Mode)
We don't use this mode very much in the sections below, but there is an alternative way of executing Python scripts that depends upon the working environment within which you are executing Python. That alternative, very similar to the way of executing a Bash, or other script file, is to include this line as the first line in the Python script file (which you've created in your favorite text editor; we used nano, and have named the nano-created file **first. py** in this example case):

Example 2.4

#! /usr/bin/env python3

You must also be sure that you have execute privilege on **first.py**, using the **chmod u+x first.py** command. Then, to execute the **first.py** script file, on the Bash command line, type the following:

$./first.py

This method uses Python3 to execute the script file.

The main advantage of the method is that, depending on which version of Python you want to run, you can place the command name for that version in the first line of the script file. For example, if you want to use Python Version 3.11.3 (if you've installed that version!) to run the script file, you could modify the first line in the script file to read:

#! /usr/bin/env python3.11

There are portability issues with this method, for example when the working environment is in conflict with what version of Python you want to execute the script file code with. But for beginners, you can ignore those issues for now.

This method of executing the Python code is sometimes called running it as a *user-written library module*.

There is another way of running a Python script, which we do *not* use in this chapter, but which is useful, and we illustrate it in the next section.

2.3.6.1 Compiling a Script File into Bytecode for Bash Execution

It is possible to run a Python3 script file that you have used the interpreter to compile into a portable form of executable code, to execute from the Bash command line. It's called the bytecode form. Here's how to do it:

In Python, the process of converting a script into bytecode is handled by the Python interpreter itself. When you run a Python script, the interpreter first compiles it into bytecode before executing it. This bytecode is then executed by the Python Virtual Machine (PVM).

If you want to explicitly generate bytecode from an already-created Python script, without using Thonny, or running Python3 itself in a terminal, you can use either the **py_compile** module from the Python3 command line, or on the Bash command line, with the **-m py_compile** command-line option, to generate the bytecode.

Do the following things to accomplish this:

0. As specified and explained above at the end of Example 2.3, how do you know what the current working directory that Thonny is using to look for script files in? You can find out, and set it to be whatever you want, by using the following Python3 commands in the Thonny Shell Area:

```
>>> import os
>>> current_directory = os.getcwd()
>>> print("Current working directory:", current_directory)
Current working directory: /home/bob
>>>
>>> os.chdir(/home/bob/Public)
```

So, for the steps below, we want to change the current working directory *for Thonny* to where we're keeping all of our Python3 script files: in */home*/bob/ Public!

1. Using the **py_compile** module:

In the Thonny Shell Area, to create a bytecode version of the script file **first. py**, type:

```
>>> import py_compile
>>> py_compile.compile('first.py')
>>>
```

This will generate a bytecode file named something like first.cpython-39.pyc, in a subdirectory of the directory that the original script file was located in (/ home/bob/Public, in our case). This subdirectory will be named __pycache__
The generated bytecode file (first.cpython-39.pyc,) can be executed directly by the Python interpreter as shown in step 3 below, without the need for recompilation. It contains the compiled bytecode instructions ready for execution by the PVM. Descend to the sub-directory __pycache__, and make sure you give yourself execute privilege on the bytecode file with the **chmod u+x first.cpython-39.pyc** command.

```
>>>
```

2. Or using the **-m py_compile** switch:

Open a terminal, to get a Bash command prompt, and set the current working directory to the directory where your Python script is located. Then run the following command:

```
$ python3 -m py_compile first.py
```

This will generate the bytecode file named something like **first.cpython-39. pyc**, in a subdirectory of the directory that the original script file was located in. This subdirectory will be named __pycache__

The generated bytecode file (first.cpython-39.pyc) can be executed directly by the Python interpreter without the need for recompilation. It contains the compiled bytecode instructions ready for execution by the PVM.

Descend to the sub-directory __pycache__, and make sure you give yourself execute privilege on the bytecode file with the **chmod u+x first.cpython-39. pyc** command.

3.   Then type the following to execute the bytecode file, outside of Thonny, or the Python3 interpreter:

$ python3 first.cpython-39.pyc

Note
The bytecode generated by the Python interpreter is specific to the version of Python you are using, as seen by the appended 39 to the bytecode filename. So, bytecode generated for a particular version of Python3 may not be compatible with earlier versions of Python.

2.3.7 Uses of Python3

Python can accomplish several kinds of programming tasks, which might be broken down into the following sample categories:

Shell scripting

Systems programming

Network and Internet scripting

Database programming

Systems administration scripting

Graphical user interface (GUI) scripting

Scientific and math programming

Data mining

In this chapter, we use all four modes of running Python shown above in the examples in Section 2.3.6, and we give a beginners' introduction to the Python language. We also follow the model of level schemes as shown in the beginning of Section 2.3, going roughly from the top of the scheme to the bottom.

2.3.8 Information on the Installation of Python

Version 3.9.2 of Python was already installed and usable by us on the Raspberry Pi OS we had deployed on our Pi4B and Pi400 hardware. But, you may need to, or want to, install a more recent version of Python3 on your system, or if you want to install a later version of the software alongside, or to even replace the version your system already has preinstalled on it. Be aware that because of variations in the way your system has been installed by you, or the system administrator, and exactly what version of the Raspberry Pi OS has been installed, the installation procedure for the latest available Python3 may have to be already done by a system administrator for you! A good example of a similar situation would be that you do not have a C compiler available, or you want to upgrade to the latest *gcc* compiler, and don't know how to do that with, or without, a package manager!

We give installation instructions for the installation of the latest Python3 (available at the time we wrote this book) below. Be aware though that it may not include, or have the stable features found with the Python3 that is already installed.

2.3.8.1 Installing the Latest Release of Python3

Follow the steps below to install the latest release of Python3:

1. Go to www.python.org/downloads/ in a web browser.

   Find the name of the latest stable release of Python.

2. For us, at the time this book was written, it was Python-3.11.3.tgz

   Remember that the version of Python3 already installed by default on our Raspberry Pi OS was Python 3.9.2.

3. Type the following commands, substituting the latest release for the one we show in Step 2:

```
$ wget www.python.org/ftp/python/3.11.3/Python-3.11.3.tgz
--2023-06-02 06:05:47-- www.python.org/ftp/python/3.11.3/
Python-3.11.3.tgz
Resolving www.python.org (www.python.org)... 199.232.144.223,
2a04:4e42:64::223
Connecting to www.python.org (www.python.org)|199.232.144.223|:443...
connected.
HTTP request sent, awaiting response... 200 OK
Length: 26455738 (25M) [application/octet-stream]
Saving to: 'Python-3.11.3.tgz'
```

Python-3.11.3.tgz 100%[===========================>] 25.23M
2.06MB/s in 12s

2023-06-02 06:05:59 (2.16 MB/s) - 'Python-3.11.3.tgz' saved [26455738/
26455738]

$ **tar -zxvf Python-3.11.3.tgz**
Output truncated…

$ **cd Python-3.11.3**
~/Python-3.11.3 $ **./configure --enable-optimizations**
Output truncated…

~/Python-3.11.3 $ **sudo make altinstall**
Output truncated…

Note
This command will take several minutes to complete, as your Raspberry Pi
system compiles the new version of Python.

~/Python-3.11.3 $

To run this latest version in Way 4 (Bash Mode) type the following:
~/Python-3.11.3 $ **python3.11**

2.3.8.2 Switching Thonny to the Latest Python

To change the version of Python used by Thonny on your Raspberry Pi, you
need to be using Thonny in Regular Mode. To switch back to Simple Mode
later, use the Tools > Options> General > UI mode > simple menu choice
in Regular Mode. Be aware that you will have to click OK in the Thonny
Options dialog box, and then restart Thonny to get back to Simple Mode!
  Follow these steps in Regular Mode to switch to the latest Python you
downloaded and installed in the last section:

1. Open Thonny on your Raspberry Pi. Switch to Regular Mode by
    clicking on the "Switch to regular mode" message in the extreme right
    corner of the Thonny Toolbar. You get a message box that opens saying
    that the Configuration has been updated, and to restart Thonny to
    start working in Regular Mode. Click OK.

2. After you restart Thonny, in the menu bar at the top, click on "Tools"
    and then select "Options".

3. In the "Options" dialog box, navigate to the "Interpreter" tab.

4. Under the "Interpreter" tab, you'll see a list of available Python interpreters. This list includes the Python versions installed on your Raspberry Pi.

5. Select the desired Python version from the list. You can choose from the available versions or click on the "Browse" button to specify a custom Python interpreter.

6. After selecting the desired Python version, click on the "OK" button to save the changes.

Thonny will now use the selected Python version as the default interpreter for running and executing your Python code.

Note
You need to have the desired Python version already installed on your Raspberry Pi for it to appear in the list of available interpreters in Thonny.

If the desired Python version is *not* listed in Thonny's interpreter options, you may need to install it on your Raspberry Pi before it can be selected.

2.3.8.3 Finding Out What Version of Python 2.7.X or Python.3.X is Installed on Your Raspberry Pi System

The easiest way of knowing what versions of Python are already installed on the Raspberry Pi you are using, is to simply type **python** and press **<Enter>** at the Bash shell prompt ($) in a console or terminal window. When we do this on our Raspberry Pi system, we obtain the following output:

~$ **python**
Python 2.7.18 (default, Jul 14 2021, 08:11:37)
[GCC 10.2.1 20210110] on linux2
Type "help", "copyright", "credits" or "license" for more information.
>>>

Also, when we typed **python3** and pressed **<Enter>** at the Bash shell prompt ($) in a console or terminal window, we got the following output on our Raspberry Pi system:

~$ **python3**
Python 3.9.2 (default, Feb 28 2021, 17:03:44)
[GCC 10.2.1 20210110] on linux
Type "help", "copyright", "credits" or "license" for more information.
>>>
The three greater-than symbols (>>>) are the Python interpreter prompt, letting you know you are in Python! To exit to the command line prompt in the terminal window, press **<Ctrl-D>** after the >>>.

The first line of responses from our system shows that Python 2.7.18 or Python 3.9.2 are installed and running on this system.

If you get an error message on the Bash command line in the terminal window, such as command not found, either Python has not been installed on your system, or you do not have access to it. You would need to then contact your system administrator to install the program or set up your working environment to give you privileges to execute it. Or if you are the system administrator, for example on your own single-user Raspberry Pi computer, you would need to install the appropriate versions of Python, and set up your working environment so that you have access to those versions of the program.

Of course, in Thonny, the version of Python3 it's using is shown at the top of the Shell Area, as seen in Figure 2.1.

Every single line of Python3 code, or every script file or program shown in this chapter can be done, by default, in Python3.

The easiest way of installing Python3 on your particular Raspberry Pi system (if it is not already installed, or if you want to upgrade to the latest release of it) is to follow the instructions given above in Section 2.3.8.1.

2.3.8.4 Getting Help

If you need help on a particular module, keyword, or topic in Python3, in the Shell Area of Thonny, at the command prompt >>>, you can always type in the function call to help as follows to get into the help system:

>>> **help ()**
Welcome to python3.9's help utility!

If this is your first time using Python, you should definitely check out this excellent tutorial on the Internet at https://docs.python.org/3.9/tutorial/.

Enter the name of any module, keyword, or topic to get help on writing Python programs and using Python3 modules. To quit this help utility and return to the interpreter, just type "quit".

To get a list of available modules, keywords, symbols, or topics, type "modules", "keywords", "symbols", or "topics". Each module also comes with a one-line summary of what it does; to list the modules whose name or summary contains a given string such as "spam", type "modules spam".

help> **quit**

You are now leaving help and returning to the Python interpreter.
If you want to ask for help on a particular object directly from the interpreter, you can type "help(object)". Executing "help('string')" has the same effect as typing a particular string at the help> prompt.
>>>

2.4 Python3 Syntax

Python3 has a rich, and useful, syntactic repertoire you can draw from in order to successfully complete the programming tasks you set out to do. In this section, we give an overview of that syntax, with several examples.

2.4.1 Printing Text, Comments, Numbers, Grouping Operators, and Expressions

To use Python3 in practical examples, as shown later in this chapter, it's absolutely necessary to first become familiar with the syntax of the language. For example, how it's used as a calculator, in "interpretative mode", to execute single lines of Python code to accomplish short, meaningful operations and tasks.

One of the first things you must know about how a calculator works is how to enter numbers and mathematical expressions on the calculator. So, with Python3, instead of listing all the syntactic rules, we will execute a number of examples to illustrate, and have you work with some of the most important of those rules.

Here are a couple of the important considerations you need to be aware of before you enter any Python code on the Python command line or into a file.

1. The rule of four: The *indentation* spaces that you place on each line of Python code are very important!

This is done automatically for you in the Script Area of Thonny, when you are entering several lines of Python code.
Since Python is a structured programming language that uses specific structures in blocks, those blocks are delimited, or defined by the indentation you give them on each line (unlike in other languages that use specific printing characters to delimit blocks). This means you must line up your blocks of Python structures vertically, starting from the left-hand side, and for our purposes, use four spaces for each indented block. For example, the following sample shows this four-space indentation constraint:

```
Block 1 head
    xxxxxxxxx
    xxxxxxxxx
        Block 2 head
            xxxxxxxxx
            xxxxxxxxx
```

<pre>
        Block 3 head
            xxxxxxxxx
            xxxxxxxxx
        end of Block 3
    end of Block 2
end of Block 1
</pre>

where Blocks 1, 2, 3, and so on, and their statements xxxxxxxxx, line up vertically with an indentation of four spaces before each block, from left to right.

2. Normal order and applicative order evaluation: The order of execution of a mathematical expression used by Python is PEMDAS: Parentheses (from inner to outer), (from left to right) Exponents, Multiplication, Division, Addition, and Subtraction. See Table 2.2 for even more details of operator precedence in Python expressions.

The first thing we want Python3 to do is to print, or echo, a line of text we type at the keyboard. This is done by typing the following at the Python3 command prompt in the Thonny Shell Area:

```
>>>print ("This is the number of fingers I am holding up:")
```

TABLE 2.2

Python Order of Evaluations

Operator	Description
()	Parentheses (grouping)
f(args...)	Function call
x[index:index]	Slicing
x[index]	Subscription
x.attribute	Attribute reference
**	Exponentiation
~x	Bitwise not
+x, -x	Positive, negative
*, /, %	Multiplication, division, remainder
+, -	Addition, subtraction
<<, >>	Bitwise shifts
&	Bitwise AND
^	Bitwise XOR
|	Bitwise OR
in, not in, is, is not, <, <=, >, >=, <>,!=, ==	Comparisons, membership, identity
not x	Boolean NOT
and	Boolean AND
or	Boolean OR
lambda	Lambda expression

This is the number of fingers I am holding up:

To add comments to a script file of Python commands, you place the pound sign(#) before (and possibly after) everything on the line you want commented. For example, in interactive mode:

```
>>> # This is a comment, which you can use to annotate your script file code.
...
>>> # Anything after the # is ignored by python.
...
>>> print "You could have comments appear like this:" # this comment is
ignored.
```
You could have comments appear like this:
```
>>> # You can also use the pound sign to comment out a piece of code:
...
>>> # print "This won't run".
...
>>> print "This will run".
```
This will run.
```
>>>
```

In the interactive session above, just press **<Enter>** on the Python command line when the ... appears.

Quotation marks are used for "string literals", or characters of text you want to include "literally" as they are in the output of an executed Python script file. To include a single quotation mark in a string literal, enclose it inside of double quotation marks. For example:

```
>>> '"Don\'t", he said.'
'"Don\'t", he said.'
>>> print('"Don\'t", he said.')
"Don't", he said.
>>> s = 'First place.\nSecond place.'# \n means newline
>>> s                              # without print(),\n is included in the output
'First line.\nSecond line.'
>>> print(s)                       # with print(), \n produces a new line
```
First place.
Second place.

Triple quotation marks are used to enclose long lines of string literals.

Next, we want to combine some text with an arithmetic expression that Python evaluates for us:

```
>>> print ("Not Ring Fingers", 7 − (1 + 1))
```

Not Ring Fingers 5
Notice that in evaluating the mathematical expression, Python evaluates what is in parentheses first by doing the addition of 1 + 1, then, from left to right, subtracts 2 from 7.

In-Chapter Exercises
Have Python evaluate the following expressions, and list what Python prints:

   3. **((7 + 5) * (3 + 2))/(6/18)**

   4. How can you change the previous expression so that it yields a numeric answer, and why?

   5. **3 + 2 + 1 − 5 + 4 % 2 − 1 / 4 + 6**

   6   What kind of operator is the percent sign (%)?

We can also use relational operators in arithmetic expressions, such as less than (<), greater than (>), greater than or equal to (>=), and less than or equal to (<=). For example:

>>> **print ("Is it true that 3 + 1 < 5 · 7?")**
Is it true that 3 + 1 < 5 - 7?
>>> **print (3 + 1 < 5 · 7)**
False
>>> **print ("Is it greater?", 4 > -2)**
Is it greater? True
>>> **print ("Is it greater or equal?", 4 >= -2)**
Is it greater or equal? True
>>> **print ("Is it less or equal?", 4 <= -2)**
Is it less or equal? False

In-Chapter Exercise

   7. What are the results of typing in the following Python statements, and why?

       >>> 5 + 7>= 6 <= 78 − 9
       >>> 5 + 7>= 6 >= 78 − 9
       >>> (5 + 7>= 6 >= 78 − 9)/8
       >>> (5 + 7>= 6 >= 78 − 9)/−8

2.4.2 Variables and Naming Conventions

An important feature of a high-level programming language like Python is providing for names that allow you to refer to computational objects. The name

TABLE 2.3

Python Keywords

and	del	from	not	while
as	elif	global	or	with
assert	else	if	pass	yield
break	except	import	print	
class	nonlocal	in	raise	
continue	finally	is	return	
def	for	lambda	try	

represents, or stands for in any particular computational environment of interest, the value or values which the object can take on; thus it is called a "variable".

Python variable names, and the names of script files as well, can contain both letters, numbers, and the underscore (_) character, *but must begin with a letter*. If you get an error message about the use of a variable name, it may be a reserved word, or keyword, in Python. Table 2.3 lists the 31 keywords that may *not* be used as variables, or script file names in a Python statement.

To get a list of keywords in your current version, type the following at the Python prompt. In our version of Python 3.9.2, we got the output shown:

```
>>> import keyword
>>> print(keyword.kwlist)
```

['False', 'None', 'True', '__peg_parser__', 'and', 'as', 'assert', 'async', 'await', 'break', 'class', 'continue', 'def', 'del', 'elif', 'else', 'except', 'finally', 'for', 'from', 'global', 'if', 'import', 'in', 'is', 'lambda', 'nonlocal', 'not', 'or', 'pass', 'raise', 'return', 'try', 'while', 'with', 'yield']

```
>>>
```

The **(keyword.kwlist)** target of the print command is an illustration of a Python method application. In the following simple example, we define some variables, and use them:

```
>>> pie = 3.14159
>>> radius = 10
>>> pie * (radius * radius)
314.159
>>> circumference = 2 * pie * radius
>>> circumference
62.8318
```

2.4.3 Functions

Python provides a programming construct called a *function,* that allows you to define your own named procedures, and lets you reuse those procedures in a modular fashion in your code. You can think of a function as a black box machine that takes named objects present before the function call or invocation as inputs, processes them inside the black box with names that are only seen inside the black box, and then spits them out as named objects available to the Python program via an assignment statement.

The general form of a function definition is:

def name (formal parameters):
    body of the function
    return (returned parameters)

where **name** is the name you give the function (make sure you are not using a Python keyword!), **formal parameters** are the named objects that are passed to the function so it can carry out some operations on them and, optionally, **returned parameters** are named objects that are used by your program.

There are two basic ways you can execute a function:

1. Use Way 1 (Interactive Mode), and by typing or copying and pasting each line of code that is the function definition into the Thonny Script Area.
2. Use Way 3 (Import Script Mode), and create the function definition in a file with a **.py** extension. Then import the file into Thonny in the Shell Area, with the **import** command.

A simple example of the first way to use a function definition in Python is as follows. Type the following six lines of Python code into the Script Area of Thonny, and then click on the Run Toolbar icon. Remember to let Thonny indent the lines as shown!

```
w = 7
x = 12
def add(a, b):
    c = a + b
    return (c)
z = add(w, x)
```

Then type the following in the Thonny Shell Area:

```
>>>z
19
>>>
```

If you want to, you can use the Thonny save Toolbar icon to save the above code in Thonny's current working director.

From this example, we can call **w** and **x** the actual parameters passed to the function definition, **a** and **b** the formal parameters used in the body of the function definition, and **c** a returned parameter.

Notice that, for the returned parameter to be used in the remainder of your Python session after the function definition, you must assign a named variable on the left-hand side of the equals sign to the function call or invocation on the right-hand side of the equals sign.

A simple example of using Way 3 (Import Script Mode) to bring a function definition into Python is as follows:

Use the text editor of your choice (we like nano) to create and save the following file, named **math1.py**, in the current working directory that is set in Thonny. Remember the Rule of Four!

Example 2.5

```
def add(a, b):
    c = a + b
    return(c)
def subtract(a, b):
    c = b - a
    return(c)
def multiply(a, b):
    c = a * b
    return(c)
def divide(a, b):
    c = a / b
    return(c)
```

Then, in the Thonny Shell Area, type the following three lines of Python code:

```
>>> import math1
>>> z = math1.add(3, 4)
>>> z
7
>>>
```

The first line you typed into the Thonny Shell Area made the named objects in the **math1.py** module available in the current session of Python3. The second line allowed you to address the **add** function from that module as **math1.add**. This is another example of the use of a Python method, and its invocation. The assignment statement on the second line in the Thonny Shell Area also allowed you to add 3 and 4 together, and assign the returned value to a variable named **z**. We will cover more about Python methods, modules, and global and local scopes in functions, in the sections below.

2.4.4 Conditional Execution

As mentioned in Section 2.3, the order in which computer programs execute includes a "branching", or conditional execution structure. Python3 uses the truth value of certain test conditions to determine whether prescribed blocks of code will be executed or not. This is implemented in Python3 with the **if** statement. The general form of the **if** statement construct is:

```
if cond1 is true:
    initial statement(s)
elif cond2 is true:
    additional statement(s)
else:
    final statement(s)
```

where:
cond1 is a test condition whose truth value determines whether the initial statement(s) block gets executed,
cond2 is a test condition whose truth value determines whether the additional statement(s) block gets executed, and
else is the default which executes final statement(s).

A simple example of the use of this structure using Way 2 (Script Mode) in the Thonny Script Area is as follows.

Remember to press **<Enter>** on the keyboard after each line you type into the Script Area in Thonny. Notice that Thonny properly indents lines in the Script Area, the requisite number of spaces, according to its structured programming rules.

Example 2.6

```
x = 1
if x == 0: # the == is a logical, or Boolean operator
    print ("x equal 0")
elif x == 1: #one or more of these optional blocks are allowed
    print ("x equal 1")
else: #the optional block
    print ("x is something else")
```

When done correctly typing the above in, click on the Run icon in the Thonny Toolbar.

```
>>> %Run -c $EDITOR_CONTENT
x equal 1
>>>
```

In-Chapter Exercises

8. If you leave out the **elif** block in Example 2.6, what prints out?
9. If you change the first line to read **x = 3**, and leave out the **else** line in Example 2.6, what prints out?
10. If you change the first line to read **x = 1.8** in Example 2.6, what prints out?

It is also possible to nest conditional execution blocks inside of one another.

For example, we'll use a variation of Way 3 (Import Script Mode) for the code execution below. Enter the following code correctly into a file named **two7.py**. Remember to indent according to the Rule of Four!

Then, in Thonny click on the Load Toolbar icon, and load the file from the default directory you created **two7.py** in, into the Thonny Script Area:

Example 2.7

```
w = 36
y = 13
z = 20
if w < 37:
    print ("w is less than 37")
    if y > 13:
        print ("y is greater than 13")
    elif y == 13:
        print ("y is equal to 13")
    else:
    print ("y is less than 13")
    if z > 21:
        print ("z is greater than 21")
    elif z == 21:
        print ("z is equal to 21")
    else:
        print ("z is less than 21")
else:
    print ("w is greater than or equal to 37")
```

Finally, click the Run Thonny Toolbar icon. The following is what should appear on your display in the Thonny Shell Area:

```
>>> %Run two7.py
w is less than 37
y is equal to 13
z is less than 21
>>>
```

2.4.5 Determinate and Indeterminate Repetition Structures and Recursion

Using the procedural/imperative model, Python3 can repeat segments of program or script file structures in two basic ways: via *determinate repetition structures* or *indeterminate repetition structures*. Traditionally, a determinate repetition structure is called *counting repetition*, and an indeterminate repetition structure is called *logical repetition*. These two methods are implemented with the **for** procedural statement, and the **while** procedural statement. Generally, if you know ahead of time (for example, at the time you are writing the code) how many repetitions of a block of code you want to execute, you use the **for** statement, and if you do *not* know (when, for example, you allow the user to input the number of repetitions as the script file is run), you use the **while** statement.

Of course, it is possible to implement the same two ways of repetition by *not* using a specific structured programming approach; for example, by using conditional execution, and unstructured switching to obtain the same results. This is not good practice, and we choose to show the structured approach in Python3.

Make sure that in the body of statements included in the indeterminate repetition block that **while** is executing, the test condition for continued execution becomes false. Otherwise, this will result in *infinite repetition*! To halt infinite repetition in an executing script file, hold down the **<Ctrl>** and **C** keys on the keyboard at the same time.

A note about Python3 style is in order at this point.

Pythonic

Proceeding from Guido van Rossum's definition of *Pythonic* in the Python Language Reference, a common technique in Python3 is to loop over all elements of an *iterable* object using a **for** statement. Many other languages do not have this type of construct, so people unfamiliar with Python3 sometimes use a numerical counter instead, such as:

```
>>>for i in range(len(money)):
... print money[i]
```

The Pythonic way is:

```
>>>for bills in money:
... print (bills)
```

The Pythonic way can be characterized as *iteration*, whereas the traditional language construct can be characterized as *counting*.

The **for** structure can repeat a block of operations on any *iterable* sequence data, such as strings, lists, tuples, or user-defined iterable objects in classes.

The general form of the **for** statement structure is as follows:

for a certain number of times
    repeat these statements

The **while** structure can repeat a block of operations as long as a test condition is true.

The general form of the **while** statement structure is:

while a certain condition is true
    repeat these statements

An object, K is iterable if it can be successfully run with the following code in Way 2 (Script Mode). This code also shows that a counting form of iteration, such as the traditional **for** loop structure, can be implemented with a **while** structure. No need to type the comments into the Thonny Script Area, and to run the code, click on the Toolbar Run Icon-

```
K = [22,33,44,55]        #Lists are iterable.
c = K.__iter__()         #c is the counter
while 1:                 #execute while true
    try:
        item = next(c)       #get the next one
        print (item)         # Do operations on each item as you count through
    except StopIteration:  #Nothing left
        break
```

```
>>> %Run -c $EDITOR_CONTENT
22
33
44
55
>>>
```

Following are two simple examples of both forms of repetition. We use Way 2 (Script Mode) to run them.

Type the following three lines of code into the Thonny Script Area. Notice that the keywords in the Python script file are in **bold** type for didactic purposes here:

Example 2.8

```
limit = [1, 2, 3, 4, 5]
for number in limit:
    print ("number of repeats %d" % number)
```

Then click on the Run Toolbar icon. Your output in the Shell area should be:

```
>>> %Run -c $EDITOR_CONTENT
number of repeats 1
number of repeats 2
number of repeats 3
number of repeats 4
number of repeats 5
```

Type the following seven lines of Python3 into the Thonny Script Area. Notice that the keywords in the Python script file are again shown in **bold** type:

Example 2.9

```
s= int(input("Enter an Integer"))
i = 0
numbers = []
while i < s:
    numbers.append(i)
    i = i + 1
    print ("numbers now: ", numbers)
```

Then click on the Run Toolbar icon. Your output in the Shell area should be as follows. When prompted for an integer, type in **6** and then press **<Enter>** on the keyboard. Your output should be:

```
>>> %Run -c $EDITOR_CONTENT
Enter an Integer 6
numbers now: [0]
numbers now: [0, 1]
numbers now: [0, 1, 2]
numbers now: [0, 1, 2, 3]
numbers now: [0, 1, 2, 3, 4]
numbers now: [0, 1, 2, 3, 4, 5]
>>>
```

Try this same script file using different input integers, each time you run it to confirm that indeterminate repetition is happening.

Another interesting, and extremely useful, indeterminate repetition method that Python3 can implement is known as *recursion*.

Basically, recursion is the repetition of a body of calculations to accumulate intermediate results, until some basic state is reached, and at that point the calculations yield the final results.

The following is an example of a recursive process that calculates the factorial of an integer, implemented in Python as a function that calls, or invokes, itself an indeterminate number of times (the Python keywords are shown in **bold** type, and we are using Way 3 [Import Script Mode] to execute the script):

Example 2.10

```
def factR(n):
    if n == 1:
        return n
    else:
        return n*factR(n - 1)
```

If you create this function definition in a file named **FactR.py** in Thonny's current working directory, then typing the following into Thonny's Shell Area will yield the factorial of the input argument 7 as shown:

```
>>> import FactR
>>> FactR.factR(7)
5040
>>>
```

In-Chapter Exercises

11. What error message do you get if you supply a real number, such as 9.76, when you run the code of Example 2.9? Why do you get this error message?

12. How can you find the factorial of a real number in Python? Such as the factorial of 3.72, for example.

2.4.6 File Input and Output

If you look back to Section 2.3.7, at the programming tasks that Python3 is capable of (such as systems programming, network and Internet scripting, database programming, systems administration scripting, GUI scripting, scientific statistical math programming, and data mining), the common thread which runs through all of those tasks is the ability to interface with the

Raspberry Pi OS via utilities that work with Linux files. For example, you may be programming a statistical analysis script in Python that perhaps has its data generated from some other program or utility stored in a file somewhere in the file structure of your Raspberry Pi system. These files can be text, Unicode text, or binary, raw 8-bit bytes.

The general form of a file operation in Python3 is:

name = open(filename, mode)
name.method(argument(s))
name.close()

where:
name is a file object name in the current procedure,
open is the keyword that opens Python3's connection to an external file,
filename is the name of the external file, which may include directory paths, and so on,
mode is a way of accessing the file, like reading from it, or writing to it,
method is one of several operations that are allowed to be performed on the open external file,
argument(s) is(are) one or more qualifiers on the operation specified in method, and
close is the termination of connection to the external file.

The mode can be **r**, **w**, or **a**, for reading (the default, meaning you do not need to specify this to open with read), writing, or appending to the file, respectively. The file will be created if it does not exist, and opened for writing or appending if it does exist. It will be truncated when opened for writing. Add **b** to the mode for binary files. Add **+** to the mode to allow simultaneous reading and writing.

The preferred way to open a file is with the built-in **open()** function. Add **u** to the mode to open the file for input with universal newline support.

In the following examples, we illustrate some simple operations on files, such as how to open, write/read from, and close them.

In the first example, we input a string of text into a named file. In the Thonny Shell Area, type the following three lines of code:

Example 2.11

```
>>> file = open('sometext', 'w')
>>> file.write('This is a line of text.')
23
>>> file.close()
>>>
```

Then, when you are in the same current directory set by Thonny, type the following line at the Bash shell prompt (shown as $):

```
$ more sometext
```
This is a line of text.
$

In the next example, we input some integer data into an external file using your favorite text editor, and then do some Python3 operations on that data. In the current directory set by Thonny, run your favorite text editor, and into a file you name **somedata.txt**, type the following four integers (one integer per line):

23
33
43
54

Then, in the Thonny Shell Area, execute the following lines of code. The variable named x1 is a *list*, which we will discuss in more detail in Section 2.4.7 below. So, the list element x1[0] is the first element of the list that has been read from the first line in the external file. The **float** and **int** functions convert the text strings in the file to real numbers and integers:

Example 2.12

```
>>> file = open('somedata.txt') #the default mode is reading
>>> x1 = file.readlines()
>>> x1
['23\n', '33\n', '43\n', '54\n']
>>> s = float(x1[0])
>>> s
23.0
>>> r = int(x1[0])
>>> r
23
>>> s + r
46.0
>>> file.close()
>>>
```

We can also write list elements, such as numbers, to an external file. For example, type or paste the following Python code into the Thonny Script Area. It uses the write method to place three lists into a file named **listw.txt**. Then, click on the Run Toolbar icon in Thonny:

Example 2.13

```
L = [1, 2, 3]
M = [4, 5, 6]
N = [7, 8, 9]
F = open('listw.txt','w')
F.write(str(L) + '\n')
F.write(str(M) + '\n')
F.write(str(N) + '\n')
F.close()
```

In the Thonny Shell area, the following appears:

```
>>> %Run -c $EDITOR_CONTENT
>>>
```

On the Bash shell commend line, where the current directory is Thonny's default set directory, in a Raspberry Pi terminal window, view the contents of **listw.txt** with the following command:

```
$ more listw.txt
[1, 2, 3]
[4, 5, 6]
[7, 8, 9]
$
```

In-Chapter Exercises

13. What commands do you use to add the first three elements of the list x1 of Example 2.12, and print that sum?

14. What are the \n characters shown on line 4 of Example 2.12?

15. What happens if you edit the file **somedata.txt**, and enter the numbers 23, 33, 43, and 54 on a single line in your text editor instead of on four different lines, save the file, and try to perform the same action in Example 2.12 on the new file **somedata.txt**?

16. After you close the file thus created, can you still access the values 43 and 54 in any way?

17. How would you specify the third element of the list x1?

2.4.7 Lists and the List Function

On the lowest level of the organizational scheme for Python3, the *list* is an object that can contain multiple elements of possibly different types. Just like a shopping list can contain different kinds of things from a store, such as food, household goods, automotive supplies, and so on, a Python3 list can be made up of different types of elements, like integers, real numbers, strings, and so on; in fact, a list can contain any type of Python3 object. For example:

```
>>> A = [ 34, 'Bob', 54.76, [4,7,9]]
```

is an expression that assigns the integer 34, the string "Bob", the real number 54.76, and another list comprised of the numbers 4, 7, and 9 to a variable named A. List indices are integers, starting with 0. So, the following statements in Python3 yield the results:

```
>>> A[2]
54.76
>>> A[0]
34
>>> A[3][2]
9
>>>
```

A 2 × 2 matrix (or array) can be specified as:

```
B = [[x, x],[y, y]]
```

Here is Python3 code to create a 3 × 3 matrix (or array) named x, of random numbers, using the list function that works on objects (please notice that your results will differ from the output shown here, since the numbers shown in the example are randomly generated!):

Example 2.14

```
>>> import random # random is a function from the Standard Library
>>> x = list(list (random.random() for i in range(3)) for j in range(3))
>>> x
[[0.1455440585876967, 0.7525092872509719, 0.30168961326498955],
[0.6967960669374997, 0.8715621457012694, 0.24960628313623423],
[0.891389814359208, 0.9591605275600708, 0.5240885874508074]]
>>>
```

2.4.8 Strings, String Formatting Conversions, and Sequence Operations

In Python3, strings and sequences are fundamental data types that are widely used for representing and manipulating collections of characters, or other values.

A string is a sequence of characters enclosed in either single quotes (' ') or double quotes (" "). It can contain letters, numbers, symbols, and spaces. Strings are *immutable*, which means that once a string is created, it can't be changed! Following are a few examples:

```
greeting = "Hello, World!"
print(greeting) # Output: Hello, World!

name = 'Alice'
print("Hello, " + name) # Output: Hello, Alice

first_letter = greeting[0]
print(first_letter) # Output: H

sliced = greeting[7:12]
print(sliced) # Output: World
```

Sequences are ordered collections of elements, where each element has an assigned index. Python3 provides several sequence types, including strings, lists, and tuples. Sequences can contain elements of different data types, and they can be mutable or immutable depending on the type. Some common operations on sequences include indexing (accessing elements by their position), slicing (extracting portions of the sequence), concatenation (combining two or more sequences), and repetition (creating a new sequence by repeating an existing one). The following are a few examples:

```
nums = [1, 2, 3, 4, 5]
print(nums[2]) # Output: 3

fruits = ('apple', 'banana', 'cherry')
print(fruits[1]) # Output: banana

combined = nums + list(fruits)
print(combined) # Output: [1, 2, 3, 4, 5, 'apple', 'banana', 'cherry']

repeated = nums * 3
print(repeated) # Output: [1, 2, 3, 4, 5, 1, 2, 3, 4, 5, 1, 2, 3, 4, 5]
```

Strings can also be treated as sequences, so you can use sequence operations on strings as well. Both strings and sequences are versatile data types in Python3, and understanding their properties and operations allows you to work effectively with text and collections of data.

2.4.8.1 Strings

As stated above, strings are a class of objects in Python3 that can represent text, and are basically seen in their single-quoted and double-quoted form, which are interchangeable. For example:

```
>>> 'program', "program's"
('program',"program's")
>>>
```

To format strings in an expression, you can use the % binary operator to format values as strings according to a specific format definition. On a line of code, on the left of the % operator, put in a format string that has one or more code types. On the right of the % sign, put in objects you want to substitute in for the types.

The operator (s % k) produces a formatted string, given a format string *s* and a collection of objects in a tuple or mapping object (dictionary). The string *s* may be a standard or Unicode string. The format string contains two types of objects: ordinary characters (which are left unmodified) and conversion specifiers, each of which is replaced with a formatted string representing an element of the associated tuple or mapping.

If k is a tuple, the number of conversion specifiers must exactly match the number of objects in k. If k is a mapping, each conversion specifier must be associated with a valid key name in the mapping, using parentheses. Each conversion specifier starts with the % character and ends with one of the conversion characters shown in Table 2.4.

The following example allows you to perform some basic operations on strings, such as *concatenating* them (adding their characters together), embedding escape sequences in them (to include special characters), finding their lengths (an integer representing their length), or *slicing* them (extracting smaller sub-string parts of them).

TABLE 2.4

String Formatting Conversions

Character	Output Format
d, I	Decimal integer or long integer
u	Unsigned integer or long integer
o	Octal integer or long integer
x	Hexadecimal integer or long integer
X	Hexadecimal integer (uppercase letters)
f	Floating point as [−]m.dddddd
e	Floating point as [−]m.dddddde±xx
E	Floating point as [−]m.ddddddE±xx
g, G	Use %e or %E for exponents less than −4 or greater than the precision
s	String or any object. The formatting code uses str() to generate strings
r	Produces the same string as produced by repr()
c	Single character
%	Literal %

Example 2.15

```
>>> a = 'programming'
>>> b = 'programmer\n'
>>> c = 'programs'
>>> print (a + ' ' + b + c)
```
programming programmer
programs
```
>>> len(a+b+c)                    #len is the length operator
```
30
```
>>> d = a[0:3] + b[3:7] + c[7]  #b[3:7] is gram
>>> d
```
'programs'
```
>>> b[3:]
```
'grammer\n'
```
>>> print (b[3:])
```
grammer
```
>>> q = c[:]
>>> q
```
'programs'
```
>>>
```

In-Chapter Exercises

18. Instead of printing the concatenated strings in line 4 of Example 2.15, what do you get echoed to you on the Shell Area command line if you just type **a + b + c**?

19. The variable c has 12 characters in it. Why are there 30 characters returned for the length of the concatenation of a, b, and c?

20. What is the first index value used to extract sub-strings from a string?

21. What is the last index value used to extract sub-strings from a string?

22. What does the indexing operation [:] shown in Example 2.15 accomplish?

23. What does a[1:3] return, and why?

2.4.8.2 Sequence Operations

Three important, and quite useful operations you can perform on sequence types of objects are *indexing, slicing,* and *extended slicing.* Objects such as strings and tuples are immutable and cannot be modified after creation. But, lists can be modified with the operators shown in Table 2.5.

TABLE 2.5

Indexing, Slicing, and Extended Slicing Operations

Operation	Description
s[n]	Returns nth element of s
s[i] = x	Index assignment
s[i:j] = r	Slice assignment
s[i:j:stride] = r	Extended slice assignment
del s[i]	Deletes an element
del s[i:j]	Deletes a slice
del s[i:j:stride]	Deletes an extended slice

The following section describes, and gives examples of some sequence operations on mutable objects.

Indexing into the sequence:
Gets components using offsets, where the first element indexed is at zero (0) offset.
Negative indices count backward from the end, where the last element is at offset −1.

s[0] gets the first element, s[1] gets the second element, and so on.
s[−2] gets the second from last element.

Slicing the sequence:
Extracts contiguous sections of a sequence, from i to j−i.
Slice boundaries i and j default to 0 and sequence length len(s).

s[1:4] retrieves elements from offset 1–3.
s[1:] retrieves from offset 1 until the end of the sequence object.
s[:−1] retrieves from offset 0 to the next to last element.
s[:] makes a copy of the sequence object.

Extended slicing of the sequence:
The third element is a *stride*, which defaults to 1, added to the offset of each element extracted.

s[::2] is every other item in the sequence.
s[::−1] is the reverse of the sequence.
s[4:1:−1] retrieves from offset 4, up to but not including 1, in reverse.

Slice assignments:
On mutable objects, deleting elements of the sequence and then reinserting new ones.

Iterable objects assigned to slices s[i:j] do not have to be the same size. Iterable objects assigned to extended slices s[i:j:k] must match in size.

Here are several interactive code examples of sequence object operations on a list of integers, typed into the Thonny Shell area:

```
>>>m = [0, 1, 2, 3, 4, 5, 6, 7, 8, 9]
>>>n = m[::2]
>>>m
[2, 6, 10, 14, 18]
>>>p = m[::-2]
>>>p
[20, 16, 12, 8, 4]
>>>q = m[0:5:2]
>>>q
[2, 6, 10]
>>>r = m[5:0:-2]
>>>r
[12, 8, 4]
>>>s = m[:5:1]
>>>s
[2, 4, 6, 8, 10]
>>>t = m[:5:-1]
>>>t
[20, 18, 16, 14]
>>>u = m[6::1]
>>>u
[14, 16, 18, 20]
>>>v = m[5::-1]
>>>v
[12, 10, 8, 6, 4, 2]
>>>w = m[5:0:-1]
>>>w
[12, 10, 8, 6, 4]
>>>
```

Here are several more code examples, again typed into the Thonny Shell Area, of some further uses of formatting expressions on different objects.

Example 2.16

```
>>>x = 400
>>>y = 75.142783
>>>z = "master"
```

```
>>>d = {'x':13, 'y':1.54321, 'z':'unive'}
>>>q = 1234567812345678
>>>print ('x is %d' % x)
x is 400
>>>print ('%10d %f' % (x,y))
400 75.142783
>>>print ('%+010d %E' % (x,y))
+0000000400 7.514278E+01
>>>print ('%(x)-10d %(y)0.3g' % d)
13 1.54
>>>print ('%0.4s %s' % (z, d['z']))
mast unive
>>>print ('%*.*f' % (5,3,y))
75.143
>>>print ('q = %d' % q)
q = 1234567812345678
>>>
```

Here are even more interactive code examples showing slicing operations on a list of integers:

```
>>>x = [1,2,3,4,5]
>>>x[1] = 6
>>>x
[1,6,3,4,5]
>>>x[2:4] = [10,11]
>>>x
[1,6,10,11,5]
>>>x[3:4] = [-1,-2,-3]
>>>x
[1,6,10,-1,-2,-3,5]
>>>x[2:] = [0]
>>>x
[1,6,0]
>>>
```

A slicing assignment may be supplied with an optional *stride* argument. The argument on the right side of the assignment statement must have exactly the same number of elements as the slice that is being replaced. Here are a few code examples of this, typed into the Thonny Shell Area:

```
>>>y = [1,2,3,4,5]
>>>y[1::2] = [10,11]
>>>y
```

[1,10,3,11,5]
>>>y[1::2] = [30,40,50]
Traceback (most recent call last):
File "<stdin>", line 1, in <module>
ValueError: attempt to assign sequence of size 3 to extended slice of size 2
>>>

2.4.9 Tuples

Similar to the list object described in Section 2.4.7, the Python3 *tuple* is a simple object that creates data structures using any other object type. Tuples support most of the same operations as lists, such as indexing, slicing, and concatenation. But, you cannot modify the contents of a tuple after creation, as you can with a list.

This is a tuple's most important feature, as a sequence object used in data structures:

It cannot be changed.
The following example uses Way 2 (Script Mode) to execute the code, and shows the creation, querying, and manipulation of tuples in a database.

Example 2.17

With your favorite text editor, create the following file of six lines (named **data.txt**) in Thonny's current working directory:

```
Conditions,23,45.8
Methods,12,11.75
Objects,40,17.1
Modules,1023,1.4
Dictionaries,45,120.71
Comprehensions,5,234.75
```

Next, type-in or paste the following code into the Thonny Script Area:

```
filename = "data.txt"
collection=[]
for line in open(filename):
    fields = line.split  (",")   #splits line by commas
    name = fields[0]   #create the fields
    uses = int(fields[1])
    value = float(fields[2])
    card = (name,uses,value)   #create the tuple
    collection.append(card)
```

```
print (collection[0])
print (collection[3][2])
sum = 0.0
for name, uses, value in collection:
    sum += uses / value
print (sum)
```

Then, click on the Thonny Run Toolbar icon.
You should see the following output in the Thonny Shell Area:

```
>>> %Run -c $EDITOR_CONTENT
('Conditions', 23, 45.8)
1.4
734.9710205576091
>>>
```

2.4.10 Sets

Another elementary object type in Python3 is the *set*, which is an *unordered* collection of objects that have no duplicate elements. The distinguishing feature of a set as an unordered sequence is that you cannot address or index into the set using the index operations on sequences we illustrated for lists and tuples. To create sets, and do some operations on them, do the following example (you can omit typing in the comments shown!):

Example 2.18

```
>>> x = set([1.0, 2.0, 3.0, 4.0])
>>> x
{1.0, 2.0, 3.0, 4.0}
>>> z = set([10,11,12,13,14])
>>> z
{10, 11, 12, 13, 14}
>>> q = set("Hello")
>>> q
{'H', 'e', 'l', 'o'}                          #no repeated elements
>>> a = z | q                                 #union of z and q
>>> a
{'l', 10, 11, 12, 13, 14, 'H', 'o', 'e'}      #ordered ascending
>>> r = set([9, 8, 7, 6])
>>> b = q | r
>>> b
{'l', 6, 7, 8, 9, 'H', 'o', 'e'}              #ordered ascending even
                                              #though r is descending!
>>> c = r | a
```

```
>>> c
{'l', 6, 7, 8, 9, 10, 11, 12, 13, 14, 'H', 'o', 'e'}
>>> c = r & a                          #intersection of r and a
>>> c
set()                                  #the empty set
>>> x.add(5.0)                         #add an element
>>> x
{1.0, 2.0, 3.0, 4.0, 5.0}
>>> x.remove(4.0)                      #remove an element
>>> x
{1.0, 2.0, 3.0, 5.0}
>>> x.update([6.0, 7.0, 8.0])          #add multiple elements
>>> x
{1.0, 2.0, 3.0, 5.0, 6.0, 7.0, 8.0}
>>>
```

In-Chapter Exercises

24. In Example 2.18, why is c finally the empty set?
25. What would the set x contain if you added three number 5.0's with only one **x.add** command? What would the set x contain if you added three number 5.0's with the **x.update** command?
26. Can you use slice assignment statements to reassign new values to elements of a tuple?

2.4.11 Dictionaries

A Python3 *dictionary* is a data structure, or "container", that acts like a table of objects that can be indexed into, where parts of it can be addressed by what are known as *keys*. The keys can be strings, or one of several distinct other Python3 objects. The container is not a sequence object, in the way that a list is. An example of dictionary creation commands, created and run in the Thonny Script Area, that uses strings as keys, is as follows:

Example 2.19

```
function = {
    "name":"operator",
    "class":"arithmetic",
    "number": 12
    }
```

Then, when you type the following in the Thonny Shell Area, you get:

```
>>> function
{'number': 12, 'name': 'operator', 'class': 'arithmetic'}
>>>
```
The keys are the strings "name", "class", and "number", the field data are "operator", "arithmetic", and 12, and the curly braces {} are the syntax that allows you to define the dictionary.

Notice that the order of how the keys and their field data is presented on output by Python3 may *not* necessarily be the same order in which you defined them!

Here is a way of extracting a value from the table **function** we created in Example 2.19, and then changing one of the data values in it. In the Thonny Shell Area, type the following:

```
>>> n = function.get("number")
>>> n
12
>>> function["class"]="logical"
>>> function
{'number': 12, 'name': 'operator', 'class': 'logical'}
>>>
```

Here is a way that lets you sort the keys in a **for** loop using the **sorted** function. Python3 has two basic ways of sorting. The **sorted** function sorts any iterable object, such as entries in a Python dictionary. The **sort** method is a **list** method that works on Python3 lists (there is no need to type in the comments shown next to the commands you input into the Thonny Shell Area. Remember, ellipses (…) indicate you've pressed the **<Enter>** key on the previous line in the Thonny Shell Area):

```
>>> K = {'x':1, 'y':2, 'z':3} #creates the dictionary
>>> K
{'x': 1, 'y': 2, 'z': 3}        #not a sequence, thus comes back in any order
>>> for key in sorted(K):
... print (key, '=', K[key]) #auto-indent by Thonny, and press Enter twice here!
...
x = 1
y = 2
z = 3
>>>
```

2.4.12 Generators

A Python functional technique of program execution, that uses the advanced programming methodologies of data flows, streams, and process pipelines, and preserves the state of the "propagation" of output as it executes in a "stepwise" fashion, is called a *generator*. A generator produces a collection of output results only when a method named **next()** in Python3 is called. The **next()** method is executed by the Python3 **yield** statement. When a collection of data needs to be created on the fly, perhaps in single steps ("stepwise"), at a particular time during program execution, the generator function is called. The **next()** built-in function steps you through, and generates the output.

Note
The techniques shown in this, and the following section are necessarily for more advanced programming applications.
    The following Example 2.20 shows how to create and invoke a generator function. It's helpful to dissect this example into its component parts, as shown on the Thonny Shell Area, as follows:

    a.   Propagation, or generation, then
    b.   Invocation with a seed value of 4, then
    c.   Invocation again with a seed value of 6, then
    d.   Output

Example 2.20

```
>>> def generadd(Q):
...     for i in range(Q):
...         yield i   #generates the next value
...         i += 1
...
>>> for i in generadd(4): #whenever function is called, #the values are
generated
...         print (i)
...
0
1
2
3
>>> z = generadd(6) #this passes 6 to generadd
>>> z               #this will show you the compiled generator object
<generator object generated at 0x284f60f4>
>>> next(z)         #the next built-in steps you through and generates
                    the value
```

```
0
>>> next(z)
1
>>> next(z)
2
>>> next(z)
3
>>> next(z)
4
>>> next(z)
5
>>> next(z)
Traceback(most recent call last):
File "<stdin?", line 1. in <module>
StopIteration
>>>
```

As a further application of generator use, the code of the following example shows how to implement generator functions, in a file named **regen.py** that you create with your favorite text editor. First create the file **regen.py** as shown, in the current directory that Thonny is using, and then use Way 3 (Import Script Mode) to do In-Chapter Exercises 27–29:

Example 2.21

```
def abc():
    a = deff()
    for i in a:
        yield i
    yield 'abc'
def deff():
    a = ijk()
    for i in a:
        yield i
    yield 'deff'
def ijk():
    for i in (1,2,3):
        yield i
    yield 'ijk'
```

In-Chapter Exercises

27. Give the exact Thonny operations that would bring the three functions from Example 2.21 into the Python3 interpreter, given that you have used Way 3 (Import Script Mode).

28. Give the exact Python3 code that would invoke the three functions from Example 2.21 on the Thonny Shell Area command line.

29. Give the exact Python3 code that would allow you to step through the invocation of the three functions from Example 2.21, to generate its output results until you reach the **StopIteration** message. List the output generated at each step through the recursion.

2.4.12.1 Generator Recursion

Recursion, which is the delay of computation until some target final state is reached, can be implemented using Python3 generator functions by defining a generator function that *calls itself within the body of its definition*. Here's an example of that kind of a recursive generator function in Python3:

```
def recursive_generator(n):
    if n == 0:
        return
    yield n
    yield from recursive_generator(n - 1)
for num in recursive_generator(5):
    print(num)
```

Save the above code in a file named **recursive.py**, in Thonny's current working directory. In this descriptive example, the **recursive_generator** function takes an integer **n** as its parameter. If **n** is 0, the function simply returns, indicating the final state of the recursion has been reached. Otherwise, it yields the current value of **n** and then calls itself again, recursively with **n - 1**, using the **yield from** statement to assign the iteration to the recursive call. But **n** is assigned the value of 5.

Using Way 3 (Import Script Mode), here's how you can use the **recursive_generator** function to generate a sequence of numbers. When you import the above code into the Thonny Shell Area, the output is as follows:

```
>>>import recursive
5
4
3
2
1
```

In this descriptive example, calling **recursive_generator(5)** generates a sequence of numbers from 5 down to 1, using recursion. The **for** loop iterates over the generated values, and prints them one by one.

Note that the use of a generator function for recursion allows you to iterate over the generated values *lazily*, i.e., one value at a time, which can be memory-efficient compared to generating the entire sequence upfront.

2.4.13 Coroutines

So perhaps to end your suspense, here's how we answered the above three In-Chapter Exercises in the Thonny Shell Area:

```
>>>import regen
>>>x = regen.abc()
>>>next(x)
1
>>>next(x)
2
>>>next(x)
3
>>>next(x)
'ijk'
>>>next(x)
'deff'
>>>next(x)
'abc'
>>>next(x)
Traceback(most recent call last)
File "<stdin>", line 1, in <module>
StopIteration
>>>
```

In the previous section, we introduced the advanced programming technique of using generator functions, which use **yield** to give output results. Python3 generator functions can also "consume" results using a **yield** statement. In addition, two new methods applied to generator objects, **send()** and **close()**, create a "framework" for objects, that consume and produce values. Generator functions that define these objects are called *coroutines*. Coroutines consume values using a **yield** statement on the right side of an expression, as follows:

value = (yield)

Using this syntax, execution pauses at this here until the object's **send** method is invoked with an argument:

coroutine.send(data)

Then, execution resumes, with **value** being assigned, or referenced to the value of data. To signal the end of a computation, we shut down a coroutine using the **close()** method. This raises a GeneratorExit exception inside the coroutine, which we can catch with a **try/except** clause.

The next example illustrates these concepts. It is a coroutine that prints strings that match a provided template pattern. Use Way 2 (Script Mode), and the Thonny Run Toolbar icon to implement this in Thonny:

Example 2.22

```
def grepper(template):
    print ('Searching for ' + template)
    try:
        while True:
            x = (yield)
            if template in x:
                print (x)
    except GeneratorExit:
        print ("Done")
```

In the Thonny Shell Area, type the following:

```
>>> q = grepper("Pythonista")
>>> next(q)
Pythonista
>>> q.send("After doing this section, you will be known as a Pythonista")
After doing this section, you will be known as a Pythonista
>>> q.send("Not a very Pythonic answer")
>>> q.send("Python makes C look high maintenance and too complex")
>>> q.close()
Done
>>>
```

When we call **q.send** with a value, evaluation resumes inside the coroutine **q** at the statement line = (**yield**), where the sent value is assigned to the variable line. Evaluation continues inside **q**, printing out the line if it matches, going through the loop until it encounters the line = (**yield**) again. Then, evaluation pauses inside **q** and resumes where **q.send** was called.

We can chain functions that **send()** and functions that **yield** together to achieve complex behaviors, similar to streaming, or pipelining. In the next example, the function **read** splits a string named "text" into words and sends each word to another coroutine. Continuing in the Thonny Shell Area, with grepper still defined:

```
>>> def read(text, next_coroutine):
...       for line in text.split():
...             next_coroutine.send(line)
...       next_coroutine.close()
...
```

Each word is sent to the coroutine bound to **next_coroutine**, causing **next_coroutine** to start executing, and this function to pause and wait. It waits until **next_coroutine** pauses, at which point the function resumes by sending the next word, or exiting with the message Done.

By continuing in the Thonny Shell area as follows, we're joining the **read** function together in a pipeline with the function **grepper**, thus creating a program that allows us to print out only the words that match a particular word.

```
>>> text = "0110 1100 0101 1000 1010 0111 1111 0001 0110"
>>> found = grepper('01')
>>> next(found)
Looking for 01
>>> read(text, found)
0110
0101
1010
0111
0001
0110
Done
>>>
```

The **read** function sends each word to the coroutine **grepper**, which prints out any input that matches its template pattern. Within the **grepper** coroutine, the line x = (yield) waits for each word sent, and it transfers control back to **read** when it is reached.

In-Chapter Exercises

30.

    (a) Put the code from Example 2.22 into a file (if you have not done so already), and using Thonny and Way 3 (Import Script Mode), invoke the coroutines **grepper** and **read** on the template "1201".

    (b) Then search the following string using that template: "0120 1201 1020", "3012 3013 3212", "12010203101213012".

    (c) What prints out on your screen when you use the proper commands, similarly to what is shown in the follow-up code to the **read** function?

31.

    (a) Put the code from Example 2.22 in a file (if you have not done so already), and using Thonny and Way 3 (Import Script Mode), invoke the coroutine **read** on the template "Python is the most Pythonic enterprise a Pythonista can practice".

    (b) Then search for the string "Python" in that template using the coroutines **grepper** and **read**.

    (c) What prints out on your screen when you use the proper commands, similarly to what is shown in the follow-up code to the **read** function?

2.4.14 Exceptions

It's worth noting that there are some very useful facilities in Thonny that can help you to debug your program or script in a "trial run", step-by-step fashion. Usually these facilities are a part of a Python IDE, or any high level language-capable IDE.

A good example of one of these facilities that we've seen in Thonny is automatic indentation. Another is Thonny's interactive step-by-step debugging tools, which are seen as icons in the Toolbar. We don't show the use of the debugging icons, but encourage you to play around with them while any of the script files in this chapter is active in Thonny's Script Area.

With that said, within the language itself, and its syntactic structures, an exception, or unexpected end to a program, is a Python3 object that represents an error. To terminate the flow of execution of a program because of some exception the interpreter has found, Python3 has two kinds of exception-handling structure that can end the program. These structures are:

1. Exception handling tht uses for example **try:...except:...else:** as shown in Example 2.23 below, and the standard exception, for example, **StopIteration**.

2   Assertions, for example using the **assert** statement.

The general form of **try:...except:...else:** is:

```
try:
    Some operations...
    ...
except ExceptionI:
    If there is an Exception, do this...
else:
    If there is no Exception then, do this...
```

The following is a simple exception test example, which, when run in the Thonny Script Area by clicking on the Run Toolbar icon, opens a new file in the current working directory, writes some content to the file, and then exits normally.

Example 2.23

```
try:
    handler = open("datafile", "w")
    handler.write("This is a data file for testing exception handling!!")
except IOError:
    print ("Error: Can\'t find file or write data")
else:
    print ("File write successful")
    handler.close()
```

```
>>> %Run -c $EDITOR_CONTENT
File write successful
>>>
```

In-Chapter Exercises

32. List five other standard exceptions, what general class of exception they signal, and what source you used to obtain their names.
33. Modify the code of Example 2.23 so that it writes the integers 1, 2, 3, 4, 5, 6, 7, 8, 9, and 10 as a string list to the file named **datafile2**.

2.4.15 Modules, Global and Local Scope in Functions

At a certain level of abstraction, everything in Python3 is a module, even Python3 itself! A Python3 module is a container, or package, which holds all the hierarchical objects, statements, expressions, and other modular components we spoke about at the beginning of this chapter, that are necessary to accomplish an intended task, or sub-task. Modules may contain function definitions, class operations, and variable assignments. Basically, there are only two types of Python3 module: a module written by you, or a module from some external library, like the Python standard library. The standard library that is built into Python3 contains over 200 modules, and there are many other module resources available online that a programmer can use so that she does not have to "reinvent the wheel", so to speak.

A schematic diagram of the modular construction of a possible Python program is as follows:

Python shell --->
   First Module.py --->
      Second Module.py, etc. --->
         Standard Library >>> **commands**
                   <---**objects** --->**results**

The following example, using the code in Example 2.5 above, shows the composition and use of a module, which happens to be a function, that you create.

If you have not already done so, type the code from into a file named **arith1. py** using your favorite text editor (or rename **math1.py** as **arith1.py**). Then type the following lines of Python code at the Python command line:

Example 2.24

```
Python 3.9.2 (/usr/bin/python3)
>>> import arith1
>>> A = arith1.add(3.5,4.2)
>>> B = A + arith1.subtract(14.78,20.45)
>>> C = arith1.multiply(B,5.0)
>>> D = arith1.divide(A,C)
>>> D
>>>
```

Notice these things about Example 2.24's code:

1. You use **import**, rather than **from...import**.
2. The methods in **arith1** are addressed, or "touched", by referencing the general syntactic form **arith1.function_name**. For example, by applying the method **arith1.add**.

In-Chapter Exercises

34. After doing Example 2.24, what result do you get if you type **b** on the Python3 command line, and why?
35. After doing Example 2.24, type **del arith1** on the Thonny Shell Area command line. Then type **D = arith1.divide(A,C)** and press <Enter> on the keyboard. What result do you get, and why?
36. Edit the file **arith1.py**, and comment out all of the return statements in the functions. Then, redo the commands shown in Example 2.24. What is **D** equal to then, and why?

A simple example of a library module from the standard library that you can import, and use to execute Raspberry Pi OS commands is given next. Type in the commands shown on the Thonny Shell Area command line (the output results given in the example may differ from what you see on your screen, depending on the specific content in the targeted directory of your system):

Example 2.25

```
>>> import os
>>> File = os.popen('pwd')
>>> File.read(50)
'/home/bob/Public\n'
>>> for line in os.popen('ls -la f*'): print(line.rstrip()) #Press Enter twice!
...
-rw-r--r-- 1 bob bob 421 Jun 10 06:47 firstclass.py
>>>
```

2.5 Practical Examples

To begin this section, it would be helpful for you to read and try to get some familiarity with the following two references in the Python online documentation for the release of Python you are using. With the purpose of getting a better "top-down" overview of how Python is structured.

1. *The Python Language Reference*— *https://docs.python.org/3/reference/*
2. Python standard library, particularly the **sys** and **os** modules.

In the previous sections of this chapter, we provided an overview of the Python3 language and its syntax via the writing and execution of small (1–25 line) script files and functions. In this section, we will detail some of Python3's practical applications in real-world computer programming with larger (25–50 line) user-written modules, functions, and scripts.

As mentioned in Section 2.3.7, Python3 can be used to accomplish tasks revolving around shell scripting, systems programming, network and Internet scripting, database programming, systems administration scripting, GUI scripting, scientific and math programming, and data mining.

We will begin by writing script files in Python3 that accomplish what Raspberry Pi OS shell scripts accomplish, with the goal of familiarizing you with some simple practical applications of Python3.

2.5.1 Another Way of Writing Shell Script Files

In this section, we do *not* go over the basics of shell scripting, but provide methods and practical examples (including the rewriting of shell scripts) of how to accomplish what shell scripting accomplishes, using Python3 language syntax and structure. The advantages of using Python3 are that it is a more robust and extensible language, with many more features and capabilities than any of the usual scripting languages, like Bash, Tcsh, or csh. One of these features is Python3 OOP, which Bash and Tcsh scripts are *not* capable of.

2.5.1.1 Rewriting Bash and Tcsh Scripts

We start with a simple example of a Bash shell script rewritten in Python3. The Bash shell script to print out whether a certain directory path exists on our file system or not is given first, and then its Python equivalent, is shown in Example 2.26. You should run both, using Way 4 (Bash Mode) for the Python3 code, and run the Bash script on the Raspberry Pi command line in a terminal. Shown below are these code samples; you should note the comparative output on your system.

Example 2.26

Bash script code

```
#!/bin/bash
if [-d "/usr/bin"]; then
    echo "/usr/bin is a directory"
else
    echo "/usr/bin is not a directory"
fi
```

Equivalent Python code

```
#!/usr/bin/python3
import os
if os.path.isdir("/usr/bin"):
    print ("/usr/bin is a directory")
else:
    print ("/usr/bin is not a directory")
```

On our Raspberry Pi system, using Python 3.9.2, we executed the Python3 code equivalent using a variation of the alternative method of Way 4 (Bash Mode). In our nano text editor, we created and named the Python equivalent **ex26.py**. We obtained the following output (remember to make the Python equivalent executable using the **chmod u+x** command!):

```
$ ./ex26.py
```
/usr/bin is a directory
$

The important thing to notice about the above Python3 code, and its execution, is that:

1. A standard library module named **os** is imported at the top of the script file.
2. **os.path** is a nested module that provides directory and pathname tools, in addition to those tools in the **os** standard library module.

In-Chapter Exercises

37. Give the exact syntax you used on the Bash command line to run the Bash shell script shown in Example 2.26.
38. Referring to the online documentation, what other **os** module from the standard library can be used to achieve the same thing as the Python3 code in Example 2.26?
39. Edit the Python3 code for Example 2.26, and substitute the path **/usr/bin/yyy** for **/usr/bin**. What output from the program do you get when you run it after making this change?

Another simple example of a Bash shell script converted to Python is as follows. Again, we ran the Python3 script using Way 4 (Bash Mode).

Example 2.27

Bash script code

```
#!/bin/bash
echo "Enter input: \c"
read line
echo "You entered: $line"
echo "Enter another line: \c"
read word1 word2 word3
echo "The first word is: $word1:"
echo "The second word is: $word2:"
echo "The rest of the line is: $word3:"
exit 0
```

Equivalent Python code

```
#!/usr/bin/python3
import sys
s = input("Enter input:")
print ("You entered:", s)
r = input("Enter another line:")
words = r.split()
print ("The first word is:", words[0])
print ("The second word is:", words[1])
rest = (r.join(words[2:]))
print ("The rest of the line is:", rest)
sys.exit() #normal exit status
```

On our Raspberry Pi system, using Python 3.9.2, we ran the Python code equivalent, using Way 4 (Bash Mode). We named the Python3 equivalent **ex27.py**. We obtained the following output, with the supplied text shown (remember to make the Python3 equivalent executable using the **chmod u+x** command!):

```
$ ./ex27.py
Enter input: Linux rules!
You entered: Linux rules!
Enter another line: Raspberry Pi rules!
The first word is: Raspberry
The second word is: Pi
The rest of the line is: rules!
Process ended with exit code 0.
$
```

In-Chapter Exercises

40. Give two examples of list indexing or slicing used in Example 2.27.

41. Give two examples of string methods from Example 2.27.

The following is another illustration of taking a Bash shell script and converting it to Python3.

Example 2.28

Bash script code

```
#!/bin/bash
echo "The command name is: $0."
echo "The value of the command line arguments are: $1 $2 $3 $4 $5 $6 $7 $8 $9."
```

```
echo "Another way to display values of all the arguments: $@."
echo "Yet another way is: $*."
exit 0
```

Python code

```
#!/usr/bin/python3
import sys
x = (sys.argv)
print ("The command name is: ", sys.argv[0])
print ("The value of the command line arguments are: ", x[1:10])
print ("Another way to display values of all the arguments: ", sys.argv[1:])
print ("Yet another way is: ", sys.argv[slice(1,15)])
sys.exit ()
```

On our Raspberry Pi system, using the default Bash shell and Python 3.9.2, we ran both the Example 2.28 Bash script code, and its Python3 code equivalent (using Way 4 [Bash Mode]). We named the Bash version **ex28.bash**, and the Python3 equivalent **ex28.py**. We obtained the following output, with the argument lists shown (remember to make the Bash script file and its Python equivalent executable using the **chmod u+x** command before you run these commands!):

$ **./ex28.bash a b c d e f g h i j k l m n**
The command name is: ./ex28.bash.
The value of the command line arguments are: a b c d e f g h i.
Another way to display values of all the arguments: a b c d e f g h i j k l m n.
Yet another way is: a b c d e f g h i j k l m n.
$

$ **./ex28.py a b c d e f g h i j k l m n**
The command name is: ./ex28.py.
The value of the command line arguments are: ['a', 'b', 'c', 'd', 'e', 'f', 'g', 'h', 'i']
Another way to display values of all the arguments: ['a', 'b', 'c', 'd', 'e', 'f', 'g', 'h', 'i', 'j', 'k', 'l', 'm', 'n']
Yet another way is: ['a', 'b', 'c', 'd', 'e', 'f', 'g', 'h', 'i', 'j', 'k', 'l', 'm', 'n']
$

Similar to the Bash shell in syntax and structure, the Tcsh shell has functional capabilities that can be implemented easily in Python3. The following is a Tcsh script file, whose syntactic structure and program functionality are converted to a Python3 script file that you should run using Way 4 (Bash Mode), similar to the above examples in this section:

Example 2.29

Tcsh shell code

```tcsh
#!/bin/tcsh
if (($#argv == 0) || ($#argv > 1)) then
    echo "Usage: $0 ordinary_file"
    exit 1
endif
if (-f $1) then
    set filename = $argv[1]
    set fileinfo = `ls -il $filename`
    set inode = $fileinfo[1]
    set size = $fileinfo[6]
    echo "File Name:   $filename"
    echo "Inode Number:   $inode"
    echo "Size (bytes):   $size"
    exit 0
else
    echo "$0: argument must be an ordinary file"
    exit 1
endif
```

Python code

```python
#!/usr/bin/python3
import os
import sys
if len(sys.argv) == 1 or len(sys.argv) > 2: #check for no/too many args
    print ("Usage: ", sys.argv[0], " ordinary file")
    sys.exit(1)
if os.path.isfile(sys.argv[1]): #bingo, get stats
    filename = sys.argv[1]
    fileinfo = os.stat(filename)
    print ("Filename inode size")
    print (" ")
    print (filename, fileinfo.st_ino, fileinfo.st_size)
    sys.exit(0)
else:                       # argument must something else!
    print (sys.argv[1], " argument must be an ordinary file")
    sys.exit(1)
```

On our Raspberry Pi system, we ran the Python3 code equivalent using Way 4 (Bash Mode). We named the Python3 equivalent **ex29.py**. We obtained the following output, where there was a file named **ex29.py** in the current working directory, but *no* file named **lab1** (remember to make the Bash script file and its Python equivalent executable using the **chmod u+x** command!):

```
$ chmod u+x ex29.py
$ ./ex29.py
Usage: ./ex29.py ordinary file
$ ./ex29.py lab1
lab1 argument must be an ordinary file
$ ./ex29.py ex29.py
Filename inode size

ex29.py 12452180 572
$
```

2.5.2 A Basic Web Server and User File Maintenance

A very useful, and practical example of using built-in Python3 capabilities on your Raspberry Pi system is the **http.server** module, that comes standard with Python3. The value of using this module, at least for an ordinary user of a Raspberry Pi system, is that you can quickly and easily implement a system service that can be programmed, configured, and controlled by that ordinary user.

Another very useful, and important aspect of an ordinary user's interaction with a Raspberry Pi system, that we cover in Section 2.3.2.2, is how effectively you can maintain the files on your system. The Python3 standard library, and many user-written libraries and modules, can help you do this efficiently on the Raspberry Pi OS. You can utilize the extensive syntax, and the multi-paradigm programming capabilities of Python3, to go far beyond the capabilities of doing operating system and file maintenance that are available in any of the shell script-creation programs.

User file maintenance consists of creating, saving, organizing, and deleting files on your system, in your own account, or globally for the entire system and its users.

2.5.2.1 Web Server Example

In this section we show an ordinary user how to create and use a web server, using a built-in Python3 module.

Example 2.30

A Simple Web Server Implemented in Python3.

The SimpleHTTPServer module that comes with Python3 is a simple HTTP server that provides standard GET and HEAD request handlers. An advantage of using the Python3 built-in HTTP server is that you don't have to install

and configure anything! The only thing that you need is to have Python3 installed on your system, which it is by default on our Raspberry Pi OS.
Step 1. To start an HTTP server on port 8000 (which is the default port), type the command:

$ python3 -m SimpleHTTPServer
Serving HTTP on 0.0.0.0 port 8000 (http://0.0.0.0:8000/) ...

This will serve files and directories to a browser, whose URL is set to your IP address (in the case of the above command, this is 0.0.0.0) and port 8000, where the files and directories are located in the current working directory when you typed the above command.

You can also change the port to some other valid port number, for instance 8096, by typing this command:

$ python3 -m SimpleHTTPServer 8096

Step 2. To share other files and directories on your network, or the Internet, in a terminal, change the current directory with the **cd** command into whichever directory you wish to have accessible via browsers and HTTP. For example:

$ cd /home/bsystebex

$ python3 -m SimpleHTTPServer
Serving HTTP on 0.0.0.0 port 8000 (http://0.0.0.0:8000/) ...
127.0.0.1 - - [11/Jun/2023 12:06:1"] "GET / HTTP/".1" 2–0 -
127.0.0.1 - - [11/Jun/2023 12:06:11] code 404, message File not found
127.0.0.1 - - [11/Jun/2023 12:06:1"] "GET /favicon.ico HTTP/".1" 4–4 -

Output truncated ...

Step 3. Then in a web browser on your Raspberry Pi system, put in either of the following two addresses:

http://your_ip_address:8000

or to the localhost:

http://127.0.0.1:8000

If you 'on't have a valid index.html file in the current working directory, then all files and directories in /home/bsystebex will be listed. If there's a valid index.html file systebex above (which in our case, there is), you will see the content of that index.html page displayed in the web browser. As long as the Python3 HTTP server is running, the terminal will update with messages as they are loaded from the server. These messages will be standard http logging information (GET and PUSH), 404 errors, IP addresses, dates, times, and a subset of the journal messages.

To terminate the Python HTTP server, in the terminal you launched it from, type **<Ctrl> + C**

```
^C
Keyboard interrupt received, exiting.
$
```

In-Chapter Exercise

42. Use the steps shown in Example 2.30 to implement and test a basic web server on your Raspberry Pi system. What security issues might arise if you have not deployed firewalls, or taken other preventative measures on your Internet-connected Raspberry Pi?

2.5.2.2 Backing Up Your Files

We will not go into the general necessity of backing up your files on your Raspberry Pi system as a part of maintaining that computer system, because the reasons for doing that should be pretty obvious to even novice users. According to Linux system professionals, there is an easy-to-remember and important set of considerations you have to make when backing up the system as an ordinary user, and perhaps even as the system administrator. This set of considerations can be posed in simple question form as "How, What, Why, When, Where, and Who?" Some of the answers to these simple questions can be dovetailed together, and we give a selected list of example answers as follows:

"How" means on the boot/system medium, to Dropbox, to a USB thumb drive manually, to another computer on your home network, automatically by *cron, systemd,* or ZFS, to another USB3-connected medium manually, totally, incrementally, via RAID, or any variant and combination of all of these.

"What" means just some of your personal files, all of them, only certain kinds of documents, your entire home directory, the whole boot/system medium, multiple external media, and so on.

"Why" means deciding on the relative importance of "What" you are backing up.

"When" means every five minutes, hourly, once a day, once a week, once a month, every time you save a particular file, and at what time exactly, like AM.

"Where" means very much the same thing as "How".

"Who" means you personally, automatically by cron, systemd, or ZFS, the designated system administrator, Dropbox.com, or some other commercial backup agent.

To give you a notion of a prudent strategy to deploy in backing up your own user files, the file that contains the words you are reading right now was archived in the following manner:

1. Saved at regular intervals to an SSD, which served as the boot/system medium on a Raspberry Pi 400.

2. Saved periodically to an externally mounted USB3 thumb drive mounted on that same Raspberry Pi 400.

3. Saved periodically to another Raspberry Pi 4B attached to the local area network.

We will use the **rsync** command to accomplish our backup strategies in this section. This command is similar to the **cp** and **rcp** commands, except that it is more efficient and faster.

Most importantly, **rsync** "synchronizes" two files or directory structures so that changes in one are reflected in the **rsync** duplicate, either locally between mounted media, or remotely over a local area network (LAN) or the Internet.

It can copy locally or to/from another host over any remote shell, particularly **ssh**. It has a large number of options that control every aspect of its behavior and permits very flexible specification of the set of files to be copied. The **rsync** command finds files that need to be transferred using a "quick check" algorithm (by default) that looks for files that have changed in size or in last-modified time. We encourage you to consult the **rsync** man page for more information.

The general forms of the **rsync** command are:

Local:

rsync [OPTION(S)...] SRC... [DEST]

Across a network:

Pull: rsync [OPTION(S)...] [USER@]HOST:SRC... [DEST]
Push: rsync [OPTION(S)...] SRC... [USER@]HOST:DEST

where **OPTION(S)** are the valid options for the **rsync** command, **SRC** is the source file or directory, and **DEST** is the destination path.

The next five examples will use Python3 standard library modules, and embed Bash shell commands in a Python "wrapper" (Linux shell command(s) embedded in Python code). The examples primarily use the Python3 **os. system** module to:

1. Back up a single file on the system medium to a mounted USB thumb drive.

2. Back up a single directory beneath your home directory on the system medium to a directory on a mounted USB thumb drive.

3. Back up a single directory beneath your home directory on the system medium to another network location on your LAN in **Push** mode.

4. Back up a directory on the system medium to a mounted USB thumb drive in a rolling, incremental scheme, that creates "snapshots" of the source directory anytime the Python3 script is run.

5. Customize a system command to show permissions of files in the current working directory that match a certain pattern.

The following simple example shows you how to use Thonny and Python3 to back up a single file on your system medium to a USB thumb drive you mounted and attached to your file system . It assumes you have an ordinary file in the current working directory named **ex28.bash**, and that the destination path on the USB thumb drive is **/media/bob/7C87-8F1D**. That path on your Raspberry Pi system will be different.

Example 2.31

```
>>>import os
>>>os.system('rsync -av ex28.bash /media/bob/7C87-8F1D')
sending incremental file list
ex28.bash

sent 331 bytes received 35 bytes 104.57 bytes/sec
total size is 225 speedup is 0.61
0
>>>
```

The following example shows you how to use Thonny and Python3 to back up an entire directory on your system medium to the USB thumb drive you have mounted and attached to your system. It assumes that Thonny's current working directory has a subdirectory named __pycache__, and that the destination path on the USB thumb drive is /media/bob/7C87-8F1D .

Example 2.32

```
>>>import os
>>>os.system('rsync -av __pycache__ /media/bob/7C87-8F1D')
sending incremental file list
__pycache__/
__pycache__/grepper.cpython-39.pyc
```

```
__pycache__/looper.cpython-39.pyc
__pycache__/looper2.cpython-39.pyc
```

```
sent 1,103 bytes received 77 bytes 2,360.00 bytes/sec
total size is 782 speedup is 0.66
0
>>>
```

The following example shows you how to use Python3 to back up an entire directory on your boot/system medium to a remote location on your local area network. It assumes:

0. You will execute Python3 on the Bash command line.
1. You have the **ssh** daemon running on both your local and remote host, and that you have successfully logged into the remote host and previously exchanged keys between local and remote host.
2. You have a directory under the current working directory named __ **pycache__**, with some files in it
3. Where a password is asked for, you type in your password on the *remote* host
4. That the destination path to the remote host is **bob@192.168.1.7:/home/ bob**

Example 2.33

```
$ python3
Python 3.9.2 (default, Feb 28 2021, 17:03:44)
[GCC 10.2.1 20210110] on linux
Type "help", "copyright", "credits" or "license" for more information.
>>>import os
>>>os.system('rsync -av __pycache__ bob@192.168.1.7:/home/bob')
bob@192.168.1.7's password: zzz
sending incremental file list
__pycache__/
__pycache__/grepper.cpython-39.pyc
__pycache__/looper.cpython-39.pyc
__pycache__/looper2.cpython-39.pyc
```

```
sent 1,103 bytes received 77 bytes 214.55 bytes/sec
total size is 782 speedup is 0.66
>>>
```

In-Chapter Exercise

43. Repeat the operations shown in Examples 2.31 through 2.33, substituting file names and directory paths on your computer system and local network for those shown in the examples. When backing up files to a USB thumb drive is finished, be sure to **unmount** that drive before removing it from the USB connector on your machine. Unless you want to use it again in Example 2.34 below.

The following example shows you how to create a rolling backup scheme of "snapshots" of a directory on your hard disk, and archive the contents of the directory to multiple (five) backup directories on a USB thumb drive you mounted and attached to your Raspberry Pi system. It is assumed that the source directory, containing some files, already exists. Every time you execute this Python3 script, it recycles (in other words, deletes) the oldest (fifth) archived directory, and creates a new full backup, using the **rsync** command. You should use a text editor to create the file below, and then to execute it, run Python3 on the Bash command line (as you did in Example 2.33 above). The destination path on our USB thumb drive is seen in the code for this Example as **/media/bob/7C87-8F1D**:

Example 2.34

```
#!/usr/bin/python3
import os
import shutil
target = "/media/bob/7C87-8F1D/"
i = 1
while i <= 5:
    temp_path = target + str(i) + "/"
    if not os.path.exists (temp_path):
        try:
            os.makedirs (temp_path)
            print ("Created " + temp_path)
        except:
            print (" Could not create " + temp_path)
    i = i + 1
print ("Deleting the oldest archive")
shutil.rmtree (target + "5")
print ("Recycle the backups")
os.rename (target + "4", target + "5")
os.rename (target + "3", target + "4")
os.rename (target + "2", target + "3")
```

```
os.system('cp -a ' + target + "1" + " " + target + "2")
os.system('rsync -av __pycache__' + " " + target + "1")
```

When we ran the code from Example 2.34 on our Raspberry Pi system for the first time, using the pathnames to the source directory for the backup, and the USB drive, as shown in the code, we got the following output:

$ **python3 ex34.py**
Created /media/bob/7C87-8F1D/1/
Created /media/bob/7C87-8F1D/2/
Created /media/bob/7C87-8F1D/3/
Created /media/bob/7C87-8F1D/4/
Created /media/bob/7C87-8F1D/5/
Deleting the oldest archive
Recycle the backups
sending incremental file list
__pycache__/
__pycache__/grepper.cpython-39.pyc
__pycache__/looper.cpython-39.pyc
__pycache__/looper2.cpython-39.pyc

sent 1,103 bytes received 77 bytes 2,360.00 bytes/sec
total size is 782 speedup is 0.66
$

Here is another example (the code of which we named **ex35.py**) of carrying out simple system administration, in this case using Python 2.7.12. It customizes a shell command to show permissions set on files in the current working directory that match a certain pattern:

Example 2.35

```
#!/usr/bin/python
import stat, sys, os, string, commands
try:
    #Getting search pattern from user and assigning it to a list
    pattern = raw_input("Enter the file pattern to search for:\n")
    #defining a 'find' string and assigning results to a variable
    commandString = "find " + pattern
    commandOutput = commands.getoutput(commandString)
    findResults = string.split(commandOutput, "\n")
    #output find results, along with permissions
    print "Files:"
    print commandOutput
    print "**********************************"
```

```
    for file in findResults:
        mode=stat.S_IMODE(os.lstat(file)[stat.ST_MODE])
        print "\nPermissions for file ", file, ":"
        for level in "USR", "GRP", "OTH":
            for perm in "R", "W", "X":
                if mode & getattr(stat,"S_I"+perm+level):
                    print level, " has ", perm, " permission"
                else:
                    print level, " does NOT have ", perm, "permission"
except:
    print "Error - check your input of file matching pattern"
```

When we ran Example **ex35.py** on our Raspberry Pi system, using Python 2.7.12, using the input shown, we got the following results:

$ python ex35.py
Enter the file pattern to search for:
*.py
Files:
2_1.py
2_16.py
2_17.py

****

Permissions for file 2_1.py:
USR has R permission
USR has W permission
USR does NOT have X permission
GRP has R permission
GRP does NOT have W permission
GRP does NOT have X permission
OTH has R permission
OTH does NOT have W permission
OTH does NOT have X permission

Output truncated...

We present a problem at the end of this chapter, Problem 2.16, that asks you to convert this Python 2.7 script file into a Python3 script file.

In summary, we used the **rsync** command to backup a file and directories from the system medium to a USB thumb drive, to a remote host on the local network, and in a rolling scheme to a USB thumb drive. We have also illustrated, using Python 2.7.12, a simple file maintenance command useful for system administration.

2.5.3 Graphical User Interfaces with Python3 and tkinter Widgets

Up until this point in the chapter, we have interacted with Python3 via a graphical IDE, basically in a text-based manner, where we typed commands into Thonny's Script or Shell Areas, or into a text editor, and executed Python 3.9.2 to view the output results as text. In this section, we will build a "widget"-based (widget is short for window gadget) GUI with Python3, where we still create the Python3 code as text, but see the resulting output of the Python3 script in the form of widget graphics. We use tkinter as the GUI interface, or toolkit. tkinter is an abbreviation for the "TK interface". And "TK", which is short for "toolkit", is a platform independent, customizable, and configurable GUI library. The Python module tkinter allows Python programs to interface with the TK libraries, to produce pictures, and other forms of graphics, on the display of the Raspberry Pi.

To accomplish this, we assume the following:

1. That you are using a GUI, desktop environment to interact with your Raspberry Pi system. After all, that's what Thonny is! A graphical IDE. Therefore, we also have a GUI capability when we program with tkinter to create Python GUI's.

2. That you have Python3.X on your Raspberry Pi system. The command line sessions, In-Chapter Exercises, examples, and questions and problems found in this, and in the following sections of the chapter, all require that you have at least a late version of Python3 installed on your Linux system.

Our coverage of GUI construction with tkinter uses Python 3.9.2, and the appropriate tkinter module for those versions of Python. Depending upon the default Python3.X you are using, and given the specific Raspberry Pi OS distribution you are executing it on, the tkinter installation instructions may vary slightly from what is shown in Section 2.3.3.1 below, but basically it will be the same.

2.5.3.1 Installing tkinter

The standard widget GUI package that works with Python3 is named tkinter in Python3.X. For you to add widget GUI components and functionality to Python, you must be able to import this component package into your Python3 session.

In this section, as much as is possible and practical given the Python3 GUI scripts we show, we add widgets from a "styled" widget set. These were available since TK version 8.5, and are named ttk widgets.

You can easily test to see if your default Python system has tkinter available. On the Python command line, type:

```
>>> import tkinter
```

If you get an error message that the module does not exist, or some similar error message, then you must install the tkinter package. To accomplish this, use the **apt** command on the Bash command line as follows:

```
$ sudo apt-get install python3-tk
```

You may also have to install the required Tcl/Tk development packages with the following command:

```
$ sudo apt-get install tk-dev
```

Then the Python build system will be enabled and build the Tkinter extension for your version of Python3. (If you've built a later version of Python3 than the one installed by default on your Raspberry Pi OS, you need to run the **configure** and **make** commands again, as was show in Section 2.3.8.1 above.)

When we ran the install of tk-dev on our system, the latest version of those development tools was already installed, but we re-ran the **configure** and **make** commands again anyway, so that the latest version of Python3, Python 3.11.3, had access to tkinter.

2.5.3.2 tkinter Toolkit Graphical User Interfaces

A GUI allows you to use a mouse, or other pointing device (such as your finger on a tablet), rather than just the keyboard, to interact with programs that are running. Generally when you use a CUI, such as during a Bash shell session, and you execute a command, the tasks that command accomplishes do so in some structured order, either in a determinate (counting-wise) or indeterminate (logic-wise) manner. Then the command eventually terminates. But the Python3 GUI programs we show in this section create screen widgets that are displayed on screen, and then the Python3 script that generates the icons and widgets "waits" for the user to do something with them.

This kind of programming structure is event-driven. *GUI programs, partcularly in X windows graphics systems, are event-driven.* We emphasize that kind of programming structure in the examples and descriptions we provide below.

A meaningful and useful Python3-scripted GUI program generally always has some form of this basic content and structure:

1. Data of some sort is produced, or already exists, for example, in the form of numbers, or database text on the Raspberry Pi. This data itself can be generated in a variety of ways. It could be generated by Python3 user-written modules placed before the GUI-constructing

components in a Python3 script, which is the style of Python3 GUI programming shown in all of our examples. It could also be input interactively while the Python3 GUI script is running. It could use preexisting data generated beforehand by some other application, or it could even use a C program that generates data within the Python3 environment, while the Python3 script is executing!

2. Widgets are created, and are organized within some encompassing window frame, and then displayed on screen to the user. These widget objects are instances of master widget classes in tkinter, and contain GUI functions that are selected for, and specify particular kinds of responses to user input, and possible data-generating application events.

3. There is a "hooking", or tying together, of the instances from Step 2 that utilize "callback" GUI functions to access the data you want to display, or otherwise modify. For example, you can use any "callable" Python3 object as a callback. These might be ordinary Python3 functions, bound methods, lambda expressions, and any other callable object.

This is the most critical, and therefore the most useful aspect, of Python GUI programming.

4. Steps 2 and 3 exist inside of an infinite event-driven loop, that processes user events. When a user event, such as a mouse button press, occurs, the event-driven loop invokes the function associated with a specific event.

5. Data is modified or produced with no apparent visible change on screen, or with graphical changes occurring on screen. This is the "request" step.

6. The loop continues to wait for events, and process them, until a possible termination event happens.

As we present in Section 2.5.3.3 next, tkinter widgets can be chosen and constructed to display and be hooked up to data using OOP, where the widgets are object instances of master classes of tkinter widgets. But the style and execution of the Python3 GUI script file itself can take on a procedural/imperative programming model approach. We choose, as much as possible, to show the procedural/imperative approach because we feel it's easier for beginners to understand, and figure out; particularly people who are *not* familiar with the OOP model of programming. Python3 does *not* have core modules that implement GUI, event-driven-programming. GUI programming is implemented using imported modules, such as those from the tkinter toolkit.

To summarize the above steps, a user presses a mouse button to signify a graphical "pick" in a widget, within an encompassing tkinter-produced frame shown on-screen. That choice, or "event", is recognized by, and acted upon by the tkinter function controlling that widget. This event may generate a "request" for graphical service, and this request displays the data or graphics within the tkinter frame. A very similar situation is present in the X window System Event-Request Model.

2.5.3.2.1 Non-Event Driven tkinter

That brings up some interesting questions: What kind of graphics is *not* event driven, and what apps or programs accomplish this way of displaying data? Basically static, non-interactive forms of computer graphics. Can you name any of those? And, is tkinter able to do this form of non-event driven processing, and exactly how?

Well, here's an answer to that last question.
As we've noted, tkinter is primarily designed for event-driven graphics programming, where the program responds to user input or system events. However, you can also create non-event driven graphics using tkinter by using a technique called "animation loops".

In a non-event driven program, you need to create your own loop that continuously updates the graphical elements.

Here's a basic example of how you can create a non-event driven graphical program using tkinter:

```
import tkinter as tk
def update_graphics():
    # Update your graphical elements here
    # This function will be called repeatedly in the main loop
    # Example: Move a shape on a canvas
    canvas.move(shape, 1, 0)
    # Schedule the next update
    root.after(10, update_graphics) # Update every 10 milliseconds
root = tk.Tk()
canvas = tk.Canvas(root, width=400, height=400)
canvas.pack()
# Create a shape on the canvas
shape = canvas.create_rectangle(50, 50, 100, 100, fill='red')
# Start the update loop
update_graphics()
root.mainloop()
```

In the above example, the **update_graphics()** function is called repeatedly using the **root.after()** method, which schedules a function to be called after a specified delay (in milliseconds). Inside the **update_graphics()** function, you can update your graphical elements as needed. In this case, the example moves a rectangle on a canvas by calling the **canvas.move()** method.

By adjusting the delay passed to **root.after()**, you can control the speed of the updates. Smaller delays result in faster updates and smoother animation, but they can also consume more system resources.

Keep in mind that tkinter is not optimized for high-performance graphics or animations! For more complex or demanding graphics, you might consider using specialized libraries or frameworks such as Pygame or OpenGL.

2.5.3.3 Basic Widget Construction Techniques

Widgets are constructed images on the screen display, and they have a unique "style", depending on the details of what information, and kind of interactivity you want them to participate in. The "style" of a widget is controlled by many complex graphical components: the X Window System, the display manager used, and the operating system itself. The tkinter module contains two versions of widgets: a default, or "generic version", which makes widgets look the same regardless of what windowing system, operating system, or display manager is running. tkinter also implements widgets that emulate a particular windowing system, operating system, or display manager's "style". Which tkinter modules you import determines which widget sets are available to generate events and "callbacks". The standard way of doing this uses the module tk to access the "generic" widgets, and the module ttk to access the "styled" widgets. You *must* import the tk module, because it allows you to create a "root", or outer-most frame window. You optionally import the ttk module if you want the "styled" widgets.

Note

As is done in some of the following examples, you can use both the tk and ttk widgets in a GUI Python3 script file.

To use the "generic" widgets, include the following **import** statement at the top of the Python3 script file:

import tkinter as tk
or:
import tkinter

To use the "styled" widgets, include the following **import** statement at the top of the Python3 script file:

from tkinter import ttk

The following two tables list the standard, pre-defined widgets in the tkinter module.

TABLE 2.6

tkinter, tk, and ttk Input Widgets

Widget Name in tk and ttk	Function
tk.Button, ttk.Button	Display a button to execute some operation
tk.Menu	Produce a top-level pulldown or popup menu.
ttk.Menubutton	Display a popup or pulldown menu of buttons
tk.OptionMenu	Display a popup menu, and a button to activate it
tk.Entry, ttk.Entry	Enter one line of text in an object
tk.Text	Display and edit formatted multi-line text
tk.Checkbutton, ttk. Checkbutton	Display on–off, or True–False selections in an object
tk.Radiobutton, ttk. Radiobutton	Display on–off selections in an object
tk.Listbox	Display one or more alternatives from a list of choices
ttk.Combobox	Display a text field with a pulldown list of values
ttk.Notebook	Manage a collection of windows and display a single one at a time
tk.Scale, ttk.Scale	Allow selection of a numerical value via a "slider" on a scale

TABLE 2.7

tkinter, tk, and ttk Information Display Widgets

Widget Name in tk and ttk	Function
tk.Label, ttk.Label	Display a fixed text string, or image
tk.Message	Display a fixed multi-line text string
ttk.Separator	Display a horizontal or vertical separator line
ttk.Progressbar	Show the relative progress of some operation
ttk.Treeview	Display a hierarchy of items as a tree

The widgets listed in Table 2.6 are used for user input. You can choose between the tk and ttk widgets. But sometimes you must use the tk version because the equivalent ttk versions don't exist.

The widgets in Table 2.7 display information, but don't allow any user interaction.

When we wrote this book, we found out the version of the tk toolkit by using the following commands in Python Version 3.9.2 running on our Raspberry Pi system:

```
$ python3
Python 3.9.2 (default, Feb 28 2021, 17:03:44)
[GCC 10.2.1 20210110] on linux
Type "help", "copyright", "credits" or "license" for more information.
>>> import tkinter
```

>>> tkinter.TkVersion
8.6
>>>

At the time we wrote this book, the best source of documentation for tkinter could be found at the following URL:

https://docs.python.org/3/library/tk.html

2.5.3.4 General Form of a Widget Call and a Primary Example

As shown in Section 2.5.3.2, there are several parts to tkinter widget GUI script file construction, but the basic parts follow this outline:

1. Generating data.
2. Constructing your widgets, using a set of universal constructor tools and the tkinter widget method set.
3. "Hooking" the data of the first part to the widget constructors of the second part, all within the context of an infinite (but indeterminately interrupted) event-loop.

In this section, we show the general form of widget instancing. We then show an outline of tkinter GUI scripting, and also a primary example of one.

tkinter widgets can be constructed to display and be hooked up to your Python3 application code, either using purely OOP, or they can be constructed using a procedural/imperative programming approach.

As stated in Section 2.5.3.2, we choose the latter approach because it's easier for beginners. By the time you do all the examples we present here, you should be able to see that OOP is an essential, but not mandatory, part of tkinter GUI programming.

The general form of using a tkinter widget is as follows:

>>> widget = Widget.method (master, option=value, option=value,...)

where:

widget is the name assigned in your Python3 script to the particular instance you are creating and using

Widget is the master instance of a widget class in the tkinter module

method is the "operation" of instancing some master instance of the widget

master is the "container", or frame, to which our instance of the widget belongs, or is attached to

option is a graphical entity or modifier that gives attributes to your particular instance

value is one of the characteristics that the option can take on

After importing the tkinter module, the first thing you need to do is create an object, which is a surrounding frame or window, for the display of your information and/or data. This is done by creating a TK object with the following generic line of Python code:

window_object_name = tkinter.Tk()

Then you create widgets you've selected for their suitability to your purposes, and add them to the frame's widget hierarchy.

For example, to create a button widget instance, you would call either the tk or ttk Button method. You need to specify the window_object_name as the first argument, as follows:

cmd_button = tk.Button(window_object_name, text="Some text".)

or

cmd_button = ttk.Button(application_window, text="Some text".)

The arguments needed to create each kind of widget vary, so you should refer to the Python3 documentation we specified in Section 2.5.3.2 for each specific widget type shown in brief in Table 2.6.

The following simple example shows a complete tkinter Python script, and the widget it creates. You should create, and then execute these six lines of code in Thonny's Script Area, and run it with the Toolbar Run icon, using Way 2 (Script mode). Line numbers are shown *for reference only* in the following code.

Example 2.36

```
1 import tkinter
2 from tkinter import ttk
3 w = tkinter.Tk()
4 w.title("Python GUI")
5 ttk.Label(w,text="My first tkinter gui window").grid(column=0, row=0)
6 w.mainloop()
```

When this widget was generated on our Raspberry Pi 400, it appeared in the extreme upper-left corner of the display screen, just below the raspberry in the Raspberry Pi menu, but we could manually move it wherever we wanted on the screen display.

To close the widget, just click on the "destroy window" button (shown in Figure 2.2 as the X in the upper right-hand corner of the widget) in your style of GUI window in which the widget was created. You may have to expand the window to see all of the window manipulation buttons, but we didn't need to do that on our Raspberry Pi 400. The following universal traits

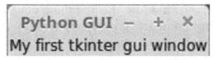

FIGURE 2.2
First Python GUI Display.

of a tkinter widget GUI script file, that are illustrated in Example 2.36 and Figure 2.2, are as follows:

1. As specified in Section 2.5.3.2, tkinter programming is event driven, meaning you invoke tkinter and put it in a *wait state*, where it waits for an event like a mouse button click on the destroy window button, or a keyboard entry, and so forth. The widgets you create, and which remain on screen, generally only do so while tkinter is waiting for an event to happen, or until you destroy the window. You can also construct exit handling events in your script to close the widget and its window.

2. Lines 1 and 2 import all tkinter modules, and the ttk styled widgets, into the current session.

3. Line 3 creates the frame within which all widgets will exist, and assigns it a name **w**.

4. Line 4 gives a title, "Python GUI", to the frame.

5. Line 5 instantiates the ttk *Label method*, assigns it a title "My first tkinter gui window", and then uses the grid geometry manager to position the label in the frame **w**. There are three geometry managers available in tkinter: "pack", "grid", and "place". The grid geometry manager, which treats every window or frame as a table of rows and columns, gives you the greatest control over where widgets and their components are placed.

6. Line 6 starts off the event-driven loop that tkinter enters, and constructs the *Label widget*, with your modifying options, on screen.

In-Chapter Exercise

44. *If necessary*, install tkinter on your Raspberry Pi system, and do Example 2.36. Then modify it to execute any other simple widget display you find interesting and useful on your system. How can you control exactly where it's placed on the screen display, when the widget is instanced?

2.5.3.5 *Hooking tkinter Widgets to Applications in Python: Examples*

Provided with the widget method set of available core widgets in tkinter, and armed with your knowledge of Python programming up to this point in the chapter, you are ready to do the following examples. The next simple example allows a user to add two real numbers as text, that has been entered interactively, on lines inside the widget. Line numbers and comments are for reference only, and are *not* executed. We again describe and explain in simple terms what each line in the code does. And, as in Example 2.36 above, you can enter the code in Thonny's Script Area, and use the Toolbar Run icon to launch it.

Example 2.37

```
1 import tkinter as tk
2 from tkinter import ttk
3 from functools import partial
  # This is the data generating module, which computes the sum.
4 def add_it(label_result, n1, n2):
5        num1 = (n1.get())
6        num2 = (n2.get())
7        result = float(num1)+float(num2)
8        label_result.config(text="Sum = %f" % result)
9        return
  # This "grids" the widget object where indicated, then returns it.
10 def mkgrid(r, c, w):
11       w.grid(row=r, column=c, sticky='news')
12       return w
13 root = tk.Tk()
14 root.title('Real Number Adder')
  # The rest hooks the adder into the grid manager widgets.
15 add1_lab = mkgrid(0, 0, ttk.Label(root, text="addend 1",anchor='e'))
16 add2_lab = mkgrid(1, 0, ttk.Label(root, text="addend 2",anchor='e'))
17 add1= mkgrid(0, 1, ttk.Entry(root))
18 add2= mkgrid(1, 1, ttk.Entry(root))
19 spacer = mkgrid(0, 2, ttk.Label(root, text="))
20 labelResult = ttk.Label(root)
21 labelResult.grid(row=7, column=2)
22 add_it = partial(add_it, labelResult, add1, add2)
23 add_but = mkgrid(1, 2, ttk.Button(root, text="Add them",command=add_it))
  # Starts the root main event loop
24 root.mainloop()
```

A line-by-line description/explanation of Example 2.37 is as follows:

Lines 1 & 2. Import all tkinter modules, and the ttk styled widgets, into the current session.

Line 3. Imports the **partial functools** function module.

Lines 4 through 9. Define the function **add_it**, that computes the real number sum.

Lines 10 through 12. Define a function that will specify grid locations for the grid manager.

Line 13. Creates the frame within which all widgets will exist, and assigns it a name: "root".

Line 14. Adds a title, "Real Number Adder", to the frame "root".

Lines 15 & 16. Construct two Label widgets, to designate the input locations for the addends.

Line 17 & 18. Allow input of both addends, and constructs them using the Entry widget.

Line 19. Places a spacer at grid position 0,2.

Lines 20 & 21. Establish a ttk label in the root window for the sum.

Line 22. Uses the Python3 **partial** function to call the **add_it** function, with values of **add1** and **add2**.

Line 23. Defines a ttk button at grid location 1,2, that calls the function **add_it** to find the sum when the button is "pressed" to generate an event.

Line 24. Starts the event loop, creating the root window and all widgets defined above.

Even though Example 2.37 uses the procedural/imperative programming paradigm, syntax, and data abstraction, after having examined the line-by-line description and explanation of it above, you should begin to see that tkinter GUI scripts are basically composed of OOP class instance objects. All of the methods applied to those instances come from the methods applied to the core widgets in tkinter.

The following example will construct a Fahrenheit-to-Celsius temperature conversion GUI with tkinter (Figure 2.3). A line-by-line description/explanation of the script follows the code. Line numbers and comments are

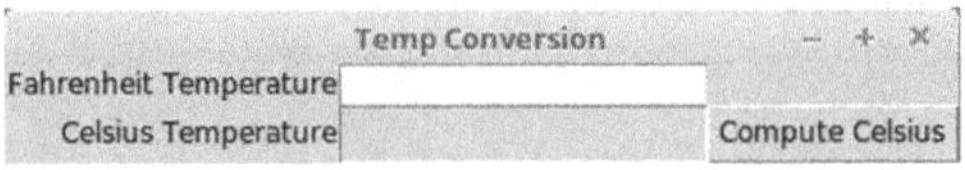

FIGURE 2.3
tk Temp Conversion Display.

for reference only, and are *not* executed. And, as in Examples 2.36 and 2.37 above, you can enter the code in Thonny's Script Area, and use the Toolbar Run icon to launch it.

Example 2.38

```
1 import tkinter as tk
2 from tkinter import ttk
# This function computes the Celsius temperature from the Fahrenheit.
3 def findcel():
4     famt = ftmp.get()
5     if famt == '':   #not double quote, 2 single quotes
6             cent.configure(text='')
7     else:
8             famt = float(famt)
9     camt = (famt - 32) / 1.8
# A method (configure) applied to cent to convert camt to a string (str(camt)).
10     cent.configure(text=str(camt))
# This grids the widget object where indicated, then returns it.
11 def mkgrid(r, c, w):
12     w.grid(row=r, column=c, sticky='news')
13     return w
14 root = tk.Tk()
15 root.title('Temp Conversion')
# The rest hooks the Temperatures into the grid manager widgets.
16 flab = mkgrid(0, 0, ttk.Label(root, text="Fahrenheit Temperature",anchor=\
    'e'))
17 clab = mkgrid(1, 0, ttk.Label(root, text="Celsius Temperature",anchor='e'))
18 ftmp = mkgrid(0, 1, ttk.Entry(root))
19 cent = mkgrid(1, 1, ttk.Label(root, text="", relief='sunken',anchor='w'))
20 elab = mkgrid(0, 2, ttk.Label(root, text=''))
21 fbut = mkgrid(1, 2, ttk.Button(root, text="Compute Celsius",command=\
    findcel))
# Starts the root main event loop
22 root.mainloop()
```

Here is a line-by-line description/explanation of the code of Example 2.38.

Lines 1 & 2. Import all tkinter modules, and the ttk styled widgets, into the current session.

Lines 3 through 10. Define the function **findcel**, that does the temperature conversion from F to C. Note that lines 5 and 6 ensure that if an empty string is entered for **famt**, then **cent** is empty as well. Line 10. converts **cent** to text.

Lines 11 through 13. Define a function that will specify grid locations for the grid manager.

Line 14. Creates the frame within which all widgets will exist, and assigns it a name "**root**".

Line 15. Adds a title, "**Temp Conversion**", to the frame "**root**".

Lines 16 through 21. Define the labels and buttons necessary for the event generation and callbacks.

Line 22. Starts the main root event loop.

Again, even though the previous example is a procedural/imperative model program design, you should be able to recognize from this line-by-line description and explanation that the underlying core widgets from tkinter are OOP classes that we have instanced as objects.

The example used methods applied to those classes, but the structure of our script file was still functional and declarative in nature.

In-Chapter Exercises

45. What functional and declarative control structure is most similar to the event loops used in the above three examples?

46. Do Examples 2.37 and 2.38 on your Raspberry Pi system. Then modify them to accomplish interesting calculations, of your own choosing, that take input in a tk GUI, and show output results in a similar fashion to the examples.

47. What is the difference between a Python method and a Python function?

48. In the grid geometry manager, where does the numbering of cells that widgets can be placed in begin, and how do the numbering indices evolve? For instance, in Example 2.38, what does grid position 0,2 mean?

49. What code would put a "quit" button in the grid cell 0,2 instead of a blank label?

2.5.4 Multi-Threaded Concurrency with Python

The first question you must ask yourself about how and why the Raspberry Pi OS functions the way it does is: Given the limited resources, and very prodigious nature of modern computer hardware, how does an operating system maximize performance and efficiency for all users of the system? And furthermore, how can user programs, such as Python3 scripts, reflect this technique?

The answer for the Raspberry Pi OS is:

First, by separating the hardware, that is, the SoC CPU and its cores, main memory, and peripheral memory, into multiple virtual machinery: in short, via *virtualization*.

Then, by executing instructions *concurrently* on this virtualized machinery—this means not in any particular sequence, and perhaps even all at once.

Finally, by making sure that the data generated and stored in the file system is *persistent* over time.

Python3, as a Raspberry Pi software tool that creates user programs and scripts, can achieve concurrency with a mechanism called *threads*, and the concurrent execution of instructions by threads. This is very similar to UNIX and Linux system programming with threads.

Similar to the Linux system programming concurrency facility, Python3 threads give you the ability to run several programs concurrently, in a single process. When you create one or more threads in your Python3 program, they are executed concurrently, independently of each other, and they can share information among them because they are using the same resources of a single process. These features make Python3 threads useful in creating Python3 applications for such things as network programming, and the creation of GUI programs.

Python3 supports threads on the Raspberry Pi OS, and any other systems that use the POSIX threads library (pthreads).

To quote from from the Python documentation:

> The Python interpreter is not fully thread-safe. In order to support multi-threaded Python programs, there's a global lock, called the global interpreter lock or GIL, that must be held by the current thread before it can safely access Python objects. Without the lock, even the simplest operations could cause problems in a multi-threaded program: for example, when two threads simultaneously increment the reference count of the same object, the reference count could end up being incremented only once instead of twice.
>
> Therefore, the rule exists that only the thread that has acquired the GIL may operate on Python objects or call Python/C API functions. In order to emulate concurrency of execution, the interpreter regularly tries to switch threads. The lock is also released around potentially blocking I/O operations like reading or writing a file, so that other Python threads can run in the meantime.

The takeaway from the above documentation, in terms of Python3 performance, is that Python3 threads *cannot* ordinarily take advantage of multiprocessor or multicore processor architectures, even the ARM architecture used in the Raspberry Pi's CPU. Thread switching can only occur between the execution of individual bytecodes in the Python3 interpreter. The frequency with which the interpreter checks for thread switching is set by the **sys. setcheckinterval()** function. By default, the interpreter checks for thread switching after a limited, but prescribed, number of bytecode instructions.

One of the many ways around this impasse is to use various Python3 extension modules. The coverage of these is beyond the scope of what we can illustrate here, and what is necessary for a beginner to have at her command. But being somewhat familiar with Python3 threads is useful even for the beginner.

2.5.4.1 Python Thread Examples Using Procedural/Imperative Programming

We show both the _**thread** and **threading** modules in Python 3.9.2, in the examples we present in this section.

Unless you absolutely need OOP tools and capabilities for Python3 in general, and specifically in the threading module, the choice is largely a matter of programmer and programming team preference, and their programming design goals/methodologies. We also cover some of the functions offered in the **threading** module in Section 2.5.5 below.

The basic _**thread** module does *not* necessarily require that you program with OOP!

It's very easy to use if you are accustomed to, and desire to, exclusively structure your programs with the procedural/imperative programming model. The procedural/imperative model is used by programming languages such as C.

The _**thread** module provides low-level primitives for working with multiple threads of control (also called *lightweight processes* or *tasks*) that share their global data space. For synchronization, simple locks (also called *mutexes*) are provided within the classes and methods of this module.

2.5.4.1.1 _**thread** *Functions Reference*

Since the basic _**thread** module is a bit simpler than the more advanced **threading** module covered later in the next subsection, we give examples of that first. This module provides a portable interface to whatever threading system is available in your platform: its interfaces work in the same way on any system with an installed pthreads POSIX threads implementation (including Linux systems and others). Python scripts that use the Python3 _**thread** module work on all of these platforms without changing their source code.

2.5.4.1.2 *Examples*

Our first example allows you to experiment with a script that deploys the main _**thread** interfaces.

The script in Example 2.39, uses Way 2 (Script Mode) to enter the code into Thonny's Script Area, and is run with the Toolbar Run icon. It starts successive, one-at-a-time-only threads. Each new thread creation is triggered by a key typed at the Python3 command line in Thonny's Shell Area, followed by pressing **<Enter>**, until you type an **x** at that console, followed by pressing a final **<Enter>**. Following is the code, and its execution in Python 3.9.2 on our representative Raspberry Pi systems.

Example 2.39

```
import _thread
def child(tid):
    print ('Started thread', tid)
def parent():
    i = 0
    while 1:
        i += 1
        _thread.start_new_thread(child, (i,))
        if input() == 'x': break
parent()
```

>>> %Run -c $EDITOR_CONTENT
Started thread 1
k
Started thread 2
o
Started thread 3
r
Started thread 4
x
>>>

What exactly is going on in Example 2.39? A single thread is being started, and then it immediately dies, and the program loops indeterminately, allowing you to create successive new threads by pressing a key on the keyboard, followed by pressing **<Enter>**. Only two thread calls are made in this example: the import of the **_thread** module, and the call to its method, **start_new_thread**, that creates a new thread. This call takes a function (or other "callable") object as a tuple argument, and starts a new thread to execute a call to the passed function with the passed arguments. It's that simple!

Following is the code of another example, which you can again use Way 2 (Script Mode) to enter the code into Thonny's Script Area, and run with the Toolbar Run icon. Its command line execution in the Thonny Shell Area is done in Python 3.9.2 on our representative Raspberry Pi systems. It iterates to create new threads that exist simultaneously, in parallel:

Example 2.40

```
import _thread, time
def counter(myId, count):              # function that will run in each thread
    for i in range(count):
        time.sleep(1)                  # simulate useful code here? why here?
        print ('[%s] => %s' % (myId, i))
for i in range(5):                     # call start_new_thread 5 times
    _thread.start_new_thread(counter, (i, 3))  # loop the newest thread 3 times
time.sleep(5)                          # prevents exit from parent too early
print ('Main thread exiting.')         # all threads are destroyed by default
```

When we execute this script file with the Thonny Toolbar Run icon, we get:

```
>>> %Run -c $EDITOR_CONTENT
[1] => 0[0] => 0[2] => 0[3] => 0[4] => 0

[1] => 1[3] => 1
[0] => 1
[2] => 1
[4] => 1

[3] => 2
[1] => 2
[2] => 2
[4] => 2
[0] => 2
Main thread exiting.
>>>
```

What exactly is happening in Example 2.40? Five threads are being created, and run simultaneously. Within each thread, the counter value, which is displayed from 0 to 4, is being printed in the Thonny Shell Area. The **time. sleep(1)** method in the function **counter** is used to "simulate" code that might be used to do some system programming task(s) at that point in the code.

In-Chapter Exercises

50. If each of the threads you start in Example 2.39 were to perform some operations, after what line in the given code would you put the lines of code that performed that work?

51. In the output of Example 2.40 shown, you will notice that the order in which the value of the **myId** variable that is printed is not always the same. Why is this true?

52. If you run Example2.40 a few times, is the order of the printed value of **myId** the same on each successive run of the program? Why or why not?

2.5.4.2 Python Thread Example Using the OOP Model

The **threading** module builds higher-level threading interfaces, on top of the lower-level **_thread** module. If you want your applications to take advantage of the computational power of the multi-core Broadcom CPU in your Raspberry Pi, you should use the multi-processing **threading** module. However, **threading** is still an appropriate model to deploy if you want to run multiple I/O-bound tasks.

2.5.4.3 OOP GUIs and Producer–Consumer Model Threads

Threads are an extremely integral part of the tk GUI toolkit, which we illustrated in Section 2.5.3. This also applies in general to GUI libraries, such as Qt. Since many of the functions of a GUI use synchronous I/O, any operation that can block, or take a long time to complete, must be spawned to run in parallel, so that the central GUI module (the main thread) is always running. Although such spawned children can be run as multiple processes, the efficiency and shared environment model of threads make them ideal for this role, since they are run in the namespace of a single process. Most GUI toolkits do *not* allow multiple threads to update the main thread in parallel- updates, and are usually restricted to the main thread.

The two important points to be made about Python3 threads in a GUI are that the main thread handles all screen graphics updates, and that GUI threads must obey the synchronization rules established for general thread concurrency according to standardized models.

All threads in a GUI generally follow what is called the *producer–consumer model*. Simply put, that's where one or more objects (the producers) are responsible for placing data into some storage pool, and one or more objects (the consumers) are responsible for removing data from that pool.

The drawbacks to the producer–consumer model are as follows:

The producer(s) cannot add more data than the storage pool can hold.

The consumers(s) cannot take from an empty pool.

The actions of all objects *must* be synchronized.

We address more of the issues of the producer–consumer model in Section 2.5.5, and give an example Python3 program in that section to illustrate the solution implemented by the model, using what are known as *condition variables*.

2.5.4.4 OOP Threads Example

The following is an example illustrating the basic methodology of using OOP and Python3 threads. We first describe, in blocks of code, what's happening in the Python3 code of the example. Then, we present the actual example code in its entirety. Finally, we show sample output when the code is run in Thonny.

It would be very instructive for a beginner to compare what the basic methodology and structure of the following OOP example is, compared with the previous Python3 thread code examples presented.

The components of Example 2.41 are shown as blocks of code as follows (the blocks are indicated as comments on the line of code that begins the block):

Block 1.
Import the Thread class from the threading module. Why do it this way? The **Thread** class of the **threading** module contains many useful methods that allow you to construct and manipulate threads. Using it avoids having to define your own functions or methods to do the same operations. Not doing it this way would mean you would have to write lower-level system programming functions to accomplish thread creation and synchronization, and then, somehow, stitch that code together with higher-level Python3 functional programming code.

Block 2.
Subclass your own thread, named **Threader**, by defining it as a child class based on the **Thread** class, and also define the constructor properties of it as function definitions.

Block 3.
Define a **.run** method in the **Threader** class. This run method is always executed when we call the **start** method of any object in our **Threader** class. The **sleep** function makes the thread inactive for a definite amount of time. This randomly timed sleep will ensure that the code will not be executed so quickly that we will not be able to notice any changes.

Block 4.
The critical block. Create three objects. Apply the **.start** method to each object, which, in turn, executes the **.run** method for each object. You need to call the

.join method built into the **Thread** class, and apply it to each object, or the program will terminate before the threads complete their execution!

Place the following code in the Thonny Script Area, and use the Run Toolbar icon to execute it:

Example 2.41

```python
from threading import Thread        #Block 1.
from random import randint
import time

class Threader(Thread):            #Block 1.
    def __init__(self, val):
        # The Constructor
        Thread.__init__(self)
        self.val = val
    def run(self):                 #Block 3.
        for i in range(1, self.val):
            print('Value %d in thread %s' % (i, self.getName()))
                        # Sleep for random time
            GoToSleep = randint(1, 5)
            print('%s sleeping for %d seconds...' % (self.getName(), GoToSleep))
            time.sleep(GoToSleep)

if __name__ == '__main__':        #Block 4.
    # Declare Threader class
    Threader_Object1 = Threader(4)
    Threader_Object1.setName('Thread 1')
    Threader_Object2 = Threader(4)
    Threader_Object2.setName('Thread 2')
    Threader_Object3 = Threader(4)
    Threader_Object3.setName('Thread 3')
    # Run the threads!
    Threader_Object1.start()
    Threader_Object2.start()
    Threader_Object3.start()
# Wait . . .
    Threader_Object1.join()
    Threader_Object2.join()
    Threader_Object3.join()
#Exit . . .
    print('Main Terminating...')
```

The output from the program is as follows, as shown in the Thonny Shell Area:

```
>>> %Run ex41.py
Value 1 in thread Thread 1
Thread 1 sleeping for 5 seconds...Value 1 in thread Thread 2

Value 1 in thread Thread 3Thread 2 sleeping for 4 seconds...

Thread 3 sleeping for 1 seconds...
Value 2 in thread Thread 3
Thread 3 sleeping for 4 seconds...
Value 2 in thread Thread 2
Thread 2 sleeping for 3 seconds...
Value 2 in thread Thread 1
Thread 1 sleeping for 1 seconds...
Value 3 in thread Thread 3
Thread 3 sleeping for 4 seconds...
Value 3 in thread Thread 1
Thread 1 sleeping for 2 seconds...
Value 3 in thread Thread 2
Thread 2 sleeping for 4 seconds...
Main Terminating...
>>>
```

Note
When we ran this script file in Python 3.11.3, we got the following Deprecation Warning messages:

/home/bob/Public/ex41.py:21: DeprecationWarning: setName() is deprecated, set the name attribute instead **Threader_Object1. setName('Thread 1')**
/home/bob/Public/ex41.py:23: DeprecationWarning: setName() is deprecated, set the name attribute instead **Threader_Object2. setName('Thread 2')**
/home/bob/Public/ex41.py:25: DeprecationWarning: setName() is deprecated, set the name attribute instead **Threader_Object3. setName('Thread 3')**
/home/bob/Public/ex41.py:12: DeprecationWarning: getName() is deprecated, get the name attribute instead **print('Value %d in thread %s' % (i, self.getName()))**
Value 1 in thread Thread 1Value 1 in thread Thread 2
Value 1 in thread Thread 3
/home/bob/Public/ex41.py:15: DeprecationWarning: getName() is deprecated, get the name attribute instead **print('%s sleeping for %d seconds...' % (self.getName(), GoToSleep))**

So if you're running Python 3.11.3 or later, you can substitute the "instead" code shown above in the DeprecationWarning messages into your script file, and be in conformance with the latest release of Python3.

In-Chapter Exercise

53. If you wanted the threads to do some actual work, in what block of Example 2.41, and exactly where in that block, would you put the Python3 code to accomplish that work?

2.5.5 Talking Threads: The Producer–Consumer Problem Using the queue Module

In computing, the *producer–consumer problem* (sometimes called the *bounded-buffer problem*) is a classic example of the use of various approaches to the synchronization of the execution of multiple threads, or processes. We addressed some of the issues involved with the producer–consumer model in Section 2.5.4. In this section, we give more details, and a worked example, to further illustrate this important computer science concept using Python3.

The problem concerns two tasks, the "producer" process and the "consumer" process, that share a common, fixed-size queue, or storage pool. The producer "produces" a piece of data, puts it into the queue and starts producing more data. Simultaneously, the consumer is "consuming" the data, i.e., removing it from the queue.

The solution to the problem, as we present it here, is to make sure that the producer will not add data into the queue when it's full, and that the consumer will not try to remove data when the queue is empty. The next time the consumer removes an item from the queue, it notifies the producer, which starts to fill the queue again. In the same way, the consumer can become idle if it finds the queue is empty. The next time the producer puts data into the queue, it activates the idled consumer.

There are a variety of approaches to the solution in Python3, for example, using locks, semaphores, event synchronization, condition objects or variables, barriers, and the **queue** module. The Python3 **queue** module has three classes that facilitate threading, and these are only different in terms of retrieval order off the queue: **Queue**, **LifoQueue**, and **PriorityQueue**. It also uses a number of Python3 methods, which have within them the "locking/releasing" mechanisms that can be applied in order for you to work very efficiently with multi-threaded process applications. We choose to implement our example solution in Section 2.5.5.2 using the **queue** module, with its **Queue** class, and its accompanying Python3 methods. Section 2.5.5.1 gives a basic overview of the **queue** module, along with its classes and methods.

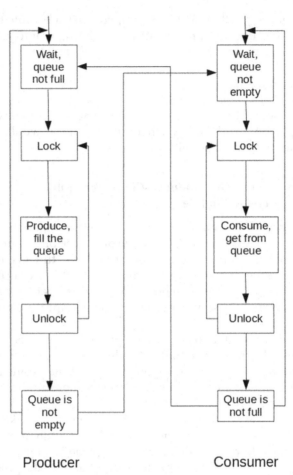

Producer   Consumer

FIGURE 2.4

Producer/Consumer Model Solution.

In all of the approaches to a solution in Python3, the threads, as executing processes, "talk" to each other, or have *interprocess communication*, while they are actively producing or consuming data.

A summary of the solution is illustrated in Figure 2.4.

2.5.5.1 The queue *Module and Its Classes and Methods*

The **queue** module in Python3 implements three OOP classes of queue, which differ only in the order in which the entries are retrieved. In a *First In First Out* (FIFO) queue, the first tasks put into the queue are the first taken out. In a *Last In First Out* (LIFO) queue, the most recently added entry is the first retrieved (similar to a "push-down" stack). In a priority queue, the entries are sorted, and the lowest-valued entry is retrieved first.

The critical feature of the **queue** module is that locks, and release mechanisms, that temporarily block or free competing threads, are implemented in the OOP "public" methods for the classes, *without the programmer having to do it!*

For your convenience, we present the **queue** module definitions, taken from the Python documentation, of the following Queue classes, and their exception handling methods:

class queue.Queue(maxsize=0)

This is the FIFO constructor for a queue. The argument for **maxsize** is an integer that defines the largest number of items that can be placed in the queue. Placement of items on the queue will be blocked if the **maxsize** has been reached; queued items must be consumed to unblock. The queue size default is infinite.

class queue.LifoQueue(maxsize=0)

This is the LIFO constructor for a queue. The argument for **maxsize** is an integer that defines the largest number of items that can be placed in the queue. Placement of items on the queue will be blocked if the size has been reached; queued items must be consumed to unblock. The queue size default is infinite.

class queue.PriorityQueue(maxsize=0)

This is the constructor for a prioritized queue. Placement of items on the queue will be blocked if the **maxsize** has been reached; queued items must be consumed to unblock. The queue size default is infinite. Note that the lowest valued entries in the queue are retrieved first (the lowest valued entry is the one returned by sorted(list(entries))[0]). Typically entries are tuples of the form- (priority_number, data).

exception queue.Empty

An exception raised when non-blocking .get() or .get_nowait() is called on a Queue object which is empty.

exception queue.Full

An exception raised when non-blocking .put() or .put_nowait() is called on a Queue object which is full.

The three Queue classes provide the public methods described in Table 2.8, which has also been taken from the Python3 documentation. Remember that a public method is accessible anywhere outside of the class.

TABLE 2.8

queue Class Public Methods

Methods and Arguments	Description
Queue.qsize()	Obtain the approximate size of the queue. No assurance that put() or get() will not block
Queue.empty()	Tests the truth value of an empty queue. No assurance that put() or get() will not block
Queue.full()	Tests the truth value of a full queue. No assurance that put() or get() will not block
Queue.put(item, block=True, timeout=None)	Adds item into the queue. If block is true, and timeout is None, blocking occurs. If timeout is a positive number, block occurs at that number of seconds, and the Full exception is raised. If block is false, put item on the queue if a space is available. If no space is available raise a Full exception, and ignore the timeout
Queue.put_nowait(item)	Same as .put, with arguments item and block=false
Queue.get(block=True, timeout= None)	Delete and return an item from the queue. If block is true, and timeout is None, block until an item is available. If timeout is a positive number, it blocks at most timeout seconds and raises the Empty exception if no item was available within that time. Otherwise (block is false), return an item if one is immediately available, else raise the Empty exception (timeout is ignored in that case)
Queue.get_nowait()	Equal to .get(False)
Queue.task_done()	Signals that an enqueued task is finished
Queue.join()	Blocks until all items in the queue have been retrieved and processed. The count of unfinished tasks goes up or down depending on whether an item is added or taken off the queue

2.5.5.2 Examples of Using the queue Module Queue Classes

The three examples we present in this section illustrate **queue** module classes and methods, and are used to construct a queue in a very simple and basic way. Example 2.42 uses the LifoQueue class to implement an LIFO queue, similar to a stack. Example 2.43 uses the PriorityQueue class to implement a queue in which the order of retrieving the elements has to do with some characteristic of each element. Example 2.44 uses the Queue class to implement an FIFO queue. They can each be executed in Thonny, using the Script Area and the Run Toolbar icon.

Example 2.42

```
import queue

q = queue.LifoQueue()
for i in range(7):
    q.put(i)
while not q.empty():
    print(q.get(), end=' ')
```

```
>>> %Run -c $EDITOR_CONTENT
6 5 4 3 2 1 0
>>>
```

Example 2.43

```
import queue as Q
q = Q.PriorityQueue()
q.put(15)
q.put(18)
q.put(4)
q.put(9)
while not q.empty():
    print (q.get(),)
```

```
>>> %Run -c $EDITOR_CONTENT
4
9
15
18
>>>
```

Example 2.44

```
import queue

q = queue.Queue()
for i in range(8):
    q.put(i)
while not q.empty():
    print(q.get(), end=' ')
    print()
```

```
>>> %Run -c $EDITOR_CONTENT
0
1
2
3
4
5
6
7
>>>
```

2.5.5.3 An Example of the Queue Class Solution to
the Producer–Consumer Model

The following Python3 code brings together much of the syntax and structure from this chapter. This final example illustrates a Python3 solution to the producer–consumer problem, using an FIFO queue with the **queue.Queue** class, in a multi-threaded program. It uses OOP, and the threading module and its methods, to start two threads: Producer and Consumer.

An overview of how we use the Queue class to obtain a solution to the producer–consumer problem, taken from the reference material, is as follows:

> The Producer places a piece of data on the queue using the **.put** method. The utility and advantage the queue module is most visible here- **.put** locks the queue, checks to see if the queue is full, and calls an internal .**wait()** to pause the producer if the queue is full. The Consumer then uses the .**get** method to acquire the lock before removing data from the queue, and .**get** checks for an empty queue. If the queue is empty, the consumer is put in a wait state.
>
> .**get()** and .**put()** also implement the notification logic to allow "talking" between Producer and Consumer threads.

What exactly is happening, step-by-step, in the code of Example 2.45 below? A brief explanation of the layout of the program, in major summary blocks, and a description of the operational heart of the code is as follows:

Block 1:
This is the initialization part of the program, where the **threading** module, sub-module **Thread**, and modules **queue, time**, and **random** are imported. In this block, we also instance a class of the **queue.Queue** class, and name it **q_buffer**.

Block 2:
This defines the function **Producer** as a class derived from the **Thread** module, and runs it as self. It specifies the range of integers that will be used as data "numbering", using the variable numbers. It specifies, in a determinate, or logical repetition loop, how we will add data, as an "actual_number", to the queue. The Producer is put to sleep for a random amount of time.

The shared namespace for **q_buffer** is established here using the **global** keyword.

Block 3:
Very similar to Block 2, this defines the function **Consumer** as a class derived from the **Thread** module, and runs it as self. It specifies, in a determinate, or logical repetition loop, how we will retrieve data, in the form of an "actual_number_gotten", from the queue. The **Consumer** is put to sleep for a random amount of time.

The shared namespace for **q_buffer** is used here via the **global** keyword.

Block 4:
Producer is started first, and then **Consumer** is started. The threads continue to be produced and consumed until a **<Ctrl> + <Z>** interrupt is sent to the running process from the keyboard.

Trace the steps through the Blocks of code we present next in Example 2.45, in preparation for completion of the In-Chapter Exercises and problems that follow. Also, in this final Python3 example, create the code in a file named **ex45.py** with your favorite text editor, and run it (and also terminate it, and the Python3 process it spawns) according to our Way 4 (Bash Mode) from the Bash command line as shown below:

Example 2.45

```
from threading import Thread  #Block 1
import time
import random
import queue

q_buffer = queue.Queue()

class Producer(Thread):        #Block 2
    def run(self):
        numbers = range(5)
        global q_buffer
        while True:
            actual_number = random.choice(numbers)
            q_buffer.put(actual_number)
```

```
            print ("Produced thread", actual_number)
            time.sleep(random.random())
class Consumer(Thread):          #Block 3
    def run(self):
        global q_buffer
        while True:
            actual_number_gotten = q_buffer.get()
            q_buffer.task_done()
            print ("Consumed thread", actual_number_gotten)
            time.sleep(random.random())

Producer().start()               #Block 4
Consumer().start()
```

Output from the above example is as follows:

```
$ python3 ex45.py
Produced thread 1
Consumed thread 1
Produced thread 0
Produced thread 4
Consumed thread 0
Consumed thread 4
Produced thread 3
Consumed thread 3
Produced thread 0
Consumed thread 0
Produced thread 4
Consumed thread 4
Produced thread 4
Consumed thread 4
Produced thread 2
Produced thread 1
Consumed thread 2
Produced thread 1
^Z
[1]+ Stopped    python3 ex45.py
$ ps
PID    TTY    TIME     CMD
50443  pts/0  00:00:00 bash
50611  pts/0  00:00:00 python3
50615  pts/0  00:00:00 ps
$ kill -9 50611
$
```

In-Chapter Exercise (refer to Example 2.45)

54. As the output of running this program one time shows, the production and consumption of data to and from the buffer is sporadic. That is, sometimes data is produced and then immediately consumed, and sometimes data is produced and not immediately consumed. Also, you will notice that if you do several runs of the program, each run may yield different patterns of production and consumption. Why is this so?

2.6 Summary

We gave a broad introduction to the Python3 programming language, using Python 3.9.2. For the beginner Python3 programmer, we illustrated all of its important programming capabilities and syntactic structures, in the context of the three predominant computer programming paradigms: *virtualization*, *concurrency*, and *persistence*. We showed the details of doing an installation of the latest version of Python3.X on a Raspberry Pi system, instead of utilizing the default installation of it that comes with your Raspberry Pi OS. We gave a brief introduction to Thonny, the Python3 IDE. We showed all of Python3's important basic syntax, including numbers and expressions, variables, statements, getting input from the user, functions, the procedural/imperative OOP programming models in Python3, functions, modules, saving and executing Python3 scripts, string and sequence operations, and error handling. We also gave many basic and practical examples, such as another way of writing shell script files, such as rewriting Bash and tcsh scripts, basic user file maintenance, backing up files, remote copying with the **rsync** command, and graphics using tkinter. Finally, we showed how various forms of thread execution are achieved in Python3, and how OOP can be deployed to accomplish them.

2.7 Ultimate Reference Glossary

A simplified and abbreviated glossary of some of the terms we have abstracted from the references in Section 2.5 follows:

Class: A template for creating user-defined objects. Class definitions normally contain method definitions which operate on instances of the class.

Expression: A piece of syntax which can be evaluated to some value. In other words, an expression is an accumulation of expression elements like literals, names, attribute access, operators, or function calls, which all return a value.

In contrast to many other languages, not all language constructs are expressions. There are also statements which cannot be used as expressions, such as **print** or **if**. Assignments are also statements, not expressions.

Immutable: An object with a fixed value. Immutable objects include numbers, strings, and tuples. Such objects cannot be altered. A new object has to be created if a different value has to be stored; for example, a key in a dictionary.

Iterable: An object capable of returning its members one at a time. Examples of iterables include all sequence types (such as a list, string, and tuple) and some nonsequence types like **dict** and **file** and objects of any classes you define with an **_iter_()** or **_getitem_()** method. Iterables can be used in a **for** loop and in many other places where a sequence is needed. When an iterable object is passed as an argument to the built-in function **iter()**, it returns an iterator for the object. This iterator is good for one pass over the set of values. When using iterables, it is usually not necessary to call **iter()** or deal with iterator objects yourself. The **for** statement does that automatically for you, creating a temporary unnamed variable to hold the iterator for the duration of the loop.

Lambda: An anonymous inline function consisting of a single expression which is evaluated when the function is called. The syntax to create a lambda function is **lambda [arguments]: expression**.

Method: A function which is defined inside a class body. If called as an attribute of an instance of that class, the method will get the instance object as its first argument (which is usually called self).

Mutable: Mutable objects can change their value but keep their class identity.

Pythonic: An idea or piece of code which closely follows the most common usages of the Python language, rather than implementing code using structures common to other languages. For example, a common usage in Python is to loop over all elements of an iterable using a **for** statement. Many other languages do not have this type of construct, so people unfamiliar with Python sometimes use a numerical counter instead:

```
for i in range(len(money)):
    print (money[i])
```

The Pythonic way:

for bills in money:
    print (bills)

Sequence: An iterable which supports efficient element access using integer indices via the **_getitem_()** special method and defines a **len()** method that returns the length of the sequence. Some built-in sequence types are **list, str, tuple**, and **unicode**. Note that **dict** also supports **_getitem_()** and **_len_()**, but is considered a mapping rather than a sequence because the lookups use arbitrary immutable keys rather than integers.

Type: The kind of object, such as integers or character strings.

Appendix 2A: Python Syntax and Command Summary

TABLE 2A.1

Python Syntax and Command Summary

Interactive Help in Python Shell

```
help() Invoke interactive help
help(m) Display help for module m
help(f) Display help for function f
dir(m) Display names in module m
```

Module Import

```
import module_name
from module_name import name, ...
from module_name import *
```

Common Data Types

Type	Description	Literal Ex
int	32---bit Integer	3, -4
long	Integer > 32 bits	101L
float	Floating point number	3.0, -6.55
complex	Complex number	1.2J
bool	Boolean	True, False
str	Character sequence	'Python'
tuple	Immutable sequence	(2, 4, 7)
list	Mutable sequence	[2, x, 3.1]
dict	Mapping	{x:2, y5}

(Continued)

TABLE 2A.1 (Continued)

Python Syntax and Command Summary

Common Syntax Structures

Assignment Statement

```
var = exp
```

Console Input/Output

```
var = input([prompt])
var = raw_input([prompt])
print exp[,]
```

Selection

```
if (boolean_exp):
    stmt ...
[elif (boolean_exp):
    stmt ...]
[else:
    stmt ...]
```

Repetition

```
while (boolean_exp):
    stmt ...
```

Iteration

```
for var in iterableable_object(sequence suite):
    stmt ...
```

Function Definition

```
def function_name(parmameters):
    stmt ...
```

Function Call

```
function_name(arguments)
```

Class Definition

```
class Class_name [(super_class)]:
   [class variables]
   def method_name(self, parameters):
     stmt...
```

Object Instantiation

```
obj_ref = Class_name(arguments)
```

Method Invocation

```
obj_ref.method_name(arguments)
```

TABLE 2A.1 (Continued)

Python Syntax and Command Summary

Exception Handling

```
try:
   stmt ...
except [exception_type] [, var]:
   stmt ...
```

Common Built-in Functions

Function	Returns
abs(*x*)	Absolute value of *x*
dict()	Empty dictionary, e.g.: d = dict()
float(*x*)	int or string *x* as float
id(*obj*)	memory addr of *obj*
int (*x*)	float or string *x* as int
len(*s*)	Number of items in sequence s
list()	Empty list, eg: m = list()
max(*s*)	Maximum value of items in s
min(*s*)	Minimum value of items in s
open(*f*)	Open filename f for input
ord(*c*)	ASCII code of c
pow(*x,y*)	x ** y
range(*x*)	A list of x ints 0 to x --- 1
round(*x,n*)	float x rounded to n places
str(*obj*)	str representation of obj
sum(*s*)	Sum of numeric sequence s
tuple(*items*)	tuple of items
type(*obj*)	Data type of obj

Common Math Module Functions

Function	Returns (all float)
ceil(*x*)	Smallest whole nbr >= *x*
cos(*x*)	Cosine of *x* radians
degrees(*x*)	*x* radians in degrees
radians(*x*)	*x* degrees in radians
exp(*x*)	e ** *x*
floor(*x*)	Largest whole nbr <= *x*
hypot(*x, y*)	sqrt($x * x + y * y$)
log(*x* [, *base*])	Log of *x* to *base* or natural log if *base* not given
pow(*x, y*)	x ** y
sin(*x*)	Sine of *x* radians
sqrt(*x*)	Positive square root of *x*
tan(*x*)	Tangent of *x* radians
pi	Math constant pi to 15 sig figs
e	Math constant e to 15 sig figs

(Continued)

TABLE 2A.1 (Continued)

Python Syntax and Command Summary

Common String Methods	
`S.method()`	**Returns (str unless noted)**
`capitalize`	`S` with first char uppercase
`center(w)`	`S` centered in str `w` chars wide
`count(sub)`	int nbr of non---overlapping occurrences of `sub` in `S`
`find(sub)`	int index of first occurrence of `sub` in `S` or ---1 if not found
`isdigit()`	bool `True` if `S` is all digit chars, `False` otherwise
`islower()`, `isupper()`	bool `True` if `S` is all lower/upper case chars, `False` otherwise
`join(seq)`	All items in `seq` concatenated into a str, delimited by `S`
`lower()`, `upper()`	Lower/upper case copy of `S`
`lstrip()`	Copy of `S` with leading/ trailing
`rstrip()`	whitespace removed, or both
`split([sep])`	List of tokens in `S`, delimited by `sep`; if `sep` not given, delimiter is any whitespace

Formatting Numbers as Strings

Syntax: `format_spec % numeric_exp`
`format_spec`
`width` (optional): align in number of columns specified; negative to left---align, precede with 0 to zero---fill
`precision` (optional): show specified digits of precision for floats; 6 is default
`type` (required): d (decimal int), f (float), s (string), e (float exponential notation)
Examples for $x = 123$, $y = 456.789$
`% x --->` ... 123
`% x --->` 000123
`%8.2f % y --->` ... 456.79
`"8.2e" %y-->` 4.57e+02
`"-8s"%y "Hello" ->` Hello ...

Common List Methods	
`L.method()`	**Result/Returns**
`append(obj)`	Append `obj` to end of `L`
`count(obj)`	Returns int nbr of occurrences of `obj` in `L`
`index(obj)`	Returns index of first occurrence of `obj` in `L`; raises `ValueError` if `obj` not in `L`

TABLE 2A.1 (Continued)

Python Syntax and Command Summary

pop([*index*])	Returns item at specified *index* or item at end of L if *index* not given; raises IndexError if L is empty or *index* is out of range
remove(*obj*)	Removes first occurrence of obj *from* L; *raises ValueError if* obj *is not in* L
reverse()	Reverses L in place
sort()	Sorts L in place

Common Tuple Methods

T.method()	Returns
count(*obj*)	Returns nbr of occurrences of obj in *T*
index(*obj*)	Returns index of first occurrenceof obj in *T*; raises ValueError if obj is not in *T*

Common Dictionary Methods

D.method()	Result/Returns
clear()	Remove all items from *D*
get(k [,*val*])	Return *D*[k] if k in *D*, else *val*
has_key(k)	Return True if k in *D*, else False
items()	Return list of key-value pairs in *D*; each list item is two-item tuple
keys()	Return list of *D*'s keys
pop(k, [*val*])	Remove key k, return mapped value or *val* if k not in *D*
values()	Return list of *D*'s values

Common File Methods

F.method()	Result/Returns
read([*n*])	Return str of next *n* chars from *F*, or up to EOF if n not given
readline([*n*])	Return str up to next newline, or at most *n* chars if specified
readlines()	Return list of all lines in *F*, where each item is a line
write(*s*)	Write str *s* to *F*
writelines(*L*)	Write all str in seq *L* to *F*
close()	Closes the file

Questions, Problems, and Projects

Chapter 0

0.1. Create a directory called Raspberry in your home directory. What command line did you use to do this?

0.2. Give a command line for displaying the files lab1, lab2, lab3, and lab4. Can you give two more command lines that do the same thing? What is the command line for displaying the files lab1.c, lab2.c, lab3.c, and lab4.c? (Hint: use shell metacharacters.)

0.3. Give a command line for printing all the files in your home directory that start with the string memo and end with .ps on a printer called upmpr. What command line did you use to do this?

0.4. Give the command line for nicknaming the command **who -H** as **W**. Give both Bash and C shell versions. Where would you put it if you want it to execute every time you start a new shell?

0.5. Type the command **man ls > ~/Raspberry/ls.man** on your system. This command will put the man page for the **ls** command in the **ls.man** file in your Raspberry directory (the one you created in Problem 0.1). Give the command for printing two copies of this file on a printer in your lab. What command line would you use to achieve this printing?

0.6. What is the mesg value set to for your environment? If it is on, how would you turn it off for your current session? How would you set it off for every login?

0.7. What does the command **lpr -Pqpr [0-9]*.jpg** do? Explain your answer.

0.8. Use the **passwd** command to change your password. If you are on a network, be aware that you might have to use the **yppasswd** command to modify your network login password. Also, make sure you abide by the rules set up by your system administrator for coming up with good passwords!

0.9. Using the correct terminology (e.g., command, option, option argument, and command argument), identify the constituent parts of the following Raspberry Pi OS single commands:

```
ls -la *.exe
lpr -Pwpr file27
chmod g+rwx *.*
```

0.10. View the manpages for each of the useful commands listed in Table 0.2. Which part of the man pages is most descriptive for you? Which of the options shown on each of the man pages is the most useful for beginners? Explain.

0.11. How many users are logged on to your system at this time? What command did you use to discover this?

0.12. Determine the name of the operating system that your computer runs. What command did you use to discover this?

0.13. Give the command line for displaying manual pages for the socket, read, and connect system calls on your system.

Advanced Questions and Problems

0.14. Following is a typical /etc/profile configuration file, this particular one is from a default installation on our Raspberry Pi OS:

```
# /etc/profile: system-wide .profile file for the Bourne shell (sh(1))
# and Bourne compatible shells (bash(1), ksh(1), ash(1), ...).

if ["$(id -u)" -eq 0]; then
  PATH="/usr/local/sbin:/usr/local/bin:/usr/sbin:/usr/bin:/sbin:/bin"
else
  PATH="/usr/local/sbin:/usr/local/bin:/usr/sbin:/usr/bin:/sbin:/bin:/\
usr/local/games:/usr/games"
fi
export PATH

if ["${PS1-}"]; then
  if ["${BASH-}"] && ["$BASH"!= "/bin/sh"]; then
    # The file bash.bashrc already sets the default PS1.
    # PS1='\h:\w\$ '
    if [-f /etc/bash.bashrc]; then
      . /etc/bash.bashrc
    fi
  else

  if ["$(id -u)" -eq 0]; then
    PS1='# '
  else
    PS1='$ '
  fi
  fi
fi
```

```
if [-d /etc/profile.d]; then
 for i in /etc/profile.d/*.sh; do
  if [-r $i]; then
   . $i
  fi
 done
 unset i
fi
```

Write an explanatory sentence in your own words describing exactly what you consider important lines in the file accomplish, including the comments (the lines that begin with the pound sign #). Examine this file on your Raspberry Pi OS. How does it compare, line-for-line, with the one above? We assume here that, by default, Bash is both the interactive and login shell on your system.

0.15. What is the default umask setting in an ordinary, non-privileged account on your Raspberry Pi OS, from both a login and non-login shell? Describe in your own words what the umask setting is, and how it is applied to newly created directories and files. Is the umask set in /etc/profile on your Raspberry Pi OS? If not, where can the umask be set most effectively on a persistent basis, for a particular single user, both in a login and non-login shell?

0.16. Assume that all users, when they log into your Raspberry Pi OS, have Bash as their default shell. What file sets the shell prompt for them on your Raspberry Pi OS? Is it the file illustrated in Problem 0.14? Describe the lines in the file that actually specify the shell prompt, and give a short description of the components of those lines. Experiment to find out which file accomplishes the actual shell prompt setting for ordinary users (for both interactive or login shells), and write an explicit description of what you have discovered.

Additionally, set the shell prompt for yourself in the current interactive shell, so that it contains the following:

A display of just the date/time.

A display of the date and time, hostname, and current directory.

A display where the entire prompt is in red text, along with hostname and current directory.

Then make those changes persistent for yourself in both login and interactive shells. Finally, undo the persistent changes.

As a follow-up, design your own shell prompt so that it contains the information you want in a useful display given your use case(s), and make that designed prompt persistent for yourself on your Raspberry Pi OS.

0.17. Give a sequential list of the exact commands you would use to make the TC shell the default login shell for your user account on your Raspberry Pi OS. Is the TC shell installed by default on your Raspberry Pi OS? Give the exact commands for installation of not only the TC shell, but any of the other four major Raspberry Pi OS shells available.

0.18. Execute all of the compound command examples provided at the web link:

https://explainshell.com/

and then use the output shown to explain all of them in your own words. Try executing the examples with meaningful arguments on your Raspberry Pi OS, if possible.

Project 1

After completing Problems 0.14 through 0.16, gather your findings together in a summary report that details the default settings (within the scope of the files you have examined and in the context of those problems) of the Bash environment on your Raspberry Pi OS. For example, which actual file takes precedence by default, and what components of the Bash environment are set in that file? What are the critical default settings in the Bash environment, and what actual files on your Raspberry Pi OS affect them?

Chapter 1

1.1 Write a brief outline of how you installed your version of the Raspberry Pi OS on your hardware, and detail exactly what special procedures you used for your particular installation, and how they may have differed from the ones presented in the current installation procedures for your version of the software. If you didn't do the installation, find out from the system administrator how the installation was done, and why it was done in that way. If you did a server install, explain how and why that was done, given the particular use case that the system had to conform to.

1.2 Do the following steps in order to complete the requirements for this problem:

a. If you have not already done so, download, install, and test the **vsftpd** service on your system.

b. Use the **adduser** command to create a new user account on your Raspberry Pi system with the following configuration (with differently assigned group and user IDs):

$ **sudo adduser ftp2**
Adding user `ftp2' ...
Adding new group `ftp2' (1004) ...
Adding new user `ftp2' (1003) with group `ftp2' ...
Creating home directory `/home/ftp2' ...
Copying files from `/etc/skel' ...
Enter new UNIX password: **YYY**
Retype new UNIX password: **YYY**
passwd: password updated successfully
Changing the user information for ftp2
Enter the new value, or press ENTER for the default
        Full Name []:
        Room Number []:
        Work Phone []:
        Home Phone []:
        Other []:
Is the information correct? [Y/n] **Y**
$

c. Test your new user account locally on your LAN by using the command **ftp 0** with username **ftp2**. Test it from the Internet. Put files in the user's account, and retrieve files from that account locally from another account, and from the Internet.

1.3 Given the steps needed to accomplish user account management shown in Section 1.5, make a table or chart of what users and groups need to be added to your system, and what their default account parameters and group memberships should be. Then, use the methods shown in Section 1.5 to accomplish user account creation, modification, and deletion from the command line. What command can you use to identify all existing groups on the system? Use the batch mode account creation technique shown in Section 1.5 to implement the users and groups from the table or chart you created.

1.4 Using the facilities available both in systemd and CUPS, add a local printer to your Raspberry Pi system with a direct USB connection. In detail, list all the steps necessary to get the printer to actually work given your installation type, and your specific hardware and system. Then print some test documents to it.

1.5 What printer commands did you use to test the addition of the printer you added to your system in Problem 1.4? In other words, what commands did you use to actually print documents on the printer you added?

1.6 What is the meaning of the term **archive**?

1.7 What is the **tar** command used for? Write an original, short, explicit, and articulate summary report that gives all its uses, in your own words. Include a detailed description of what you would use it for on your Raspberry Pi system.

1.8 You want to create a **tar** archive of a project that contains several directories, sub-directories and files, and save the archive on a USB thumb drive mounted on your system so that you can distribute the archive to your friends.

    a) What is the pathname to a USB thumb drive mounted on your system?

    b) How would you designate a USB thumb drive as the destination for where the tar archive would be created, as an argument to the **tar** command?

1.9 Give a command line example of creating a **tar** archive of your current working directory.

1.10 Give the explicit commands for compressing and keeping a **tar** archive of a "backups" directory in your home directory.

1.11 Give commands for restoring the backup file in Problem 1.8 in a directory named ~/backups.

1.12 Give a command line example of copying your home directory to another directory called home.back, so that access privileges and file modification times are preserved.

1.13 Why is the **tar** command preferred over the **cp -r** command for creating backup copies of directory hierarchies?

1.14 Suppose that you download a file, Pibook.tar.Z from an ftp site. Give the sequence of commands for restoring this archive and installing it in a directory named ~/Pibook on your Raspberry Pi system.

1.15 Use the **tar** command to create a compressed archive of a directory of your choosing in a new directory you create named mybackups under your home directory. Name the compressed archive **something.tar.gz** where something is the name of the directory you chose to backup. Show the command lines that you used to perform these tasks.

1.16 Use the **tar** command to restore the compressed tar archive ~/**mybackups/something.tar.gz** you produced in Problem 1.15 into a new directory named **mirrors** under your home directory. Show the command lines that you used to perform these tasks.

1.17 Use the **rsync** command on your Raspberry Pi system to back up your entire home directory, on whatever medium it exists, to a USB thumb drive mounted on the hardware.

1.18 Repeat Problems 1.8 through 1.11 using the **rsync** command instead of the **tar** command.

1.19 Use the the Pi Menu Accessories > SD Card Copier choice to make a bootable clone of your Raspberry Pi OS boot/system medium, onto a USB3 thumb drive. Make sure the target USB thumb drive has a large enough capacity to achieve the cloning! To test the clone, gracefully shut down your system, and remove the original boot/system medium. Then replace it with the cloned target, and restart the system.

1.20 Execute the steps of the user and group creation methods shown in Section 1.5 in detail for your Raspberry Pi system, according to the following constraints:

   a. New user accounts must be on a medium that is different than the system/boot medium.

   a. Your system's capabilities to accommodate additional persistent media.

   b. Your security model, in terms of how it isolates users and groups from one another.

   c. Your system performance model, as it affects users and groups,

   d. How many users and groups you plan to accommodate, and on what media into the future.

Advanced Questions, Problems, and Projects

1.21 Using the systemd cgroups methods of Section 1.14.1.2.2, "Persistent Cgroups and Setting Their Resources", and the constraints imposed by your particular use case, first examine and assess the most critical and important applications default use of the system resources of CPU and memory on your Raspberry Pi system. Then, give the applications that you believe warrant greater "weight" in accessing the CPU and memory than what they have by default. For example, if you are running a server that uses nginx to serve web pages, how can you give the nginx application, and its worker processes, more weight in accessing the CPU and system memory? How does the number of CPU cores that your Raspberry Pi has affect your redistribution of CPU usage, and how can you modify that redistribution to take advantage of those CPU cores? That might include taking advantage of CPU affinity, if the application you want to give more weight to is a system program written and developed by you. This Advanced Problem may be more applicable when the Raspberry Pi 5, and its hardware complement, becomes available.

1.22 After downloading and installing Webmin, as shown in Volume 1, test a connection to Webmin, both from the local machine, and over an intranet or the Internet from another computer system. What URL did you use to gain access to Webmin on the local machines web browser? What URL did you use to gain access to Webmin from another machine on an intranet? What URL did you use to gain access to Webmin from another machine on the Internet? List several precautionary steps you could take to ensure that no one else on the Internet can log into your system's Webmin interface?

1.23 After reading through Volume 1, Section 1.5, "Creating and Managing RAID Arrays Using mdadm on the Raspberry Pi OS", complete all of the steps shown in the example in that section on your Raspberry Pi system. Use the appropriate package management commands at Step 1 to install mdadm on your Raspberry Pi OS.

1.24 Examine the cups.service systemd service unit file in /lib/ systemd/system, and write a short paragraph-long description, in your own words, for why CUPS is either active or inactive when no powered-on printers are attached to the system. This question assumes that CUPS is installed on your system, according to the requirements shown in Volume 1, Section 1.6, and that it is enabled at system boot.

1.25 After reading through and executing the commands shown in Section 1.14, "Traditional Process Control", answer the following questions:

   a. Use the **top** command on your system to list the top processes running. What are they?

   b. $ **top -d 10**

top - 16:00:58 up 7 days, 23:49, 2 users, load average: 0.21, 0.26, 0.22
Tasks: 230 total, 1 running, 229 sleeping, 0 stopped, 0 zombie
%Cpu(s): 1.3 us, 1.1 sy, 0.0 ni, 97.6 id, 0.0 wa, 0.0 hi, 0.0 si, 0.0 st
MiB Mem: 3793.3 total, 451.8 free, 816.7 used, 2524.8 buff/cache
MiB Swap: 100.0 total, 99.0 free, 1.0 used. 2700.1 avail Mem

PID	USER	PR	NI	VIRT	RES	SHR	S	%CPU	%MEM	TIME+	COMMAND
723	root	20	0	397920	158504	57664	S	4.8	4.1	78:23.62	Xorg
140309	bob	20	0	905328	432960	124392	S	2.5	11.1	1:19.07	soffice.bin
907	bob	20	0	687348	85200	62232	S	1.8	2.2	24:08.90	mutter
307	root	-2	0	0	0	0	S	0.4	0.0	9:37.14	v3d_render
913	bob	20	0	1276928	91456	63728	S	0.4	2.4	6:22.77	lxpanel
305	root	-2	0	0	0	0	S	0.3	0.0	8:22.81	v3d_bin
140124	root	20	0	0	0	0	I	0.3	0.0	0:05.95	kworker/2:3-mm_percpu_wq
99	root	-51	0	0	0	0	S	0.2	0.0	31:09.55	irq/37-mmc0
15	root	20	0	0	0	0	I	0.1	0.0	7:20.06	rcu_preempt

914   bob   20   0   1084720 108600   73856 S   0.1   2.8   1:56.17   pcmanfm

Output truncated...
In the above **top** command display, what are the top processes running, and why?

    1.26 Put a particular, single unprivileged user on your Raspberry Pi system into the sudoers file. Give that user access to the resources dictated by your particular system security model.

    1.27 For User Specifications in the sudoers file found on your system, describe briefly what privileges are given by each entry.

    1.28 Is it possible to directly run a non-Linux operating system inside of an LXC/LXD container? Give a couple of example container instances, or templates, that are available for LXC/LXD.

    1.29 Define *synthetic file system* in your own words, and as verbosely as possible.

Then answer the following questions:

    a) Do the contents of the pseudo and special purpose file systems, in the virtual layer we have partitioned the Raspberry Pi storage scheme into, exist across boots, or are the data structures that define them, and their specific content, created anew each time the system boots and is restarted?

    b) Are their data structures and content fixed immutably at the time the system is built, or does their content vary across time, and how?

In your answers to the above questions, list several examples of pseudo and special purpose file systems, what function(s) they perform, how you can discover which parts of them are either volatile, persistent, or both to whatever degree, and how you can know which ones are fixed, and how, when the system is built, if that's the case.

Project 1
Do an installation of the Raspberry Pi OS onto an older X86 architecture computer that you have available, using the instructions shown in Section 1.2.2. What benefits does this confer, in terms of economy, performance, and utility, for you personally, given the use cases you might be putting this hardware to?

Project 2
On your Raspberry Pi hardware, using mdadm, mirror two externally mounted, USB3 thumb drives that have user's home directories on them.

The assumption in this project is that the source directories and files that you want to mirror and back up are created and maintained on one of the thumb drives. *Not on the system disk.* This is congruent with the recommended storage model in this chapter!

Use the RAID capabilities provided by mdadm to accomplish "automatic" backup of the source disks and partitions on them.

In particular, use the method of RAID 1, mirroring, available for mdadm, to achieve the automatic backups of directories and files which you want backed up. Then, write a report, presenting the exact and specific commands that you used to provide the tactics you employ using mdadm to accomplish the goals of this project, in a verbose, explicit, and articulate report format.

Project 3

Install the latest version of Ubuntu Linux on your Raspberry Pi hardware, using the instructions shown in Section 1.2.4. What benefits does this confer, in terms of economy, performance, and utility, for you personally, given the use cases you might be putting this operating system to?

Hint: Ubuntu allows you to use ZFS on your hardware.

Project 4

Install the latest version of any other available Linux OS on your Raspberry Pi hardware, generally using the instructions shown in Section 1.2.4 as a guide. What benefits does this confer, in terms of economy, performance, and utility, for you personally, given the use cases you might be putting this operating system to?

Project 5

What is the Linux Logical Volume Management (LVM), and why would you want to deploy it on your Raspberry Pi system? Is it possible to install the system itself with LVM as the default? Is LVM already installed on your Raspberry Pi system?

After answering these questions, add an external USB3 medium to your system, and manage it with LVM as a volume in conjunction with the original storage complement on your system. What advantages does this confer, given your particular use case(s).

Project 6

Execute all of the example code listed under EXAMPLES on the man page for **user_namespaces**. Copy and paste the Program source for the C module provided into a file, and compile and link that source to execute it. Use the reference materials above that example to provide background information for the execution of that code on your Raspberry Pi system. This will give you a good introduction to Linux namespaces.

Project 7
Install the Kernel-based Virtual Machine (KVM) on your Raspberry Pi system, and use it to create and launch a virtual machine image of an operating system of your choice. We provide the following commands to guide you during the beginning of installation and use of KVM:

```
$ sudo ls -lh /dev/kvm
$ sudo apt intall virt-manager libvirt0 qemu-system
$ sudo usermod -aG libvirt-qemu $(whoami)
$ sudo virsh net-start default
$ sudo virsh net-autostart default
```

Project 8
Besides the common system administration tasks we have selected to present in this chapter, there are numerous extensions, and also many additional tasks, that Raspberry Pi OS administration encompass.

From the following list of additional tasks, choose one, or several of the items shown, and either fully implement the details of that item, or items, on your Raspberry Pi system. The item(s) you select might be very relevant to the particular way you use your Raspberry Pi. If you choose *not* to implement any of the items, do a personalized research report that would allow you to achieve implementation of particular items of interest to you at some future date, given how your use case might change beyond what it currently is.

1. Creating, configuring, and running a "lite" version of the Raspberry Pi OS (akin to a server, text-interface-only edition) from a persistent USB3 thumb drive.

2. Doing an advanced, text-based installation of that server with a discretionary higher level of complex configuration than what we have illustrated in this chapter.

3. Maintaining a large user base across multiple machines and networks, possibly using NFSv4 ACLs.

4. Configuring customized partitions onto which the operating system is installed, or using higher levels of RAIDZ, LVM, or multi-partitioned, multi-boot environment disks with multiple operating systems on them. Possibly using Zvols as a means of partitioning your storage media.

5. Using commercial backup software.

6. Hand-building the Raspberry Pi OS, or applications software systems, from Github source, or using advanced package repository resources and configurations.

7. Using your Raspberry Pi system exclusively to stream media via NAS to a single display surface, or to multiple displays.

8. Doing the common system administration tasks we illustrated in this chapter on Ubuntu Linux, or on another Linux distro of your choice.

9. Write and administer, or install, malware-fighting programs.

10. Implementing a secure full LAMP stack, in preparation for Internet-facing your system(s).

11. Create a hubless SAN using NVMe devices over Ethernet.

Project 9
Following up on what we present in this chapter, completely list and detail what the pre-installation considerations for three distinct, and personally chosen, use cases of a Raspberry Pi hardware platform would be. For example, a public-facing web server that uses Docker containers running nginx. Then implement one of those use cases on actual Raspberry Pi hardware. Use our set of minimal recommendations for post-installation tasks as a guide to begin to fulfill the requirements of this project.

Project 10
Attach a Sense HAT to your Raspberry Pi, and incorporate it via Python programming into whatever use case you see fit.

Project 11
This project involves using Webmin, systemd timers, cron, and a shell script file, to do a system-wide backup of the Raspberry Pi OS.

Webmin can be used to execute systemctl timers, allowing you to schedule and manage tasks or services on your Linux system. Follow these steps to use Webmin to configure and control systemctl timers to achieve that backup/archive tactic:

0. Ensure that you have Webmin installed on your Linux system by following the official documentation for your distribution. Once installed, access the Webmin interface through a web browser.

1. Configure a systemctl timer: In Webmin, you can use the "Scheduled Cron Jobs" module to configure systemctl timers, as follows:

    a. In the Webmin interface, navigate to the "Scheduled Cron Jobs" module.

    b. Click on "Create a new scheduled cron job".

    c. Set the desired schedule for the timer (e.g., daily, weekly, etc.) and provide the appropriate systemctl command to execute. For example, to start or stop a service, use commands like:

To start a service: **systemctl start service-name**

To stop a service: **systemctl stop service-name**
Note

Also set the command that will execute your backup script (e.g., /path/
to/backup-script.sh).

Specify the desired schedule (e.g., daily, weekly, etc.) and set the command
to execute your backup script (e.g., /path/to/backup-script.sh, see
below in 3).

    d.   Save the cron job configuration.

2.   To do verification and monitoring of the backup, once the systemctl
timer is configured in Webmin, you can verify its functionality by
manually triggering the timer, or waiting until the scheduled time
of its execution. Monitor the execution of the timer and check if the
desired service starts or stops as expected.

3.   Here's an **rsync** script that can be automated via the Webmin, systemctl
timers, and cron operations illustrated above, to backup your entire
system:

```
#!/bin/bash
SOURCE="/path/to/file system"
DESTINATION="/path/to/backup/location"
TIMESTAMP=$(date +%Y%m%d%H%M%S)
BACKUP_FILE="backup_${TIMESTAMP}.tar.gz"

rsync -a --exclude=/proc --exclude=/sys --exclude=/dev "$SOURCE" \
"$DESTINATION"
tar -czvf "$DESTINATION/$BACKUP_FILE" "$DESTINATION"
```

Chapter 2

2.1 Type in the following Python3 code, with the indentation shown, and
note what error messages you get. Then, after each error message,
type in the proper indentation, until you can execute all eight lines of
code.

```
x= 23
if x==27:
print ("no go")
    print ("why?")
```

```
        elif x ==26:
        print ("still a no go")
        else:
    print ("why?")
```

2.2

    a. Take the code shown in Example 2.6, and convert it to a function script file that can be executed using Way 3 (Import script mode). Name the function script file **testcase.py**. Save it in the current working directory. The function should allow you to enter different values of x as an input argument each time it is invoked, and print out results on screen.

    b. How is the function brought into and invoked in Python3? Test it with several values of x.

2.3

    a. Take the code shown in Example 2.7 and convert it to a function script file that can be executed using Way 2 (Script Mode) in the Thonny Script Area. Then, in Thonny, name it **nested.py,** and save it in the current working directory. The function should allow you to enter different values of w, y, and z as input arguments each time it is invoked, and print out the results on screen.

    b. How is the function brought into and invoked in Python3? Test it with several values of w, y, and z.

2.4 From the following pseudo-coded plan,

```
for i ← 1 to length(A)
    j ← i
    while j > 0 and A[j-1] > A[j]
        swap A[j] and A[j-1]
        j ← j - 1
```

write and test a script file, using Way 2 (Script Mode), that:

    a. Allows the user to pass a list of individual numbers (real or integer) held in a list **A** in random order, as arguments to it, and that

    b. Uses for and while repetition structure(s) to sort the numbers from list **A** into ascending order, so their values can print out from low to high, left to right on the screen.

2.5 Create a function script file in Python3 that uses Way 3 (Import Script Mode) to execute it. Name it **factIter.py,** and have it calculate the factorial of an integer number using the "while" indeterminate repetition structure. Test it in the Thonny Shell Area with several integer values to the script file.

2.6 Give a definition of list comprehensions, and how the comprehension functional component in Python3 works on lists, sets, and dictionaries.

2.7 Similar to Example 2.14, write a Python3 function script file that uses Way 3 (Import Script Mode) to execute. It must deploy the list function, and when invoked in the Thonny Shell Area, allows you to input integer numbers for the indices of the matrix, and output the resulting random number matrix.

2.8 Convert the Python function script file you created in Problem 2.7 into a new Python function script file that writes the random number matrix to a file named **matrixout.txt**, similarly to what is done in Example 2.13.

2.9

    a. Convert the script file from Example 2.17 into a new Way 3 (Import Script Mode) function script file that obtains the filename as an input argument to the function.

    b. Rename the data.txt file that Example 2.17's script file worked on to **data2.txt**. Test your new function script file with the filename **data2.txt**.

    c. What are the values of **collection[2]**, **collection[2][1]**, and **collection[1][1]**? How can you obtain these on the Python3 command line after your new function script file has run?

2.10 Using Way 2 (Script Mode) to execute it, create a Python3 dictionary that represents a 3 × 3, two-dimensional matrix of real numbers of your choice. In the same script file, have it print out the elements of the matrix as:

row 1

row 2

row 3

2.11 After doing Example 2.18, and using the Python3 standard library reference documentation, find and make a list of some of the basic set operations available in Python3 (giving the basic syntax for each).

2.12 Similar to Examples 2.12 and 2.23, and using Way 3 (Import Script Mode):

    a. Write a Python function script file that takes a filename as an argument, and

    b. uses a robust set of **try:...except:...else:** error handling statements in it to test the filename, and

    c. opens the file named in a, reads a collection of integers from the file into a list, and

d. converts all of the list elements to integer numbers, and
e. produces a new integer list of the squares of all the integers, and finally
f. prints the list of the squares of all the integers.

Then, test the function for your error handling statements with erroneous file names, or names of files that are not in the current working directory.

2.13 Modify the code in **arith1.py** from Example 2.24 so that the variable **c** is declared as a global variable in all four functions (add, subtract, multiply, and divide). For example:

def add(a,b):
    global c
    c = a + b
#NO RETURN STATEMENT!

Then:

a. Save the file as **arith2.py**.
b. Import **arith2**, and redo In-Chapter Exercise 34.
c. Explain the results you get when you type >>>**arith2.c** in the Thonny Shell Area at any particular point after you have imported and invoked the file **arith2** with some numeric arguments.

2.14 Take a Bourne shell script that you've named **cmdargs_demo**, which is as follows:

```
#!/bin/bash
echo "The command name is: $0".
echo "The number of command line arguments passed as parameters \
is $#".
echo "The values of the command line arguments
are: $1 $2 $3 $4 $5 $6 $7 $8 $9 $10 $11"
echo "Another way to display the values of all of the arguments \
is: $@".
echo "Yet another way is: $*".
exit 0
```

and convert it to Python3 code that runs using Way 2 (Script Mode) in Thonny. Your Python3 conversion should find the byte sizes of all ordinary (regular) and dot (.) files in the directory specified as an argument to the command, and add them up to print a total. It should skip over subdirectories. It should include the branching structure for error handling statements from the original Bourne shell script.

Hint: The following line of Python3 code adds up, or accumulates, the running total of file byte sizes of ordinary and dot files in the directory specified:

```
x = sum(os.path.getsize(f) for f in os.listdir(directory) if os.path. \
isfile(f))
```

2.15 Following Example 2.34, substitute your own selected directory name on your Raspberry Pi system as the source for backup, and back up all the files in that selected directory to a mounted USB thumb drive on your system, in a rolling scheme of three directories. Then, make changes to the source files and directory on the hard drive, and run the script file again to see how the changes have been synchronized in the files and directory on the USB thumb drive.

Once you have tested this script file, use the proper systemd commands in a Python3 script file constructed in Thonny to run it at a specified increment of time, such as daily at 5 AM, once every 6 hours, etc.

2.16 You are tasked by your boss to convert a Python 2.7 system administration script file into a Python3 script file, to assist in doing system administration at your company. She provides this Python 2.7 script file as the one seen in Example 2.35. Your Python3 script file must execute using Way 2 (Script Mode). She also requests that you improve the output of search pattern results; therefore, you are not bound to format your output strictly in the way the Python 2.7 script file does, but your Python3 script file must supply at least the same information. She insists that your Python3 script file must also do appropriate exception handling; for example, it should *not* work on hidden files, or on files which are subdirectories of the current working directory.

What pattern-matching characters can you use with your Python3 script file, such as the wildcard characters (sometimes called globbing patterns), etc.?

2.17 Beginning with the tkinter script shown in Example 2.38, add Python3 and tkinter code to allow the user to do not only Fahrenheit-to-Celsius conversions, but also Celsius-to-Fahrenheit conversions. The layout of the widgets in the tkinter GUI for this problem can look similar to the example that we provide below for reference.

2.18 Add a single operating system call to the Example 2.39 code that executes the **ps** command. Every time you press <**Enter**>, and start a new successive thread, that thread should execute the **ps** command with output to the Thonny Shell Area.

2.19 Add a single operating system call to the Example 2.40 code that executes the **ping –c 5 google.com** command. Every thread will then ping google.com "simultaneously".

2.20 Write a program using Python3 threads that pings 10 different hosts of your choice, simultaneously.

2.21 Starting with the Python code from Example 2.45, rewrite the program so that an indeterminate number of values are produced by the producer and consumed by the consumer. Termination of the program can be achieved with **<Ctrl-Z>** if necessary.

2.22 Modify the code of Example 2.45 so that it can achieve the following, in three separate Python scripts:

    a) Start two producer threads that fill the buffer for five iterations each, and one consumer thread that iterates 10 times to consume all data in the buffer produced by the producer threads.

    b) Start one producer thread and three consumer threads, so that all data produced is consumed.

    c) Start three producer threads that fill the buffer for a number of iterations specified from within the script file interactively at run time each, but only have one consumer thread that executes until all produced data in the buffer is consumed.

Index

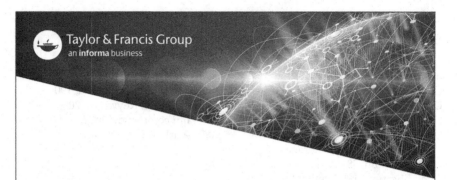

Printed in the United States
by Baker & Taylor Publisher Services